THE VEDANTA AND MODERN THOUGHT

THE VEDANTA AND MORDERN THOUGHT

W. S. URQUHART, M.A., D. LITT.

GYAN PUBLISHING HOUSE
New Delhi - 110002

THE VEDANTA AND MODERN THOUGHT

ISBN :9788121200493

Published in 2014 in India by
Gyan Publishing House
5, Ansari Road, Daryaganj,
New Delhi - 110002
Phones : 011-47034999, 9811692060
e-mail : books@gyanbooks.com
website : gyanbooks.com

Laser Typesetting at : Vinayak Printers, Delhi
Printed at : Salasar Imaging System, Delhi

TO

PROFESSOR W. L. DAVIDSON, LL.D.

EMERITUS PROFESSOR OF LOGIC AND METAPHYSICS IN THE UNIVERSITY OF ABERDEEN

AND

PROFESSOR W. R. SORLEY, LL.D.

FORMERLY PROFESSOR OF MORAL PHILOSOPHY IN THE UNIVERSITY OF ABERDEEN, AND NOW KNIGHTBRIDGE PROFESSOR OF MORAL PHILOSOPHY IN THE UNIVERSITY OF CAMBRIDGE

MY TEACHERS IN PHILOSOPHY IN THE UNIVERSITY OF ABERDEEN

AUTHOR'S PREFACE

IN the ever-increasing mass of literature which has been devoted to the criticism and appreciation of Indian thought, a tendency to extremes has constantly manifested itself. On the one hand we find amongst outside critics signs of a disposition to undervalue the results of Indian speculation. Over-zealous attempts are sometimes made to derive from alien sources the most important elements in Oriental philosophy, and when such attempts are shown by serious scholars to be almost altogether impossible, recourse is taken to a superior and slightly patronizing attitude in which, no doubt, expressions of depreciation are politely avoided, but the place of genuine and sympathetic appreciation is occupied by intermittent ejaculations of wonder as to how a people who have not had the benefits of the cultural inheritance which the superior critics themselves enjoy, should have been capable of so much as has actually been accomplished in India. Needless to say, the feeling which is aroused by an attitude of this kind amongst those upon whom judgement is thus summarily passed, is one of irritation rather than of gratitude.

The other extreme is undiscriminating admiration. Under the influence of this mood, writers, both in the East and in the West, vie with each other in asseverating that everything that is good comes from the East, and that nothing is good which does not come from the East. It is only by Eastern windows that 'when daylight comes, comes in the light'. Moved by a spurious kind of cosmopolitanism or by an almost childish desire to vindicate their own broadmindedness, certain Western philosophers of the type here indicated have gone the length of declaring that the Orient has a monopoly of spirituality, that the West is blatantly materialistic, and that all the more important elements in early European philosophy may be traced to the Eastern influences which moulded the precursors of Plato, or to the currents of philosophic thought which moved from East to West in the centuries immediately preceding or immediately succeeding the commencement of the Christian era. Three-quarters of a century ago Cousin described the East as 'the native land of the highest philosophy', and Schopenhauer earlier gave utterance to the unrestrained generalization that 'in the whole world there is no study so beneficial and elevating as that of the Upanishads'. Writers of a later date have to an even greater extent allowed their enthusiasm to overwhelm the undoubted elements of truth which are contained in such assertions. Opinions of this sort have, of course, been eagerly welcomed by some Indian writers, who have perhaps a keener relish for the compliment which appeals to patriotism than for the valuation which depends upon a balanced judgement. We come across, e.g., such statements as the following: 'India has given to humanity the main outlines at least of the whole of the philosophy and religion of the world.'[1] Although, however, such sweeping statements are by no means isolated, it would be altogether unfair to suggest that judgements of this kind are passed without qualification by the generality of Indian writers on philosophy.

A more temperate and tenable position is taken up, e.g., by Prof. S. N. Das Gupta, who claims only that 'most of the problems still debated in modern philosophical thought occurred in more or less divergent form to the philosophers of India'.[2] It cannot certainly be contended that in the course of the world's history India has been responsible for the only philosophical thought worthy of the name, but it may be argued with a considerable amount of justification that, at a very early period in intellectual development, the greater philosophical problems had presented themselves to the Indian consciousness and had received penetrating and illuminating treatment. India has had,

[1] Prof. Drivedi, *Introduction to the Māṇḍūkya U.* II.
[2] Das Gupta, p. viii.

and still has, a most important contribution to make to the thought of the world, and is well qualified to make this contribution by the intensity with which throughout the centuries she has devoted herself to her philosophical and philosophico-religious task. Rarely has metaphysical speculation afforded to any people so absorbing an interest. As Prof. Radhakrishnan says: 'In many other countries reflection on the nature of existence is a luxury of life. The serious moments are given to action, while the pursuit of philosophy comes up as a parenthesis. In ancient India philosophy was not an auxiliary to any other science or art, but always held a prominent position of independence.' [1]

A study of the Vedānta leads to many general reflections on the relations between philosophy and religion, and in particular to the questions how far such a philosophy can satisfy religious needs and how far it can be regarded as a preparation for Christianity. I have tried to set forth some conclusions as to these and allied problems. Śaṅkara has been taken as the typical philosopher of the school, for reasons which appear to me to be satisfactory; and the general trend of opinion amongst Indian writers and thinkers themselves would appear to justify this concentration. It has been my endeavour to carry out my task in a spirit of fairness, and to avoid the mistake of merely working towards a foregone conclusion. And I have no hesitation in saying that such studies as I have been able to make in Indian philosophy have confirmed me in the faith that God has not left Himself without a witness in the characteristic thought of India, that much of it is unconsciously anticipative of Christian thought, and that Jesus Christ will one day be recognized there also as the 'light which lighteth every man that cometh into the world'.

Amongst the many books which have been consulted, I have

[1] Radhakrishnan, I. 22.

found the first volume of Prof. Radhakrishnan's *Indian Philosophy*, the first volume of Prof. S. N. Das Gupta's *History of Indian Philosophy*, and Dr. J. N. Farquhar's *Outline of the Religious Literature of India* specially useful as works of reference. Dr. Farquhar, also, and the Rev. E. C. Dewick have given me much help in the preparation of my manuscript for the press. I should like to express finally my great indebtedness to my wife for many useful suggestions and for much assistance in reading both manuscript and proofs.

W. S. URQUHART.

SCOTTISH CHURCHES COLLEGE,
CALCUTTA, 1928.

CONTENTS

I. Introductory. The Affiliations and the Importance of the Vedānta. Vedantic Ideas in the Vedas . . . 1

II. Anticipations of Vedantic Ideas in the Upanishads. The Vedānta Sūtras. The Gītā. The Kārikās of Gauḍapāda 21

III. Śaṅkara and Rāmānuja: Their Lives, their Commentaries, and their Traditional Philosophical Significance 50

IV. The Approach to Śaṅkara's Central Teaching. Preliminary Conditions. His Conception of Authority. The Idealistic Attitude. His Relation to Buddhism 73

V. The Ultimate Unity. The Two Orders of Knowledge. The Place of Works 101

VI. The Doctrines of *Māyā* and *Avidyā*. Relation to Kant. The God of Qualities 128

VII. The Destiny of the Individual Soul. The Place of Ethics in the Vedānta 156

VIII. Some Comparisons between the Vedānta and Modern Philosophical Thought 191

IX. The Religious Value of the Vedānta, and Some Conclusions 215

INDEX 251

ABBREVIATIONS

Aiyar: C. N. Krishnaswami Aiyar, *Life and Times of Śaṅkara*.
Carpenter: Dr. J. Estlin Carpenter, *Theism in Medieval India*.
Das Gupta: Prof. S. N. Das Gupta, *A History of Indian Philosophy*.
Deussen, *S. V.*: Deussen, *System of the Vedānta*, Chicago, 1912.
Deussen, *P. U.*: Deussen, *Philosophy of the Upanishads*.
Farquhar: Dr. J. N. Farquhar, *Outline of the Religious Literature of India*.
Goreh: Nehemiah Goreh, *Mirror of Hindu Philosophical Systems*.
Griswold: Dr. H. D. Griswold, *The Religion of the Ṛigveda*.
Happel: Happel, *Grundanschauungen der Inder*.
J. R. A. S.: *Journal of the Royal Asiatic Society*.
Kirtikar: Vasudeva J. Kirtikar, *Studies in Vedānta*.
Müller, *S. S.*: Max Müller, *Six Systems of Indian Philosophy*.
Pal: D. N. Pal, *Śaṅkara the Sublime*.
Pringle-Pattison: Prof. Pringle-Pattison, *The Idea of God*.
Radhakrishnan: Prof. S. Radhakrishnan, *Indian Philosophy*.
Schopenhauer: Schopenhauer, *The World as Will and Idea* (trans. by Haldane and Kemp).
S. B. E.: *Sacred Books of the East*.
S. B. H.: *Sacred Books of the Hindus*.
Sen: Mr. P. N. Sen, *Philosophy of the Vedānta*.
Shastri, B. K.: Prof. B. K. Shastri, *The Bhakti Cult in Ancient India*.
Shastri, K.: Prof. Kokileswar Shastri, *The Advaita Philosophy*.
Shastri, P. D.: Prof. P. D. Shastri, *The Doctrine of Māyā*.
U.: Upanishads.

I

INTRODUCTORY. THE AFFILIATIONS AND IMPORTANCE OF THE VEDĀNTA. VEDANTIC IDEAS IN THE VEDAS

A COMPARISON between Eastern and Western philosophy should aim at proving, not that one is superior to the other, but rather that the one may be supplemented or corrected by the other. When the prevailing points of view are different and origins and methods so diverse, it is to be expected that the resulting philosophies will present strikingly contrasted virtues and limitations, and that fullness of truth can be reached only through co-operation. Max Müller, e.g., was acutely conscious of the narrowness of conception which might arise from an exclusive nurture on the thought of the Jews, the Greeks, or the Romans, and felt that from India especially we might derive 'that correction which is wanted in order to make our inner life more perfect, more comprehensive, more universal, in fact, more truly human'.[1] Thus, in seeking for that unity which is behind all the diversity of the history of thought, we must not be too anxious to discover unity at the expense of diversity. Such haste has led to many futile efforts to establish affiliations and derivations which are hardly warranted by the facts. Similarities indeed there are, fundamental and impressive, but the differences must also be clearly kept in view, if the fullness of the co-operative work of the human spirit is to be realized; and these differences, as Emerson reminds us,[2] are no more surprising than the variety of the acts of one man in which we recognize the same character.

The broad and deep similarities between Greek and Indian thinkers have frequently been noted, so that there is not much risk of our forgetting them. Many recent writers have found an almost complete accord, e.g. between the Vedānta and the abstract philosophy of the Greek Eleatics. For Parmenides, amongst the latter, the only reality is the one and indivisible Being, destitute of qualities and superior to all distinctions of place and changes in time. And did not Plato, equally with his

[1] India, *What Can It Teach Us?*, 6. [2] Essay on *History*.

Eastern fellow searchers after truth, seek for an eternal beyond change and an essential reality behind appearances—a universal Being in which all particularity is merged? Yet even in regard to that ultimate reality which was the common object of search, there are important differences between Indian and Greek conceptions. The Hindu philosopher seemed from the first to rebel against the thought of limits, whereas for the Greek, except at a very early stage, the unlimited seemed to be metaphysically undesirable. He sought above all for clarity and precision of conception, whilst to the Indian mind the one which was the goal of his endeavour was attractive just because of its vagueness, and because it could not properly be described either as Being or non-Being. The Indian thinker could not intellectualize this Being, and did not wish to do so, but only to grasp it by intuition, under an overpowering sense of that *mysterium tremendum* which a recent writer has emphasized as the essence of the religious consciousness.[1] The Being of the Vedānta has indeed many points of similarity to the Being of Plato, but the latter does not emphasize so earnestly, or rest so contentedly in, a transcendent reality, and it is with a certain amount of reluctance that he falls back on the aid of those myths through which alone he feels that he can hint at its character. Thus, when he relies on philosophy alone, the Being of Plato tends to become more fully intellectualized than the Being of the Vedānta. Plato obtains a logical, if not an actual, transition from the One to the Many, whereas the Eastern philosopher is content with a vaguer fundamental unity from which there cannot be a logical transition to the multiplicity of the world, and in contrast to whose impenetrable vastness the particularity of ordinary experience is best explained by being left unexplained. In fact it is even doubtful whether in an Indian connexion we are justified in making use of the phrase *mysterium tremendum*; for this might be taken to suggest a Reality which might some day be explained, whereas the Indian thinker was rather inclined to the idea of a reality which he neither hoped nor desired to explain.

It can, perhaps, be said with truth that it is in the philosophy of religion that India has made her greatest contribution to the

[1] Cf. Otto, *Das Heilige, passim.*

thought of the world. Nowhere is it altogether possible to draw a hard-and-fast line between the philosophy of religion and philosophy in general, but this distinction is least of all admissible in India, where it might be said that the conditions and intensity of the search for a solution of life's problems and the character of the solutions offered alike invite to a religious attitude. The almost despairing realization of the need for deliverance, together with the indefiniteness of the Reality which is conceived to be the only refuge, predisposes the searcher to a mystical mood and makes it impossible for him to be content with coldly intellectual satisfaction. The very grading of our experiences in such a way as to place deep sleep above the dreaming consciousness, and this again above the waking consciousness, in itself indicates a disposition towards mystic and abstract unity. The Indian mind is, like Newman's, subtle in analysis, but it is also simple in belief, capable of a concentration of the whole being upon an ideal of unity with a degree of intensity which is rarely equalled elsewhere, and which is of itself sufficient to carry the human spirit across the border-line—if there be a border-line—between philosophy and religion. As Prof. Das Gupta says, 'The systems of philosophy in India were not stirred up merely by the speculative demands of the human mind, but by a deep craving after the realization of the religious purpose of life.'[1] And the more intense statement of Deussen is also justified: 'No people on earth took religion so seriously, none toiled on the way to salvation as they did. Their reward for this was to have got, if not the most scientific, yet the most inward and immediate expression of the deepest secret of being.'[2]

The Hindu regarded one-pointedness (*ēkagratā*) as the indispensable condition of intellectual penetration into the deep mysteries of the universe; and, although this qualification may be difficult for outsiders to appreciate, and the application of it may lead to certain extravagances and peculiarities, it undoubtedly illustrates the facility with which the philosophy of India connects itself inextricably with religion. Its use is allied with an inclination and aptitude for a quiet and contemplative life, and with a preference for the intuitive to the discursive in

[1] Das Gupta, I. 71.
[2] Deussen, *S.V.*, 49.

method and for intensity to extensity in the resulting knowledge. It favours passivity more than activity, and indicates a belief in the service to thought which may be rendered by the 'quiet in the land'.

We may say that, under the conditions described, the prevailing tendency of thought is in the direction of a pantheism of an idealistic character. India has been described as 'radically pantheistic and that from its cradle onwards'; and its pantheism has been more continuous than in any other country. This means a readiness to find close at hand the materials for both philosophical speculation and religious devotion, and strengthens the alliance between the satisfactions of the mind and of the spirit. Every bush may be afire with God and every natural event a manifestation of His indwelling, and, subjectively, religious devotion and speculative insight are through pantheism brought very close together.

Further, the alliance between philosophy and religion is also favoured by the contemplative passivity which we have noted as a characteristic of the Indian attitude. From this arises a certain conservativeness, and a readiness to look to the past rather than to the future, expressing itself often in a belief in a golden age set far back in a period of remote antiquity. This again connects itself with a reverence for the authority of tradition and an intense appreciation of the value of even the smallest details of the sacred lore. This reverence attaches itself frequently to ritualistic formulae. Take, e.g., the importance assigned to the syllable *Om* (or *Aum*). We have here not a meaningless catchword or charm, but a symbol indicative of a whole philosophical position. It is analysed and re-analysed to the fullest possible extent, and everything of possible value is extracted from it. It is used alike as a guide to concentration and as the herald of a prophetic vision of the highest truth. Similarly, but in a broader way, the reverence for tradition, religiously valued, is seen in the constant endeavour to relate philosophical conclusions to the pronouncements of the earliest literature; and the consequence of this is to link up speculation with that period in the world's history when religion and philosophy had hardly begun to differentiate themselves from each other.

Thus there are many reasons which would lead us to look for both a religious origin and a religious design for philosophy in India; and when we turn more particularly to the philosophy of the Vedānta we find that our expectations are fully justified.

The very term *Vedānta* is an illustration of the tendencies we have just been indicating. There are many possible meanings, as we shall see, but even if we take account of only the primary and almost mechanically literal meaning—'the end of the Veda'—there is here suggested a desire to connect the speculative ideas with the body of religious literature which has the greatest claim to antiquity, and therefore the greatest authority. But this also involves the linking up of the ideas with the popular religion which the literature enshrines. The etymology itself indicates that at the end of the process of satisfying the requirements of ritual, at the end of the explanation of the significance of the ceremonies, *then* might come the deeper speculations. Thus, from the first, speculation could be secured against the charge of being merely academic, and the foundations at least were laid for the Indian conception of the closest possible union between religion and philosophy. In a comparison between Hinduism and Buddhism Dr. J. Estlin Carpenter says with truth: 'The forces of Hinduism were rooted in a remoter past, they were intertwined more closely (than those of Buddhism) even with the localities as well as with the habits of the popular religion, they sprang more directly out of the common heart, they appealed more directly to the common mind.'[1] This generalization may be applied to later developments as well as to earliest origins.

In the *Mahābhārata*, XII. 55, the term 'Vedānta' is taken to denote the Upanishads, and this may be regarded as its primary reference. It expresses the essential ideas of the Upanishads, and, through the Āraṇyakas and the Brāhmaṇas, reaches back to the very oldest extant religious literature of India, viz. the Vedas. For the Upanishads were the concluding part of the Āraṇyakas, and contained the essential doctrines in which the theosophical interpretations contained in the latter might be regarded as finding their culmination. The Āraṇyakas, again, were the hand-books—to speak metaphorically—and contained

[1] Carpenter, 117.

the most useful parts, or the most valuable interpretations, of the Brāhmaṇas. They were 'Brāhmaṇas appointed for the vow of an anchorite', and through them the Vānaprastha, or 'dweller in the woods', might be assisted in preparation for his hermit life. Their background was formed by the Brāhmaṇas, which were ritual text-books belonging to a later and less original age than that of the Vedas, embodying sacerdotal tradition, and elaborating the ideas of the Vedas into a complex, cumbrous, and ever-growing ceremonial. Finally, passing still farther up the stream of time, we come to the Vedas, comprising in the *Ṛigveda* the ancient and beautiful hymns to the gods which are amongst the most cherished possessions of Indian literature, and showing affinities with that body of ideas which is common to Indo-European thought in general and perhaps to primitive thought throughout the world. Yet, while we use the word 'primitive', we must be careful in connexion with the *Ṛigveda* not to allow it to convey any hint of disparagement, for these hymns present to us exceedingly wonderful intuitions of the Divine, all the more impressive because they are so near to the beginnings of the religious thought of the world.

The Vedas comprise also the *Sāmaveda*, a book of chants to be sung by the priests at the time of the Soma worship; and the *Yajurveda*, which contains formulae, partly in prose and partly in verse, designed for use at the various sacrifices. To these must also be added the *Atharvaveda*, later and less important than the other Vedas and considerably different from them in thought and feeling, inasmuch as it shows traces of magical and superstitious ideas which had crept in from a lower stratum of thought, and were perhaps both cause and effect of a growingly pessimistic mood.

Thus by an unbroken chain the Upanishads are connected in a backward direction with the Vedas; but as the truth contained in the Vedas is considered to be inexhaustible, we must also look forwards, and regard as a continuation of the chain every effort towards putting this truth in a more serviceable form or towards giving a fuller interpretation of it. Therefore the Vedānta will comprise not only the Upanishads and their predecessors, but also their successors. The Upanishads are later summarized in the *Vedānta Sūtras*, a collection of aphorisms in which the salient points of the Upanishads are emphasized. They are of the nature of succinct summaries for memorizing, serving the purpose of notes for discussions continued from century to century in the different schools. While these summaries might have been intelligible to those who had taken part in, or were familiar with, the discussions based upon them, they could not but be somewhat obscure to others not so privileged. Thus they were practically useless without the commentaries which followed at a later date. In one sense, therefore, the culmination of the Vedānta is to be found in commentaries such as those of Śaṇkara, who flourished about the ninth century, and Rāmānuja of the twelfth century, and many others, whose activities, of very varying degrees of importance, extended as far down as the seventeenth century.

To this whole development the name Vedānta is, as a rule, given, but variations in the application of the term should not be left unnoticed. As we have seen [1] the primary application of the term is to the Upanishads, but in the view of Prof. S. N. Das Gupta, the *Sūtras* 'form the original authoritative work of the Vedānta'.[2] To these and the Upanishads, the Gītā is added as a third authoritative source-book of the Vedānta philosophy. Further, when the age of the commentators arrives, there is a natural tendency to claim exclusive importance for one or other of them. Usually Śaṇkara obtains the pre-eminence. Mr. P. N. Sen, e.g., says: 'The philosophy of Śaṇkara has now been unalterably identified with the Vedānta philosophy; it is the Vedānta *par excellence*.'[3] Rāmānuja, of course, has also his votaries, though not perhaps to the same extent. The question of the importance of the various periods and contributors relatively to each other will come up for later discussion. In the meantime it is sufficient to notice that the name is not improperly applied to the whole course of the development. On the whole it would seem that the most common average usage throughout India is to allow this wider reference to the whole development, but at the same time to assign to the philosophy of Śaṇkara the central place in the field of the Vedantic consciousness, and this will be, for the most part, the practice followed in this book.

[1] *Supra*, p. 5. [2] Das Gupta, I. [3] *Philosophy of the Vedānta*, 6.

We have found that the literal meaning of Vedānta is 'end of the Veda', but allied meanings are 'dogma of the Veda', 'final aim of the Veda', &c. It does not seem necessary to decide between the claims of these various meanings, because the later may be seen to arise out of the primary by an entirely natural development of thought. The primary meaning would direct attention especially to the Upanishads, the philosophical speculations which *come at the end* of the ritual formulae and directions found in the Brāhmaṇas, or, more exactly, as a subsequent stage of the concentrated form in which these formulae appear in the Āraṇyakas. But these speculations, when the thought of their temporal sequence is transcended, might very well be taken as the essence of essence, the central doctrine, to express which—or to call forth the expression of which—was the aim or final purpose of the Veda. In the case of the individual pupil, also, what he learnt at the end of his course, what the Guru might communicate to him with a considerable air of secrecy and impressiveness in those days immediately preceding separation which have special significance for all masters and pupils, would naturally seem to be the most valuable of all the instructions given during the years of training and that for which the whole process had simply been an anticipation. To have introduced at an earlier stage distinctions of value between the various parts of the total body of instruction, distinctions, in other words, selective of certain truths as worthy of being raised to the rank of central dogmas, or even to have made the idea of such distinctions explicit at all, might not have been judicious, inasmuch as it might have led to a neglect on the part of the pupil of the necessary preparatory stages. But there is not the same difficulty if it is supposed that the distinction might have emerged according to the unconscious logic of events by which a situation only gradually yields up its full significance. And the historical process is not altogether different from the process as it goes on in the mind of an individual pupil. People in general are at first interested only in the succession of events and take them as they come; it is only later that their significance emerges and is realized. Thus whatever stands at the end of any process comes gradually to be regarded as containing the essential meaning of the process and as constituting the aim at which the whole process is directed. If, further, at any special period in the development this essential meaning is strikingly, even if unsystematically, set forth, the resulting situation will be that, during subsequent periods, the further interpretation of the central meaning will be the predominant concern of thinkers. Thus, by considering the matter along these lines, we can easily understand that the term Vedānta will cease to invite attention most of all to its temporal aspect and will come to indicate rather a purposeful and sustained endeavour to penetrate to the very depths of the mysteries alluded to in the earliest sacred books and to set forth the results of investigation in doctrinal statements possessing ever-increasing clearness, consistency, and comprehensiveness.

In the Vedānta, as well as in other Indian philosophies, we may notice a remarkable unity of development more closely knit than in Western philosophy. In connexion with the latter a conspicuous philosopher generally adopts the plan of enunciating a fairly complete system of thought. This may to a certain extent be elaborated by his immediate successors, but before very long the system as a whole is superseded by another system which may, indeed, grow out of its predecessor, but regards it rather as affording material for criticism than as possessing continuing authority. For the Western philosopher it is true that our little systems have their day and cease to be. On account of the fundamental similarities of human nature there will, of course, be repetitions of the old in the new, but such repetitions are not deliberate and in any case tend to be discouraged. In India the case is very different. Throughout the centuries a school of philosophy continues to be dominated by certain leading ideas, and free development, though it is not absent, is of comparatively subordinate importance. The Sūtra form of literature lent itself especially to this kind of combination of old and new according to which the old unmistakably controlled, although it did not entirely exclude, the new. As has been already indicated, the *Sūtras* were summaries for memory or notes for discussion, fully intelligible only to those who had taken part in the discussion. Inasmuch as they were *only* notes, a certain amount of freedom of treatment and therefore variation was possible, but the main lines of thought were dominatingly fixed by the *Sūtras* and by the more authoritative of the ancient teachers.[1] The newer teachers would not feel at liberty to depart from the *Sūtras* or to contradict the older teachers in regard to any important issue. Reinterpretation alone was possible, with the limited object of adjusting the traditional doctrines to opposing tendencies which had emerged at later dates or of introducing topics on which the earlier teachers had kept silence. It was of fundamental importance that authority should be maintained and tradition respected, and thus the philosophical task consisted to a large extent in the repetition and elaboration of earlier views.

Thus the unity of Eastern philosophy as compared with Western might be illustrated by the poetical unity of alliteration as contrasted with the less obvious but more organic unity of blank verse. Or, perhaps, in temporary disregard of the fact that it is maintained through centuries, the Indian unity might be compared to that of a single individual as he grows from infancy to manhood, in contrast with the unity of successive generations of men within a single system of national or racial development. Prof. S. N. Das Gupta points out with justice that 'it is not possible to write any history of *successive* [2] philosophies of India, but it is necessary that each system should be studied and interpreted in all the growth it has acquired through the successive ages of history from its conflicts with the rival systems. . . .' Earlier in the same paragraph, and perhaps with special reference to the Vedānta, he says: 'A system in the Sūtras is weak and helpless as a new-born babe, but if we take it along with its developments down to the beginning of the seventeenth century, it appears as a fully developed man, strong and harmonious in all its limbs.' [3]

It may easily, we think, be maintained that the Vedānta is the most important and most widely influential amongst Indian philosophies. Its 'boldness, depth, and subtlety of speculation,'[4] have attracted the attention of students everywhere, and it is fundamental in the thought of the simpler people. Other systems have arisen in opposition to it, have had temporary success,

[1] We may compare this with certain conditions which obtain in Indian music. The *rag*, which is a fixed form, dominates the structure of any new composition, but, nevertheless, allows considerable freedom for variation.

[2] Italics mine. [3] Das Gupta, I. 64. [4] *S.B.E.* XXXIV, p. xiv.

and have left their mark upon the body of Vedantic theory itself. But from the earliest dawn of antiquity to the present day the Vedānta has more than held its own. Max Müller claims that it is 'clearly the native philosophy of India'.[1] It may be claimed to be the first growth of philosophic thought upon the soil of India. Even in the Upanishads traces of other philosophies are few and far between, and in still earlier literature such indications are practically non-existent, whereas 'strictly Vedantic concepts meet us at every step in the Hymns, the Brāhmaṇas, the Āraṇyakas.'[2] More than sixty years ago Nehemiah Goreh could speak of other philosophies as having no adherents whilst the Vedānta was 'held by a large majority of Hindus'.[3] What was true then is still true to-day, provided that we look for signs of its prevalence not only in articulate philosophical expression, but in the more subtle thought and practice-forms which hold an often unacknowledged sway over the community.

Having referred briefly to the affiliations and importance of the Vedānta philosophy, we may now turn our attention to a fuller consideration of the emergence of the fundamental ideas in the earliest religious literature. The remainder of this chapter will be taken up mainly with the ideas in the Vedas which seem to be anticipatory of Vedantic doctrine.

The Vedas are regarded in India as of fundamental religious importance. According to one Indian writer, a man is an atheist if he disbelieves in the Vedas, but not necessarily so if he disbelieves in God. The dates of the books are variously stated. By strictly orthodox Brahmans they are regarded as eternal, but the word eternal may be modified so as to signify 'age-long', and the date of origin retracted only so far as the beginning of the present mundane age, i.e. to over one hundred billion years ago.[4] Even when only calculable periods are considered, there is great diversity of opinion. Tilak and Jacobi favour a very early date, not later than 3500 B.C., basing their conclusions both on astronomical data and on the normally observed slowness of development in India. Other scholars—Max Müller in a former generation and Professors Berriedale Keith and Hopkins at

[1] Müller, *S.S.* 115. [2] Ib. 115. [3] Goreh, 217.
[4] Cf. Griswold, 67; Das Gupta, 10.

the present day—favour dates between 1200 and 800 B.C. It cannot be said that there are sufficient data to enable us to reach a definite conclusion, and the matter can hardly be settled without further archaeological investigation and discovery. In any case we are concerned here not with minute details possibly affected by conclusions as to dates, but with certain broad tendencies which prepare the way for the leading conceptions of the Vedānta. We shall confine our attention chiefly to the *Ṛigveda*.

The religion of the Veda is for the most part one of light and joyousness, an expression of the trustfulness succeeding to the unreasoning terror of evil spirits which is a frequent accompaniment of animistic religion. The terrors of the darkness have been forgotten as by a child awakening to the light of the morning and to the presence of protecting friends. The benignant forces of nature are relied upon to triumph over the destructive; and, if occasionally malignant demons should appear, there are assuredly forces in nature of sufficient potency to overcome them and ready to assist those who are careful to worship in the appointed way. The attitude in general is one of simple trustfulness and rather easily satisfied materialism. 'Lead thou us, O Agni, to increasing riches.'[1] 'O Uṣas, waken up for me the sounds of joy, send us the riches of the great,'[2] are amongst the characteristic prayers. The ethical sense cannot be said to be very fully developed. What is uppermost in the mind of the worshipper is omission or error in sacrificial ceremony rather than a consciousness of sin. In the hymns addressed to Varuṇa, indeed, there is much searching of heart and frequent confession of sin, but this deity hardly maintained a place of supremacy in the Vedic pantheon, and in any case the sins confessed are ceremonial rather than moral, sins of ignorance rather than sins of wilfulness, social rather than personal.[3] 'In whatever way we have sinned against the gods, in whatever manner we have *through ignorance neglected thy work*, Oh, do not destroy us for these sins' and again, 'O Varuṇa, deliver us from the sins of our fathers.'

The gods who are worshipped belong to the three regions of the heavens, the air, and the earth. In Dyaus, the earliest of the

[1] *Ṛigveda*, I. 13. [2] Ib. 48. 1. [3] Cf. ib. VII. 89. 5.

gods, there is indicated a slight personification of the sky, and this is carried farther in relation to the other gods of the same region, e.g. Varuṇa, the source of steadfastness, all-seeing, following the flight of 'the birds that fly through the heaven', 'sovran of the sea, and knowing the ships that are thereon'. To Uṣas, the radiant goddess of the dawn, as she awakens the joy of the morning and puts to flight the terrors of darkness, many hymns of great beauty are addressed. Viṣṇu also appears in this group of gods, but holds a comparatively subordinate place amongst the Vedic gods generally. Amongst the gods of the atmosphere, or middle region, Indra, almost entirely beneficent in his activities although later to become the god of war, and Rudra, the terrible one, the god of the thunderbolt, are the most important, and they are surrounded by a crowd of minor deities, such as the Maruts, or storm-gods, Vāta, the god of the wind, and Parjanya, the god of the rain-cloud.

The chief deities of the earth are Agni, Soma, and Yama. Agni is the god of the sacrificial fire, and is described as the youngest of the gods, because he is born anew whenever the sacrificial fire is lit. He is perhaps not strictly an earth-god, as he has also easily intelligible affinities with the air and the sky and with their typical deities, Indra and Sūrya. The magical and medicinal qualities of the *soma* plant supply the characteristics of the god of this name. Personification is perhaps carried farthest of all in connexion with Yama, the god of death. Only later does he become an altogether sombre deity. In the *Ṛigveda* he is the pioneer of the path to the world beyond; and, although the approach to him is made difficult by reason of many perils, and he himself appears at times to be jealous of human aspirations after immortality, he is, on the whole, a kindly dispenser of bliss in the realms of the departed.

But what is of most importance for our present purpose is the evidence we may gather from the Veda of that growing conception of unity, joined perhaps with a tendency in a negative direction, which we may take as a definite anticipation of the subsequent general trend of Indian thought. In this connexion we may recall the differences already noted between Greek and Indian thought—the contentment of the latter with vagueness as contrasted with the definite personifications of the former.

The gods of the Veda had the indefiniteness of the natural forces with which they were associated, rather than clearly distinguishable characters. Thus their functions are easily interchangeable, and it becomes possible that the individual gods, instead of distributively representing each a particular quality, may represent groups of qualities several of which they possess in common. Then, by an unconscious process of generalization, the view will be entertained that the gods, seeing that they possess common qualities, are one in essence. Attention will gradually be directed beyond the particularity of the gods towards this essence and especially towards that god who is supposed to embody it most completely. One god will thus become supreme in the consciousness of the worshipper, not with the permanent primacy of a definite hierarchy, nor even with the temporary priority which is indicated by the term *henotheism*. We hesitate to accept unreservedly this favourite term of Max Müller, because it seems to suggest too definitely a comparison of the god selected with other gods who are deliberately disregarded, whereas the true state of the matter seems to be that the nature-form which occupies strikingly the centre of consciousness also occupies more or less vaguely the whole field of consciousness, and the other gods are not simply assigned to a lower rank but left out of account altogether.

But what we wish to emphasize is the earnestness and at the same time the vagueness of the religious search after unity. Dissatisfaction with sheer particularity is manifested in various ways. As already indicated, the gods are grouped into three roughly defined classes, and certain of them, such as Agni, are regarded as having affinity with all three classes. Further, the physical immensity of the deities worshipped, as, e.g., the sky and the air, will tend to strengthen the feeling of all-pervadingness and universality. Conceptions, such as that of the All-gods, the gods taken collectively, the 'fellowship of gods',[1] 'the heavenly folk',[2] will be laid hold of to break down the barriers of particularity. Also, general creative activity may be personified, as in connexion with Prajāpati, and another creative deity called Viśvakarman. In association with the latter there is developed an interesting distinction between efficient and

[1] Cf. *Ṛigveda*, VII. 35. 11. [2] Ib. X. 57. 5.

material cause, and men are found to be beginning to concern themselves with the original material (corresponding roughly to the Greek 'hyle') out of which the 'sole God' has fashioned the earth and the heaven, or with the more poetical form of the question, 'Whereon he stood when he established all things.'[1]

Perhaps in studying the idea of sacrifice we may reach a fuller appreciation of the Vedic conception of the underlying unity of all things. We have to attempt to replace ourselves in that mental attitude which was, e.g., at the back of the mystery religions in the centuries immediately preceding the Christian era, when the distinction which we moderns make between inner and outer, between symbol and fact, was less definite, and when, sensed in a mystical mood, 'the things of earth are in sympathy with the things of heaven.'[2] The sacrifice has to be viewed in its entirety, as an intricate ritualistic system of devices, every detail of which has to be followed with the most scrupulous attention, but which, when properly manipulated, affords the worshipper the opportunity of increasing the hidden forces of the world—what Oldenberg calls the 'zauberfluidum' and of 'tapping' them for his own advantage or that of his society. The sacrifice is—to adopt a Vedic metaphor—'the thread spun out to reach the gods', 'drawn out with threads on every side, the man extends it, and the man unbinds it; even to the vault of heaven hath he outspun it'.[3] What the worshipper gives to the priest may be conceived as having or acquiring independent value and as added to the fundamental reality of the world. We are not even to regard it as offered to the gods to propitiate them. It is rather a latent power which is older and deeper in the heart of things than the gods themselves, and the latter are invoked only that the sum of conditions may be completed which is necessary for the efficacy of the sacrifice. If all the rules are meticulously followed, the results of the sacrifice will emerge by necessary law, and in this conception of inescapable consequences we may perhaps find the germ of that idea of *Ṛita*,[4] or order of the universe, which again becomes

[1] Ib. 81. 4.

[2] Cumont, *Mysticisme Astral*, 242, quoted in Angus, *The Mystery Religions and Christianity*.

[3] *Ṛigveda*, X. 130. 1.

[4] Prof. Keith holds that *ṛita* originally meant the *physical order* of the universe. Cf. his *Religion and Philosophy of the Veda*, 85.

the foundation of the doctrine of Karma, so important in subsequent Indian philosophy. The conception of an underlying mysterious force or essence is also deepened metaphysically, and may not unjustifiably be taken as reappearing in the belief in the *purusha*, the mighty giant who submits to the dismemberment of himself for the sake of the production of the world. Here the sacrifice has become not merely a means of access to the constitutive principle of the universe, but itself that principle. Through the operation of a sacrificial act the world is evolved, and therefore sacrifice is fundamental.

We may gain some light also upon the subjectivity and idealism which are characteristic of later Indian thought if we turn back again from the ritual of the sacrifice to the attitude of the worshipper towards it. We must avoid mechanizing the ritual to such an extent as to detach it altogether from the subjective devotion which seeks to find expression in it, or from the fundamental sense of being in the presence of that *mysterium tremendum* of which Prof. Otto speaks. If we seek to understand the aspiration of the worshipper, we may conceive it as having at first almost a physical basis, showing itself in that agitated outbreathing which is the accompaniment of great emotion and which some modern psychologists have so closely identified with the actual emotion. The breath may be quite simply considered as dispersing and losing itself in the wider atmosphere of the external environment; and, if we can take the further step of imagining the breath as becoming articulate in prayer and can at the same time keep in mind the extremely faint line of demarcation in early thought between the physical and the psychical or spiritual, we shall find ourselves almost in a position to grasp the idea of the transition by which prayer comes to be regarded as having efficacy in the objective world and as being itself a phase of the fundamental reality of that world. Are we not here also almost within sight of the original underlying conception which may serve to unite the various meanings assigned to the word *Brahma*? The breath of aspiration which becomes vocal in the spells and incantations of the priests and the chants of the singers and finds symbolic expression in some of the material of the ritual, such as the smoke of the sacrificial fire, is discovered also to be not alien to the spirit of man, but of the same substance and character with that spirit. We may see here further the earliest conditions of the emergence of the idea of the *Ātman*, in its meaning of the 'vital breath' of man, which has at the same time the closest connexion with the innermost essence of the objective external world.[1] We do not think it unreasonable to suggest that such fused and confused conceptions as these may be the earliest sources from which some of the fundamental ideas of Indian philosophy have emerged and in course of time become gradually crystallized.

In more immediate connexion with our present subject we must take account also of what might be described as a process of internalizing the sacrifice. The conception of *tapas* appears occasionally in the *Ṛigveda*. Later on it attracted to itself the idea of mortification or penance, but here it has little more significance than 'fervour' or 'heat', suggesting the sacrifice of devotion which goes on internally and at the same time its kinship with that power of heat by which the Primal Being generated the objective world. However slightly spiritual the conception may be, it at least serves to turn the attention inwards as well as outwards and to hint at a dawning consciousness that the soul of man may be as important an element in ultimate reality as the underlying forces of the external world. We are encouraged at least to an interpretative use of this psychophysical conception, and prepared, in however slight a degree, for the idea that at the root of existence there is something more than the merely material and that the ultimate essence of the universe may have a spiritual aspect. In view of all this it will seem in no way strange that in the *Ṛigveda* we should come across such a flight of metaphysical speculation as is to be found in Book X, 129. 4:

> Within it at first arose Desire,
> Which was the primal seed of mind;
> The root of Being in non-Being Sages
> Searching by wisdom in the heart discovered.[2]

We may also trace the beginnings of a conception of the intrinsic value of knowledge, arising probably out of the idea that the knowledge of the ritual of the sacrifice is of supreme

[1] Cf. Das Gupta, 26.

[2] Prof. P. D. Shastri's translation.

importance as giving access to and control over the mysterious essence of reality. We are here on the lines of an advance to the fuller idea that knowledge itself may constitute reality; and, when the content of the effective knowledge is also taken account of, there emerges the notion of a law or principle hidden beneath the immediate appearances of things. Beneath Being there is something which is not-Being in the ordinary sense of the word, inasmuch as it is not the product of merely ordinary experience. Here there is at least the beginning of a negative procedure of thought. We describe the fundamental reality in negative terms so long as we are looking at it from the empirical point of view, and beside this negation there is the still more significant consciousness that, though we call the ultimate reality non-Being, yet just because it is fundamental, it is also Being in a far more satisfying sense than the ordinary Being of which we are aware in our usual experience. This tendency towards negation as well as towards unity in Vedic thought deserves further consideration by reason of its later importance. Prof. B. K. Shastri points out with emphasis that the fundamental contrast between the Vedic and the Upanishadic attitude to life was that, whereas the former was positive and held to the idea that life was to be lived, the latter was negative and had arrived at the consciousness that 'life must pass through a phase of *no life* to reach fuller life'.[1] Whence has come this change from the earlier joyous positive of Vedic times? Perhaps one reason may lie just in the subjective effect of this growing sense of unity amongst the gods to which we have referred. As the gods worshipped became fewer in number and at the same time more overwhelming by the immensity and extent of their power, the worshippers would inevitably feel farther separated from their deities. Correspondingly, as the world became more rationalized, it would seem to the simpler minds to be emptier of friendly intimate powers, and therefore less desirable—something to be negated. Further, in the attitude to sacrifice which we have attempted to describe, a hint of negative tendency may be discovered. With the associated magic and incantation there is closely connected the idea of ecstasy, of being caught up into a mystical excitement, and of being, therefore, detached

[1] B. K. Shastri, p. xii.

from the ordinary world. In order to participate, through the sacrifice or other ritual, in the fundamental reality, sometimes conceived of as a semi-magical, almost physical, fluid, the worshipper is led to depress his faculties as a whole or sacrifice the higher to the lower. The ascetic and orgiastic worshipper is the best magician, if not the best mystic. But if we depress our *higher* faculties, it is exceedingly natural to go farther and learn to depreciate or negate our experience as a whole. And to this may be added, on the one hand, that growing consciousness of the complexity and distressfulness of human life with which the dawning—only the faintest dawning, we admit—of the idea of transmigration may have had something to do; and, on the other hand, that disappointment of childlike trust in the first appearances of things which is the inevitable accompaniment of the natural development of the human mind. It does not take long anywhere for men to learn that the mystery of reality lies deeper than the grasp of our senses. An unmistakably vivid consciousness of negation is close at hand, whenever reflection emerges, and the speculations to which we have already referred in connexion with the *Ṛigveda*, X. 129, are but the metaphysical aspect of a more popular and universal tendency.

There seem, therefore, to be in the *Ṛigveda* evidences of a tendency towards unity and of an inclination towards negation, sufficient to justify us in finding in the earliest sacred books at least the germs of what were afterwards to be the fundamental ideas of the Vedānta philosophy. It is not necessary to consider the other Vedas to any great extent. The *Sāmaveda* and the *Yajurveda* are for the most part derivative from the *Ṛigveda*. The *Atharvaveda* belongs to a lower level of thought and is rather outside of the main stream of development, although it is not without influence even upon the Upanishads.[1] Its authors, for the most part, inhabit a world of magic and incantation. The great gods have gone from it, and the smaller gods have arrived in the guise of a horde of capricious spirits who require to be placated by the constant performance of intricate rites, which rites themselves are found gradually to be acquiring value as independent forces of the hidden world.

[1] Cf. Prof. Ranade, *Indian Philosophical Quarterly*, I. 4 and *Das Licht vom Osten*, 4.

Sin has dropped from the moral to the physical or magical level. It may attach to a man without his consent after the manner of a contagious disease, and the remedy for it is degraded to the same level and consists mainly of magical devices. As Bloomfield says: 'The notion of expiation extends also to circumstances inherent or accidental, which cannot and do not involve personal responsibility. Expiation assumes the character of cure or correction of inauspicious conditions and accidents.'[1]

It is interesting to observe that in the description of the *vrātya*, or wanderer, found in the fifteenth book of the *Atharvaveda*, Prof. Hauer sees a foreshadowing of the negative attitude and magical claims of the later Yogi, and these may be placed over against a certain philosophical background, however vague and shadowy this may be. The Vrātya, who 'seems to be a kind of Brahmacārin, or, at any rate, one who has entered the Brahmanical community after having been converted from an Aryan but non-Brahmanical tribe',[2] manifests a desire to enter into unity with the original ground of things through ascetic ecstasy and a negation of ordinary experience; and at the same time the claim is made that through magical practices supernatural power may be obtained, and the influence of the soul of the worshipper be extended to the confines of the world.[3] We find also a more elevated, but still very dim, conception of Brahma as the prayer of the worshipper and at the same time the supreme principle of the world.[4] It will therefore not be out of place to suggest that in the *Atharvaveda*, as well as in the *Ṛigveda*, there are indications of that consciousness of fundamental unity, combined with a negative attitude to ordinary experience, which we have already noted in connexion with the earlier book, and which was to become dominant in later thought. To the further development of these ideas in the Upanishads and succeeding literature we shall turn in the next chapter.

[1] Bloomfield, *Atharva Veda*, 84.
[2] Ib. 94.
[3] Cf. Hauer, in *Das Licht vom Osten*, 56.
[4] *Atharvaveda*, V. 1.

II

ANTICIPATIONS OF VEDANTIC IDEAS IN THE UPANISHADS, THE VEDĀNTA SŪTRAS, THE GĪTĀ, AND GAUḌAPĀDA'S KĀRIKĀS

IN this chapter we pass to a further stage in Indian thought, at which the development of the fundamental Vedantic ideas (especially those of a consciousness of ultimate unity and an apparent necessity for negation in the search after it) becomes much fuller and more impressive. It is difficult, if not impossible, to treat of the Upanishads in separation from the Sūtras, in which they were summarized—and some would say transformed—and also the Commentaries in which they were amplified and interpreted. They have been described as the kernel of the whole of Post-Vedic Indian philosophy, and it is proverbially difficult to separate the kernel from the remainder of the fruit. Further, the Upanishads have not self-subsistency in the sense that they present us with a clear-cut and definite system of thought which may stand separate examination. From the philosophical point of view they contain anticipations rather than completions of doctrine; they are inspirational rather than dogmatic. Their aim, as Prof. Radhakrishnan says, is 'not so much to reach philosophic truth as to bring peace and freedom to the anxious human spirit'.[1] They make no claim to independence or definiteness or coherence, and therefore surrender themselves easily and unresistingly to later summarizing or expositional treatment. Yet we must not on this account presume to undervalue their importance. They occupy a central position in the history of Indian philosophy. Not only do they, as we have seen, provide materials for future development, but they link themselves closely with the past and gather up its wisdom. They carry forward the tendencies and expound the implicit doctrines discoverable in the Vedic Hymns, and by no means break continuity altogether with the Brāhmaṇas, although they adopt a remarkably free attitude to the authority of the ancient scriptures in general, and undeniably break fresh ground. They mark a transition from ritualistic and physical to philosophical and psychical

[1] Radhakrishnan, I. 138.

categories. As Prof. Das Gupta says: 'The passage of the Indian mind from the Brahmanic to the Upanishad thought is probably the most remarkable event in the history of philosophic thought.'[1] On the whole it may be said that their significance is more prospective than retrospective, and it is important for our present purpose to note that, while they are not without influence upon all phases of Indian philosophical thought, and also supply intellectual inspiration to popular religion and to sects both high and low, they have a closer relation to the Vedānta than to any other school of thought. Indeed they are frequently regarded as containing the essence of the Vedānta, although frequently, as we have seen, the term Vedānta has both a narrower and a wider interpretation. And in connexion with the claim of the later Commentaries to constitute the special basis of the Vedānta, we may notice that the occupation of the commentators would be largely gone, had not the Upanishads supplied them with material for their discussions and a point of departure for their speculations. It may be added also that in the Upanishads themselves the name Vedānta is used as indicative of the philosophy contained in them.[2]

The fundamental meaning of the name Upanishad seems to be derived from the root *sad*, 'to sit,' and *upa*, 'near,' with the prefix, *ni*, having adverbial and intensive significance; the whole combination thus yielding the idea of 'sitting very near' to the teacher and listening intently and respectfully to him. From this it is easy to pass to the idea of the *doctrine* conveyed by the teacher; and when we take account also of the generally esoteric tendency of the teaching and the exclusive character of the audience, we arrive at the resultant meaning of 'secret doctrine'. Śaṅkara, however, in his introduction to the *Taittirīya Upanishad*, gives an interpretation which has special significance in relation to the character of his philosophy. He favours a derivation from the root *sad*, 'to destroy,' although he does not altogether abandon the idea of 'nearness' or 'approach'. His meaning apparently is that the doctrine would destroy ignorance and thus open the way of approach to God. In general, however, the conception of 'secret doctrine' would seem to correspond to the most common use of the term.

[1] Das Gupta, 31.

[2] Cf. Farquhar, 60.

According to tradition, an enormous number of Upanishads was at one time or other in existence. Weber suggests as many as 250, but Prof. Radhakrishnan is content with the more modest number of 108. For our purposes we may confine our attention mainly to the eleven which were commented on by Śaṅkara. These were the *Aitareya*, *Taittirīya*, *Chhāndogya*, *Bṛihadāraṇyaka*, *Kena*, *Kāṭhaka*, *Īśā*, *Muṇḍaka*, *Śvetāśvatara*, *Praśna*, and *Māṇḍūkya*. But in addition to these, account should also be taken of the *Kaushītaki*, the *Mahāṇārāyaṇa*, and the *Maitrāyaṇa*. The oldest and most authoritative Upanishads are in prose, and are pre-Buddhistic and non-sectarian. The earliest group, composed of the *Aitareya*, the *Kaushītaki*, the *Chhāndogya*, the *Kena*, the *Taittirīya*, and the *Bṛihadāraṇyaka*, were probably in existence by 500 B.C. They are linked very closely to the Brāhmaṇas, but arrive definitely at a philosophical point of view and are indeed more purely speculative than some of the later treatises. Within this group Deussen is inclined to assign temporal priority to the *Bṛihadāraṇyaka* and the *Chhāndogya*. The second group consists of the *Kāṭhaka*, the *Īśā*, the *Śvetāśvatara*, the *Muṇḍaka*, and the *Mahānārāyaṇa*; and the period covered by them is from 500 B.C. to the middle of the third century B.C. There are tendencies in a theistic direction, and emphasis is laid upon the importance of Viṣṇu and Śiva. Brāhmans appear to have a supremacy to which they had not attained at the period of the earlier works; and, in general, caste distinctions are more rigidly drawn. Greater stress also is laid upon the practice of Yoga, asceticism, and self-discipline. The *Śvetāśvatara*, in particular, contains references to the emergence of philosophical schools, and makes use of the technical terms and characteristic doctrines of these schools. To the third group may be assigned the *Praśna*, the *Maitrāyaṇa*, and the *Māṇḍūkya*. The *Maitrāyaṇa* seems to be contemporary with the earlier form of the *Gītā*, and may be placed in the second century A.D. It contains references to the Sāṅkhya and Yoga philosophies, and its tone is profoundly pessimistic. The *Praśna* is slightly earlier and the *Māṇḍūkya* slightly later than the *Maitrāyaṇa*.[1]

[1] Prof. Ranade has recently investigated the problem of Upanishad chronology and places the whole of the Upanishad development between

As we consider the transition from the Vedas to the Upanishads, we may refer again to the tendency referred to in the last chapter which indicates a background of growingly sombre character. A full sense of the gravity of the problems which have to be dealt with has been developed, although it is only with difficulty and very gradually that these problems come to be treated from a purely philosophical point of view. The heart is still not sufficiently at leisure from itself to permit of the calmness and detachment necessary for pure speculation. Deliverance rather than salvation is the end aimed at, and the remedy for the ills of life is sought in religion rather than in philosophy.

The religion of the Vedas was predominantly joyous, but by the time we reach the Upanishads, the sky has become overshadowed. We have already indicated in the last chapter some reasons for the change. We have seen that the tendency away from polytheism in the direction of pantheistic unity may have deepened the shadows which lay upon life. The kindly and familiar deities had withdrawn themselves from the world, and their erstwhile worshippers felt lonely in the midst of the physical immensities which had served to develop and strengthen the sense of unity.

On the other cause to which we referred in passing, a little more may be said. The transmigration theory was gradually introduced into India during this period, probably, though not certainly, from alien sources. At first the doctrine would seem to satisfy the desire for persistence and would have a comforting effect as a relief from the fear that death might be the final end. But, as the negative tendency grew stronger, and other causes still to be mentioned contributed to this strengthening, and consequently the ideas of escape and deliverance came more and more to occupy the centre of consciousness, these ideas

1200 and 600 B.C. He divides the principal Upanishads into the following five groups, with a rough, but by no means strict, chronological sequence:

I. *Bṛihadāraṇyaka* and *Chhāndogya*.
II. *Īśā* and *Kena*.
III. *Aitareya*, *Taittirīya*, and *Kaushītaki*.
IV. *Kāṭhaka*, *Muṇḍaka*, and *Māṇḍūkya*.
V. *Praśna*, *Maitrāyaṇa*, and *Māṇḍūkya*.

Cf. 'The Background of Upanishadic Philosophy', in the *Philosophical Quarterly*, Vol. I, p. 5.

would again find reinforcement in the thought of a succession of lives. Continuance of existence under such conditions would simply be an additional source of misery. Escape becomes a more difficult and more hopeless problem when a practically unending series of lives has to be reckoned with; and the pessimism which has attached itself to the experiences of a single life becomes infinitely increased.

Various other causes, not of course peculiar to India, may have contributed to the darkening of the background. The deadening effect of despotism, with its accompanying depressing contrasts between wealth and poverty, came to be obvious causes at a later period, and there may have been anticipations of such conditions even in the centuries under review. The effect of the climate of the plains of India may also be noted. As the number of centuries increased which separated the Aryan settlers from the period of their immigration, the lassitude engendered by sub-tropical conditions may have diminished their zest for life, may have induced a mood of passive acquiescence rather than of struggle, and disposed them in general to seek for deliverance rather than victory.

Throughout the Upanishads we find indications of this sombre background, and indications of a perplexed, almost pathetic, yearning after deliverance. In the *Kāṭhaka Upanishad*[1] we are told that 'the wise man ceases to *grieve* when he knows the distinction of the Self from the senses'. Human experience is found to be of a fleeting and unsatisfactory character, predominantly painful. It is repeatedly suggested that the state we are to flee from is one of misery, and the object of our striving is to free ourselves from old age or death or grief. 'There is no bliss in anything finite.'[2]

In drawing attention to this pessimistic background we are not, of course, forgetful of the general consideration that it is in a 'divine discontent' and a dissatisfaction with the actual that all philosophy originates. If, however, the preliminary view of the problems to be solved is excessively gloomy, this frequently exercises a demoralizing influence upon the solutions arrived at. Philosophy comes to be regarded as providing a means of release rather than a system of constructive thought. Instead

[1] II. 6. 7.

[2] Cf. *Chhāndogya U.* VII. 26. 1.

of being occupied with a patient investigation of the world which has presented the problems, attention is diverted from this world, and the rapidity with which a solution can be arrived at becomes all-important. The mind is thus left with insufficient freedom for pure and independent speculation, and, under the urgent influence of religious motives and practical needs, arguments are accepted which are admittedly not cogent from an intellectual point of view. Under the influence of the idea of escape, recourse may be had, e.g., to the doctrine of two orders of knowledge, so related that instead of the lower order gradually yielding up its problems and contradictions for solution on the higher plane, a quick transition is permitted from the one to the other, with consequences that are disastrous to philosophical consistency. Dr. Hauer definitely finds in causes of this sort one explanation of the negative character of Upanishad philosophy. He holds that, if the identification of the human soul with the world-principle had been purely metaphysical, this would have led to an affirmatory spiritualizing of the world. But this, however, has been expressed only occasionally in the Upanishads, and for the most part the religio-mystical attitude has led to that denial of the world which was an anticipation or accompaniment of Buddhistic negation. If the sense of need had not been so clamant and urgent, the character of the solution would probably have been different.[1]

On the other hand, while it seems necessary to stress in some degree the pessimistic character of the primary attitude, we must not overlook an actual and vigorous speculative interest. The Upanishads are dominated by a sense of a mystery which is attractive as well as terrifying, and by an intense desire to penetrate this mystery. Intellectual curiosity is a strong motive alongside of the desire for deliverance. 'Tell us what there is in the great hereafter,' says Nachicetas in the *Kāṭhaka Upanishad*,[2] and one of the searchers after truth in the *Chhāndogya Upanishad* is asked whether he has 'sought for the instruction by which the Unheard becomes heard, the Unintelligible intelligible, and the Unknown known'.[3] In the same Upanishad one of the teachers

[1] Cf. Hauer, in *Das Licht vom Osten*, 91.

[2] I. 1. 29.

[3] VI. 2. 5.

is said to have shown his pupil 'the back of the other side of darkness',[1] and the oft-repeated refrain of the *Bṛihadāraṇyaka Upanishad*, indicative of the spirit of the Upanishads as a whole, is 'Lead me from darkness into light, from the unreal to the Real'.

The very name 'Upanishad', if we adopt the prevailing interpretation, indicates a tendency to speculative construction. Further, the state from which deliverance is sought is described in an intellectual manner, not merely as a state of misery but as a state of error. The inquiries of which the results are set forth are, moreover, undertaken at a period of life when the active duties of the householder are supposed to be completed, and the seeker after truth is no longer disturbed by the cares of the world and is free to enter upon a period of quiet contemplation and study of the ultimate mysteries. Also it has to be remembered that, at the period of the great Upanishads, there was, perhaps, greater freedom from the bonds of traditional authority than at any other period in the history of Indian thought. The authority of the Vedas was still strong, but it was not so excessive as to necessitate a purely scholastic procedure and an incessant repetition of traditional ideas.

The Upanishads link themselves to previous thought through their great interest in the mysteries and power of the sacrifice, in the consideration of which we have found one of the earliest hints of a sense of underlying unity. In the sacrifice the worshipper feels himself to be in contact with the hidden forces of the world, with the power which is even more fundamental than the power of the gods. The Upanishads lay increased emphasis upon the monistic suggestions which are here involved, but make a more definite and more sustained transition from the external to the internal, and from the objective to the subjective. They lay hold upon such suggestions as we find in *Ṛigveda*, I. 164. 4, 'Where was the vital breath, the blood, the Self (Ātman) of the world?' They place full stress upon the double implication, both physical and spiritual, contained in the notions of *Brahman* and *Ātman*, and upon the internalizing of the sacrifice through the help of the conception of *tapas*. Indeed

[1] VII. 26. 2.

the possible identification of *Brahman* and *Ātman* becomes almost a central principle of investigation and the tendency in the direction of a negation of anything that hinders this identification is discovered to be greatly strengthened. The two main aspects of Upanishad thought may indeed be stated as (1) a negative movement towards a denial of the particularity of the world of our ordinary experience, and (2) a more positive movement towards the identification of the human spirit and the divine, governed by the hope of reaching an absolute unity. It is impossible, however, to separate these two movements, save for the temporary purposes of exposition.

We have found the germ of a negative movement in the Vedas, perhaps especially in the hardly more than physical idea of a participation in a semi-magical fluid. When transferred to the subjective side of the relationship, and plunged in a psychical atmosphere of ecstasy, this same tendency reappears in the depression of faculties usually regarded as higher, so that the emotional aspiration which remains may obtain contact with the physical hidden energy. But, as we have seen, the denial of the higher activities, which is thus suggested and encouraged, may very easily extend to a depreciation of our powers of ordinary experience in general, and it is by no means easy to eradicate this negative tendency when once it has manifested itself.

We have already hinted at some of the probable causes of the transition from the outer to the inner. We have noted the growing importance even in the Vedas of a *knowledge* of the sacrifice. It was thought to be exceedingly dangerous to make any mistake in the performance of the elaborate ritual, and, consequently, meticulously exact knowledge was regarded as placing enormous power in the hands of those who had acquired it. Emphasis was transferred from the action performed in the sacrifice to knowledge of how to perform it. Further, there was a tendency in the direction of identifying the knower with that which he knew. The subjective consciousness of the priest would thus be conceived of as having effective contact with the mysterious power of the sacrifice with which he had to deal; and the question would naturally arise as to whether the fundamental power or essence of things might not be found in consciousness just as well as in the objects with which it was so intimately connected.[1]

But when attention is thus directed internally to consciousness, it is important that this should be left as simple and untrammelled as possible. If it is felt as a power, its effectiveness must not be allowed to be unduly distributed. The immediate data of the senses, with their resulting disturbing intrusions of objects in space and time, must not be allowed to distract us. If we are to reach the fontal unity, we must attempt to crush together the details of the world, so that, coalescing, they may fit into this unity. Differences of value must be disregarded, and things of both higher and lower importance must be negated. He who thinks is one, and therefore the victory must remain with unity.[2]

All change and all associated plurality must be regarded as a matter of 'names and forms'. By the medieval nominalists of Europe names were held to give fictitious reality to general notions; but in the Upanishads it is to individual objects that they give this fictitious support. We need not at this stage stop to inquire into the degree of fictitiousness thus involved. It is sufficient to say that naming is the other side of an individualizing tendency the effect of which is unreal if the individuals thus constituted are taken as separate from the whole, but which may have a certain amount of justification if the unity of the whole is at the same time firmly grasped. The attainment of the conception of the merely nominal character of particulars ought, however, at least to have the result of diminishing our interest in these particulars, decreasing our centrifugal desires, and thus contributing to our peace of mind and subjective sense of unity.

It comes to this, that if we are to deny the world we must have some metaphysical justification for so doing. The world as a whole cannot properly be denied unless it is found to be of an illusory character. As we shall see later, it is not easy to decide how far the Upanishads themselves can be taken to support a doctrine of illusoriness, but there are at least anticipations of the conception of *māyā*. In the *Śvetāśvatara Upanishad*,[3] e.g., we read, 'The one God regulates nature and the Self. By meditating on Him the world-illusion is completely removed.'

[1] Cf. Hauer, *op. cit.*, 86. [2] Cf. *Māṇḍūkya U.* II. 25. [3] I. 10.

Our deliverance is wrought through the destruction of our ignorance, by rising from *aparā vidyā* (lower knowledge) to *parā vidya* (higher knowledge), and we can reach the best understanding of the position if we formulate the conception that the term *avidyā* (ignorance) may be applied not only to the mistaken mental attitude of the knower, but also to what is known. It involves not only the negative idea usually associated with ignorance, but also the more positive idea of 'false knowledge'; in other words, it includes not only empirical ignorance but empirical knowledge.

From this the transition is easy to regarding *avidyā* as a cosmical principle. It becomes the source not only of our belief in an ordinary world but of the ordinary world in which we believe. The world of ordinary experience is explained by a principle which suggests a negative way of dealing with this world, and, consequently, a depreciatory valuation of it. And this cosmic principle gains metaphysical importance by being more or less vaguely related to God. The *Śvetāśvatara Upanishad* describes it as 'the own power of God concealed by its emanation'.[1] The exact relation of this cosmic power to God and the metaphysical standing of its products give rise to some of the most important problems of later Vedantic philosophy. The central problem is just whether the things of the ordinary world are altogether to be deprived of reality, or whether only their particularity is to be denied. But whatever conclusion may later be arrived at, we may agree that there is in any case sufficient opportunity for such denial or depreciation as will afford a discipline preparatory for the second phase of the Upanishad philosophical movement, viz. the identification of the Self of the individual and the Self of the Universe; and to this we must now turn.

The principle of procedure is that in discovering the deepest nature of our own selves, we shall also discover the fundamental nature of the universe. 'The light which shines above the heaven, higher than all, higher than everything, beyond which there are no other worlds, that is the same light which is within man.'[2] All our difficulties, both theoretical and practical, come from our failure to reach this identification, and the attainment of it ought to be the object of all our searching. Here is the

[1] I. 5. [2] *Chhāndogya U.* III. 15. 7.

secret of the universe, and here is the foundation of our peace. 'He who knows Brahman is Brahman.' 'That which is that subtle essence (the root of all) in it all that exists has its self. It is the True. It is the Self, and thou, O Svetaketu, art it.' [1]

The fundamental formula is *tat tvaṁ asi*—'That Thou art'—a formula which expresses succinctly the equation of the individual self with the Universe, and of the Universe with the Self in the highest sense, the result being a pure undifferenced unity, or, at least, a unity in regard to which all differences are on the point of being transcended. Another formula with much the same meaning is *ahaṁ Brahma asmi*, 'I am Brahman.'

Sometimes the formula has been mistakenly compared to the Greek *γνῶθι σεαυτόν*, but we must carefully notice that while the Greek formula may inculcate a thorough study of the nature of the individual self, the Upanishad formula is concerned with the conception that the true self of each individual, when thoroughly known, is discovered to be not at all individual. As soon as we reach the essence of the individual self, the equation of it to the universal Self, and the identification of Ātman and Brahman, is found to be inevitable. The two terms are recognized as reciprocal. Probably the interpretation of their relation afterwards adopted by Śaṅkara may be accepted also as giving a true account of the Upanishad position. 'Brahman', he says, 'denotes the term to be defined (*viśeshyam*) and Ātman that which defines it (*viśeshaṇan*), that by Brahman the limitation implied in Ātman is removed, and by Ātman the conception of Brahman as an (external) divinity to be worshipped is condemned.' [2] Dr. Hauer of Tübingen takes much the same view. 'Thus came about the mingling of the two ideas, to the advantage of both. Brahman becomes wholly dissociated from the realm of the magical, and the Ātman attains infinity.' [3]

We reach this identification by passing through various stages, and we may first of all trace the process as it takes place in the experience of the individual who is striving to reach the inner essence of his soul. The exposition may be based on *Chhāndogya Upanishad* VIII. We are first asked to consider

[1] *Chhāndogya U.* VI. 8. 7. Cf. also VI. 9. 4; VI. 10. 3, &c.

[2] Cf. Śaṅkara's Commentary on the *Chhāndogya U.*, reproduced in Deussen, *P. U.* 86.

[3] *Op. cit.*, p. 91.

the stage of ordinary waking life, and Prajāpati, in conversation with Indra, explains that the Self is 'the person who is seen in the eye', i.e. the ordinary bodily or material self (Vaiśvanara) dwelling in a cosmical environment to which the name Virāṭ is given. Indra, however, is not satisfied with this explanation, and his attention is next turned to the dreaming state, in which only the mind is active, in more or less complete independence of the body. To this corresponds the cosmical world-power, Hiraṇyagarbha, or soul of the world. We should notice here the complete reversal of our usual experience; as a rule we put the waking state above the dreaming state, but in this scheme the latter occupies the place of greater honour. Yet, even at this stage of dreaming, the soul has not got rid of the limiting conditions of individuality. Although it 'moves about happy in dreams, immortal, fearless ',[1] it is yet dependent on bodily experiences for the materials presented to its consciousness. Hence we must rise to the third stage of dreamless sleep, at which we attain to independence of the environment and even of our own individuality, and become enfolded in the prājna Ātman—the true self, the universal subject of thought. In *Kaushītaki Upanishad* III. 3 we are helped to understand this by a comparison with a dying man and the gradual infolding of his faculties. All the distractions which have disturbed us are merged in an absolute unity, and no wishes except the wish for the self are left. The cosmical parallel of this stage is said to be Īśvara, but here we must conceive of Īśvara in his most indefinite phase, almost before the cosmical ignorance has begun to operate.

Yet, especially in the later Upanishads, there are hints that even this state of dreamless sleep is not the highest stage. It is too negative and is also transient and liable to interruptions breaking in from waking experience. The highest stage cannot therefore be left dependent on what might be called the accident of deep sleep, but must be assigned a more positive basis in profound contemplation which we may voluntarily induce and can secure against disturbance. We desire to reach a state of being which shall be 'coincident with absolute wakefulness', and shall in a measure approach the self-luminousness

[1] Cf. *Chhāndogya U.* VIII. 80.

of Brahman. This highest state, or *turīya*, cannot, of course, be described, because of the nearness of its approach to Brahman, and because Brahman is indescribable. In any case the highest experience of identity is self-sufficing with a satisfaction that we could only lessen by any attempt to put it into words. Sometimes even a fifth state, *unmanī*, is hinted at, which has been described as the fourth state 'arrived at maturity'.

In a slightly more detailed way the soul's ascent to God is described under the figure of the five *sheaths* (*kośa*), and in this connexion also we have the same mingling of psychological and cosmical conception. There is (1) the *annamaya* sheath, or sheath of food, at which stage the self is identified with the material body. Then comes (2) the *prāṇamaya* sheath, or sheath of breath, in which we reach fullness of physical life, and the organism is regarded in its dynamical rather than in its statical aspect. This life fills the outer sheath, and is to be regarded as akin to the universal life or world-force. In penetrating to (3) the *manomaya* sheath, we enter the psychical region. But we remain at the level of the purely empirical self, and are more concerned with the contents of consciousness than with the activity of underlying them. We are still entirely dependent on external impressions; religiously we are under the control of authority, and ethically we aim merely at private and personal ends. So, (4) we must transcend this purely empirical level and reach, through the *vijñānamaya* sheath, to the self that is above particular impressions and desires. We must lay hold of the Reason that underlies all our mental activity and attain the understanding that this Reason is not merely individual, but universal. Yet, though this is the highest point which the intellect or reason can reach, it is not the central reality itself. We are still under the conditions of duality; we still distinguish ourselves from the objects of our thought. We cannot be satisfied until we penetrate the (5) *ānandamaya kośa*, or sheath of bliss, where subject and object are one, where individuality is destroyed and absorption is complete, where we close with all we flow from, soul with soul. Now nothing remains but Brahman, grasped by us through pure intuition, and Brahman is fullness of joy.

We have traced the stages of this intense and earnest search after unity. The process seems to have been very largely negative, and what degree of reality may still attach to the experiences of the various stages will have to be further discussed in connexion with the final interpretations of the Vedānta. The question immediately presents itself whether even at the end we have reached reality or only blank nothingness? We may say at once that we have *not* reached an Absolute which can be described through the forms of sense-experience or even through the categories of the understanding. Brahman stands too near to us for characterization; we cannot stand apart from Him and view Him as an object. Nor should we attempt to do so, for Śaṅkara's later warning against ascribing subjective qualities to the object seems but an echo of *Bṛihadāraṇyaka Upanishad* III. 4. 2, 'Thou couldst not see the true seer of sight, thou couldst not hear the true hearer of hearing, nor perceive the perceiver of perception, nor know the knower of knowledge. This is thy Self who is within all.' To impose predicates upon Brahman is only a temporary expedient similar to the operation of the goldsmith who mixes alloy with the gold so that he may work upon it; and the confusion which results when we attempt to apply finite predicates will open our eyes to their inadequacy. Contradictory predicates, though both true in a limited sense, should finally be regarded as cancelling each other, and so setting us free for higher operations of speculation. We may, e.g., apply the predicate of Being, but we shall find that this is not Being in the empirical sense. 'Thought' in Brahman is not the mental activity to which we ordinarily apply the term. The consciousness ascribable to Brahman cannot include the relation of duality of subject and object. Brahman is neither internally nor externally cognitive, neither conscious nor unconscious.[1] All that we can say from the ordinary point of view about the mental character of Brahman is that Brahman is at least not *lower* than thought. The predicate of 'bliss' also is largely negative. It means complete deliverance from what is not bliss, complete freedom from the distractions, confusions, and miseries arising from our connexion with the empirical world.

Thus, in the failure of attempts to describe the Absolute of

[1] *Māṇḍūkya U.* V. 7.

the Upanishads, we seem to be compelled to lay our hands upon our mouths and take refuge altogether in negation, in the formula *neti*, *neti*—'it is not so, it is not so.' But it must not be thought that we have reached the negation of Brahman himself. In theory, at least, we have reached ultimate Reality and not ultimate nothingness. It is true, of course, that some will say that it is *only* in theory that we have escaped negation, and that, in passing from the knowable to the Unknowable, we have entered the realm of blank darkness and silence from which there is no return.

We are not yet in a position to decide whether or not this criticism is justified, but surely all would agree that even if the intellect may fail in the adequate expression of religious truth, this does not mean utter failure, but that above the workings of the intellect we must postulate the flashing insight of intuition. What intuition can give us it may not be possible to put into words, but yet, notwithstanding our silence, we may be in contact with the deepest reality. Most competent scholars refuse to admit that the Upanishads reach only negation. Prof. Radhakrishnan, e.g., says, 'It was not the intention of the Upanishads to make of the deeper self an abstract nothingness. It is the fullest reality, the completest consciousness, and not a mere negative calm, untroubled by any unrest and unpolluted by any blot or blemish. The logic of thought has in it a negative movement, where it rises by repudiation of the finite, but this is only a stage in the onward march. By the negative process the self has to recognize that its essence is not in its finitude or self-sufficiency. By the positive method it finds its true self, in the life and being of all. All things exist within this true self.' [1] It is possible that this interpretation is correct, but the question of its validity is just the main problem of the later developments of the Vedānta philosophy.

Meanwhile, it is sufficient to note that in the Upanishads themselves there are, placed alongside of the negative movement, certain tendencies in the direction of a more positive rehabilitation of the world of ordinary experience. Those who were most persistent in denying the reality of the world, found, nevertheless, that they had to make some efforts to live within

[1] Radhakrishnan, 163.

it, or at least to adjust their thought to it. Further, as Prof. Radhakrishnan puts it, 'The spiritual sense of the masses could not be satisfied by these abstractions of the Upanishads.'[1] They, and some of the philosophers along with them, were dissatisfied by a conclusion so remote from ordinary fulfilments of human aspiration, and by the somewhat artificial methods by which it was indicated that such a conclusion could be practically reached. The *avidyā* theory also contained within it certain disconcerting inconsistencies. Thus it came about that by means of symbols and metaphors they sought to re-establish the ordinary world, whilst yet, by emphasis upon the fact that they were *only* symbols, something of the essential character of the idealistic position could be retained. When, however, symbols were once admitted, it was very difficult to select any which did not implicitly suggest the reality of the external world. Even the metaphor of the Self as that into which all things pass 'as the ocean is the one thing into which all waters flow'[2] implies the reality of the rivers both before and after they enter. Brahman is said to penetrate the world as the salt pervades the water, but surely the water has also a reality, otherwise the salt could not pervade it. In fact, the symbols are in general found to be expressive of a doctrine of emanation, and much of the cosmology of the Upanishads is devoted to setting forth the various stages of emanation.

Thus, in regard both to the characterization of the ultimate unity and its expression in the world of concrete existences, we may say that the Upanishads at least leave it an open question whether they insist on a negatively idealistic position or permit a positive affirmation of the world. There can be no doubt, however, that the fundamental concept of the Upanishads is that of unity, and the prevailing motive is a search after this unity, discoverable as akin to the soul of man. As Dr. Barnett puts it, 'The principle of the Upanishads is monism, spirituality, and human likeness.'[3]

A short note may be added as to the conditions under which, from the point of view of the Upanishads, this relentless search after unity was undertaken. It is said in the *Kāṭhaka Upanishad* I. 5. 14, that 'the path to the Self is hard, like the sharp edge of

[1] Radhakrishnan, 275. [2] Cf. *Brihadāraṇyaka U.* IV. 5. 12.
[3] Cf. *Brahma-Knowledge*, 19.

a razor'. The conditions may be divided into external and internal. As regards the former, we may note that the aspirant must belong to the proper class. Those who venture to teach the Vedas to Śūdras are threatened with terrible penalties. Women are, as a rule, excluded from the privileges of the teaching. Even Yājñavalkya, after subjecting his wife to long discussions on the subject of immortality, leaves her behind when he goes into the forest, evidently not considering that she is worthy to accompany him. The meaning of Upanishad which is generally accepted, viz. 'secret doctrine', suggests a body of truth which is to be communicated only to a very few. Sometimes the circle is still further narrowed through the idea that the teacher has a monopoly in certain doctrines, and his rights seem to be handed on from one generation to another by a kind of apostolical succession. In any case, instruction by a teacher was considered absolutely necessary, and this instruction was spread over a long period. The conditions no doubt ministered to the development of many estimable qualities, but can hardly have been altogether favourable to intellectual freedom and healthy criticism.

Besides the authority of the teacher, we have to take account also of the authority of the Vedas and, in general, of the closeness of the relations by which the Upanishads were linked with the past. Opinion on this point seems to have been by no means uniform amongst the authors of the Upanishads. The *Chhāndogya Upanishad*[1] suggests that the Vedas need be studied only in the odd moments left over from other tasks; and the older Upanishads generally seem to regard them merely as means to an end, which means might be discarded when the end had been attained. In the later Upanishads, however, as the influence of the Brāhmans increased, the study of the Vedas acquired greater importance, and the attitude taken up towards them came to resemble very much that of the medieval European scholastics in relation to the stereotyped doctrines of the Church.

Another condition which might be described as external—inasmuch as it was not under the control of the aspirant—is connected with a vague doctrine of election. The searcher after

[1] VIII. 15.

truth has to take up a more or less passive attitude in reference to the Self. He not only searches for the Self, but it might also be said to search for him and to choose him. The *Śvetāśvatara Upanishad*, e.g., says that knowledge is 'by grace of the Creator',[1] and the *Kāṭhaka Upanishad* teaches that the Self 'is attainable by him alone whom it chooses'.[2] It should be noted, however, that, although Deussen, Max Müller, and Pandit Tattvabhushan approve of this translation, Gough favours a translation which indicates a more active attitude—'If he chooses the Self, it is attainable by him.'

As regards internal conditions, it may be said generally that success in the quest is dependent on moral conditions. The soul must be purified from vagrant desires, and works must be relegated to their proper place. The short *Īśā Upanishad* contains the prayer, 'Keep us free from crooked evil, and we shall offer thee praise', and the *Bṛihadāraṇyaka Upanishad* describes the ideal student as one who has become 'quiet, subdued, satisfied, patient, collected'. Cf. also the *Kāṭhaka Upanishad* II. 24, 'He who has not first turned away from frivolity, who is restless and uncollected, in whose heart there is not peace, cannot through searching reach him.'

There is great diversity of opinion as to the place of works in the religious and philosophic quest, but on the whole the view seems to be that works, though necessary as a preparatory discipline, cannot have permanent value. They lead only to a lower and transitory felicity; they do not 'cling to a man'. Yet there is apparent not infrequently a fear lest men may be tempted to conclude prematurely that the preparatory stage has been passed, and it is indicated that those who fall into this danger enter into greater darkness of soul than those who trust to works alone.[3] We should also remember that when we are exhorted to 'cease from works' and betake ourselves entirely to contemplation, the contemplation which is enjoined is not entirely passive, but is frequently strongly contrasted with mental inactivity and sluggishness of mind.

[1] III. 20. [2] II. 23.

[3] Cf. *Īśā U.* 12 and *Bṛihadāraṇyaka U.* IV. 4. 10.

Vedānta Sūtras

The *Vedānta Sūtras*, otherwise known as the *Brahma Sūtras*, or the *Śārīraka Sūtras* (which latter term signifies that they are concerned with the 'embodied soul' of Brahma), are regarded as constituting, along with the Upanishads and the *Gītā*, the *Prasthānatraya*, or 'Canon' of the Vedānta. We are at once faced with the problem as to whether the *Sūtras* can be considered, as it were, in their own right. As has been pointed out above,[1] they had a place in the development of Indian philosophy which is strikingly suggestive of the character of that development. They were intended to be a collection of short sayings in which the essence of the Vedānta was to be preserved; or, as Śaṅkara puts it—in a phrase which is non-committal as regards their determinative value—'they string together the flowers of the Vedānta passages'. Above all they aim at brevity. Their compilers are twitted with 'delighting as much in the saving of a short vowel as in the birth of a son', and Dr. Macdonnell says further, 'The prose in which these works are composed is so compressed that the wording of the most laconic telegram would appear diffuse compared with it.'[2] The *Sūtras*, as we have seen, served the purpose of a compressed material suitable for memorizing, and were the foundation for notes of discussions continued through the centuries in the different schools. As we have also seen, they would be difficult of understanding even for those who took part in the discussions and almost completely unintelligible for others. Various opinions are held on the question as to whether the unintelligibility was intentional or not. It may have been due to deliberate esotericism, a determination to keep the precious truths sacrosanct from the so-called unworthy. Deussen holds that the obscurity cannot 'be sufficiently explained either by striving after brevity or a predilection for characteristic ways of expression. Rather must we admit that the composer or composers intentionally sought after obscurity, in order to make their work of treating the secret doctrine of the Veda inaccessible to all those to whom it was not opened up by the explanations of a teacher.'[3] But it

[1] p. 9. [2] *Sanskrit Literature*, 56.
[3] Deussen, *S. V.* 27.

is possible also that the obscurity may have been the result merely of that spirit of academic aloofness which steals over all close corporations of scholars and renders them almost unaware even of the existence of those who are outside the privileged groups and unaccustomed to its peculiar terminology. But whatever the motive may be, there is no doubt about the obscurity. Words are omitted without the slightest compunction, and even those that are left are not key-words to the cryptic sentences, but merely mnemonics, serving the purpose of assisting the memory of a well-drilled pupil rather than of illuminating the understanding of an investigator coming freshly to his task.

Thus the *Sūtras* served mainly as lines of communication between the old and the new, securing by their traditional prestige and their compact serviceableness that the old should, to a large extent, dominate the new, but yet, because of their merely schematic character, permitting, within certain limits, considerable variety and development in interpretation. From this it comes about that although, taking advantage of the opportunities afforded by mere outlines, the *Sūtras* may selectively omit certain aspects of doctrine and emphasize others, and thus acquire a distinctive character of their own, yet for the most part their vagueness and unintelligibility will lead to their surrender into the hands of commentators. If the *Sūtras* cannot be understood without the help of these later expositions, it follows that the work of the commentators who explain will gradually acquire greater importance than that which they are explaining. For this reason it might seem hardly worth while to attempt at this stage any detailed discussion of the *Sūtras* themselves, and advisable to pass on at once to the dominating commentaries and view the *Sūtras* merely in the light of the ostensible expositions.

Yet it would be a mistake to go too far in this direction. We have spoken of the *Sūtras* as lines of communication, and we might be satisfied with a barren metaphor of this kind if we could establish a definite starting-point of the lines, and also a definite ending. We could then indicate the main purport of the *Sūtras* by giving as full an account as possible of the data from which they proceed and of the final interpretations in which their doctrines are consummated. But this is just what we cannot do, and the problem is much more complex. The Upanishads, which the *Sūtras* set out to interpret, are very far from presenting a definite system of doctrine allowing of only one possible summary. As a matter of fact the Upanishads supply material for many different systems of philosophy and for very varying interpretations, and it cannot be decided *a priori* which system or which interpretation the *Sūtras* are likely to favour. Moreover, when we look to the other end of the line of communications, we find that the *Sūtras* are susceptible of, and have actually been given, many different interpretations, and that, therefore, it is impossible to select any one commentary, as, e.g., Śaṅkara's, and say dogmatically that it may be accepted without question as the only continuation of the real meaning of the *Sūtras*. Deussen, indeed, says without hesitation that Śaṅkara is throughout in agreement with the *Sūtras*, but other scholars, possessing equal if not greater authority, declare that Śaṅkara and the *Sūtras* contradict each other on many important points, and that other commentators, as, e.g., Rāmānuja, give more trustworthy expositions of the essential meaning of the *Sūtras*. In view of such difference of opinion, therefore, it would seem necessary to attempt a slight and purely provisional characterization of the *Sūtras* in order that we may be able at a later stage to place Śaṅkara and Rāmānuja in a proper relation to them.

Deussen describes the relation of the *Sūtras* to the Upanishads as similar to that of Christian dogmatics to the New Testament.[1] This comparison is perhaps rather misleading in view of the conciseness of the *Sūtras* and the tendency to expansion manifested by at least some systems of Christian dogmatics. The comparison suggested by Dr. Carpenter would seem to be more serviceable. He says, 'The Sūtras have a distinct resemblance to the books of "Sentences" which served as the foundation of theological teaching in the medieval schools of Europe. They were based on Scripture and the Fathers, and ran a parallel course in time with Indian production, leading off with those of Isodore of Seville (560–636). Most famous was the collection of Peter the Lombard, *Magister Sententiarum*,

[1] Cf. Deussen, *S. V.* 21.

whose work was completed between 1145 and 1150, in four books dealing with God, the creation, the virtues, the seven sacraments, and the "last things". It gained immense popularity and became the accredited text-book in almost every theological school. Numberless commentaries were devoted to its elucidation, no fewer than 180 being written in England.'[1]

The dates of the *Sūtras* have been very variously estimated. Deussen[2] puts the date very late. He lays great stress on the connexion between Bādarāyaṇa (the reputed author of the *Sūtras*) and Jaimini, the author of the most important book on the Karma Mīmāṁsā. Bādarāyaṇa and Jaimini repeatedly quote each other by name, and this suggests to Deussen that what we now have is a composite work edited by Vyāsa, who might possibly be connected by a kind of apostolical anticipation with Śaṅkara, and be only some two hundred years earlier than his commentator (who flourished about the ninth century). Thus the date which Deussen favours would be about A.D. 600. Deussen also lays stress on the priority of the *Gītā* to the *Sūtras*, on which point, however, he is definitely contradicted by Max Müller,[3] who argues that the apparent quotations from the *Gītā* may well be from other sources, and holds as his general opinion that Bādarāyaṇa is not dependent on any authorities which can be assigned to a period later than the Christian era. Jacobi dates the *Sūtras* between A.D. 200 and A.D. 450.[4] Prof. S. N. Das Gupta pushes the date back to the second century B.C. He holds that an earlier date is impossible because of the references to many other systems contained in the *Sūtras*. But he would fain go farther, and it is almost with reluctance that he consents to so late a date. Some Indian scholars would go as far back as 500 B.C. It seems necessary, however, to leave room for a considerable amount of development between the date of the early Upanishads and the composition of the *Sūtras*. Thibaut holds that the 'collection of Sūtras was preceded by a long series of preparatory literary efforts of which they merely represent the highly condensed outcome'.[5] Dr. Farquhar is in agreement with Thibaut, and also takes the view that a long succession of scholars is behind the author, the names of seven

[1] Carpenter, 299. [2] Cf. *S. V.* 21. [3] Müller, *S. S.* 111.
[4] Cf. *J. A. O. S.*, 1911, p. 201. [5] Cf. *S. B. E.* XXXIV, p. xii.

of these appearing in the work itself.[1] He also offers the more particular view that a compendium was in existence about the beginning of our era, and that this was the precursor of the *Sūtras* as we now have them. In this way he would explain the reference in the *Gītā* to 'well thought out verses of *Brahma Sūtras*',[2] and incidentally dispose of Prof. Das Gupta's contention that the *Brahma Sūtras* (as we have them) were already regarded as an authoritative work by the dualists and therefore might quite naturally be referred to in the *Gītā*. On the whole, the evidence points to a comparatively late date, certainly not earlier than the Christian era. But, whatever the exact date may be, there are traces of the existence already of many diverse views. References are found, e.g., to three different views of the relation of the soul to God: one, associated with the name of Āśmarathya, that the soul is neither absolutely different from God nor absolutely the same; a second, associated with Auḍulomi, that the soul, while temporarily different, is by release altogether merged in Brahman; and a third, associated with Kāśakṛitsna, that the soul is absolutely non-different from Brahman.[3]

In regard to the special teaching of the *Sūtras* it may be said that they treat the Upanishads with great reverence, and, like them, emphasize the religious and moral conditioning of philosophical inquiry.[4] On the whole their tendency is towards a dualistic and theistic modification of the strictly monistic position which may be taken as fundamental in the Upanishads, and which was afterwards more strongly developed by Śaṅkara. They favour the interpretation afterwards adopted by Rāmānuja rather than Śaṅkara's own doctrine. They do not draw a firm distinction between two orders of knowledge or between a Brahman without qualities and a Brahman with qualities, and they show little sympathy with an extreme interpretation of the *māyā* doctrine. Whether this tendency in a theistic direction is due to the influence of the *Gītā* or itself contributed to the particular character of the latter, will, of course, be decided differently according to the view taken of the chronological

[1] Cf. Farquhar, 126.

[2] *Gītā*, XIII. 4.

[3] Cf. Thibaut, *S. B. E.* XXXIV, p. xix, and a corresponding paragraph in Farquhar, 128.

[4] Cf. *Sūtras*, I. 1. 1.

relation between the *Sūtras* and the *Gītā*. It seems probable that they belonged to much the same school of thought, and general considerations at least prepare us for the view that Śaṅkara, and perhaps one or two of his immediate predecessors, found it necessary to give expression to a reaction against the dualistic tendencies of the school of thought associated with the *Sūtras*.

The Gītā

To a very brief characterization of the teaching of the *Gītā* we must now turn. It had its place, as we have seen, as a member of the *Prasthānatraya*, or 'Canon', of the Vedānta, and therefore must be considered in any survey of the development preparatory to Śaṅkara's teaching. It is more of a poem than a treatise, and its importance is not, strictly speaking, philosophical, but lies rather in the influence which it had upon popular thought, and in the expression which it gave to the theistic and slightly dualistic elements latent in the speculations of the Upanishads. As was suggested in the last paragraph, it does not seem to be essential to decide whether its dualism is preparatory to that of the *Sūtras* or is itself strengthened by the teaching of the latter. Thibaut takes the former view and Prof. Das Gupta the latter.[1] But whatever may be the proper decision on this point, it can easily be seen that the composite character of such a work as the *Gītā* would naturally give encouragement to dualistic tendencies.

As regards the inter-relation of its elements, we may either take the view that the poem was a late Upanishad, somewhat similar in type to the *Śvetāśvatara Upanishad*, and containing the outlines of the generally monistic teaching of the Upanishads and that this monism was then brought into relation with the teaching of the Bhāgavata sect, whose worship centred in Kṛishṇa, regarded as an embodiment of Vishṇu. Or the matter may be viewed from the other side, and, with Prof. Garbe, it may be said that the poem shows evidences of the transformation of primitive trust in a warrior leader such as Kṛishṇa into faith in a personal supreme spirit. Kṛishṇa becomes identified

[1] Cf. *S. B. E.* XXXIV, p. cxxvi, and Das Gupta, 422, and for further discussion of date, Farquhar, 91, and Urquhart, *Pantheism and the Value of Life*, 379.

with Vishṇu or Vāsudeva, the latter being either a popular designation of the former or the name of a deity already almost identified with him. But Vishṇu (or Vāsudeva) is also on the point of being identified with the impersonal non-qualitative Brahman—the subject of the more severely monistic doctrine of the Upanishads. Thus, from whatever direction we view the process of modification, Vishṇu obtains the elevation which results from identification with the Absolute, and at the same time the Absolute is prevented from receding into these depths of negation and unapproachability which are suggested by some aspects of Upanishad teaching. The All-God becomes associated with qualities which constitute him a definite object of worship, and from him the world-process emerges—as a real emanation and not simply as an illusive shadow-play.

To a certain extent the tendency in the direction of realism and even dualism may be ascribed to the influence of the Sāṅkhya philosophy. The writer of the *Gītā* was not unaffected by the desire to adjust his teaching to the requirements of this philosophy, especially in its readiness to assign independent existence to matter, and many of his practical precepts owe much to the conception of external and resistless physical might. He does not of course go so far as consciously and definitely to admit the validity of this conception, but we cannot but see traces of pre-occupation with such a view, and the effect of it is indicated in the inclination towards a realistic view of the world.

Practically, as Prof. Das Gupta points out, the '*Bhagavadgītā* tried to mark out a middle path between the austere discipline of meditative abstraction, on the one hand, and the course of duties of sacrificial action . . . in the life of a new type of Yogin on the other, who should combine in himself the best parts of the two paths, devote himself to his duties, and yet abstract himself from all selfish motives associated with desires'.[1]

Thus on a rapid and conjunct view of the *Prasthānat raya* or 'Canon' we are left with an impression that no one tendency can claim absolute ascendancy, but that, if monism and a certain degree of negation seem to prevail in the Upanishads, in the other two members of the canon there are at least signs of a

[1] Das Gupta, 227.

dualistic tendency of sufficient strength to make it intelligible that in the minds of some a renewed emphasis on monistic principles would seem to be necessary. As we trace the development further, we find such an emphasis in Gauḍapāda and his *Kārikās*.

Gauḍapāda

Gauḍapāda is a noteworthy figure in the tradition which Śaṅkara inherited. There does not seem to be sufficient reason to doubt the authenticity of the name or to place the date of the work attributed to him so early as to render quite impossible his historical connexion with Śaṅkara. The Gauḍapāda with whom we have to do is the reputed author of a poem known as the *Māṇḍūkya Kārikā*, and should not be identified with the earlier author of a commentary on Īśvara Kṛishṇa's *Sāṅkhya Kārikās*, as Max Müller seems to suggest.[1] Our Gauḍapāda was connected by direct links of historical anticipation with Śaṅkara, and the latter speaks even of having come under the direct influence of Gauḍapāda. It would therefore probably be correct, if we accept the usual dating of Śaṅkara (to be discussed later), to place Gauḍapāda about the end of the eighth century A.D.

His work—the *Māṇḍūkya Kārikā*—is one of the earliest embodiments of the doctrine of strict monism. Śaṅkara cordially welcomes him as a predecessor and declares that to him is due the credit of recovering and restating the absolutist creed which he holds to be the true teaching of the Veda. In reverential language Śaṅkara thus refers to his preceptor: 'That great guru . . . on finding all the people sinking in the ocean made dreadful by the crocodiles of rebirth, out of kindness for all people, by churning the great ocean of the Veda by his churning rod of wisdom, recovered what lay deep in the heart of the Veda, and is hardly attainable even by the immortal gods.'[2]

It is acknowledged on all hands that Gauḍapāda was greatly influenced by Buddhistic teaching, and it is indeed possible—as alleged by some—that he may have been himself a Buddhist. Prof. Poussin says of him that it is impossible to read his verses

[1] Müller, *S. S.*, 224.

[2] Quoted by Das Gupta, 423.

'without being struck by the Buddhistic character of the leading ideas and of the wording itself'.[1] He seems to have used the Buddhist doctrine of the 'void' as a key to the interpretation of the teaching of the Upanishads, and it has been suggested, as, e.g., by Prof. Das Gupta,[2] that he selected one of the smallest Upanishads—the *Māṇḍūkya*—and at the same time one that had much to say about dreams, as the basis of his Commentary, in order that he might not be drawn aside by the multiplicity of details in the larger Upanishads from his main purpose of concentrating attention on this truth of illusion.[3] It must not be supposed, however, that Gauḍapāda used this small Upanishad simply as a peg on which to hang Buddhistic teaching. To whatever extent others may differ from him in the interpretation of it, we must in fairness believe that he regarded Buddhistic doctrine as suggesting to him an interpretation which could actually be found in the Upanishad, and was, indeed, its fundamental truth.

It is significant of Gauḍapāda's attitude that the word *māyā*, which was in previous literature of very rare occurrence, is to be found in no fewer than sixteen passages in his *Kārikā*, and one of the four chapters is entitled *Vaitathya*, or 'unreality'. His view is that we may discuss, if we like, theories of creation and cosmogony, but it is of little importance which we adopt, for, after all, all plurality, and indeed all creation, is a dream, and the truth lies in the One. Cf. *Māṇḍūkya Upanishad* II. 10, 'Therefore this false notion arises from some cause due to ignorance, and so it is unreal, and would cease when instruction is imparted by a Teacher. This is the saying of the wise, that "when One is known, the Two cease to exist". The illusion is so extreme that it can hardly have that degree of actuality which demands destruction; having practically no reality, it does not stand in need of 'burning' or removal. We do not require spades and shovels to remove a morning mist; and when

[1] Cf. *J. R. A. S.*, Vol. X, p. 134.

[2] P. 429.

[3] Cf. especially *Māṇḍūkya U.* I. 7, 'others think that the creation is like unto a dream or an illusion.' Madhva's comment on this is that people of this class are 'ignorant'. Prof. S. C. Vasu suggests also that it is ridiculous to think that the Almighty should revert to illusion. It is only, he argues, a hypnotist, who cannot actually produce an object, who is compelled to create an illusion. Cf. *S. B. H. Māṇḍūkya*, 12.

truth arises, the world-illusion disappears, as the morning mist fades away before the rising of the sun.

The world of ordinary experience is to be placed in the same category as dreams. There are indeed many differences between the phenomena of dreams and those of waking reality, but they have in common the condition of 'being seen'. Both of them are, in other words, the product of imagination. Further the subject or conceiver of these inner states is itself unreal, at least in its supposed distinction from the All. Truth lies most of all in the Void, in the infinite of empty space (the *ākāśa*). Spaces enclosed in the jar or in the individual life, may appear to be separate, but when the jar is broken or the illusion of the *jīva* is dispelled, then follows complete merging in the whole of characterless being. No duality remains anywhere; all particularity is mere illusion and magic. The world of becoming is full of puzzling contradictions, and, in true Parmenidean fashion, Gauḍapāda holds that it can be understood only when it is completely denied. The ordinary experiences of birth, life, and death are popular superstitions, and the sage who is worthy of the name will penetrate the illusion. The categories of causality, &c., cannot properly be used, for they immediately reveal insuperable contradictions and absurdities. If, e.g. you admit, with the Sāṅkhyans, that cause and effect are inseparable, the logical result of such identification is that the effect will have to be regarded as unoriginated like the cause and the cause will be impermanent like the effect.

So, he urges, let us by wisdom seek to penetrate the illusion. In and by consciousness is generated the illusion of both perceiver and perceived, and our consciousness is not separate from the eternal consciousness. Thus the power of illusion may be traced back to God Himself, unreality may be placed at the very heart of things, and everything except the one be dissolved in the conception of cosmic deception. The variety and forces of the world, and the life which we live within it, will all alike be emptied of meaning. Our life may be compared to the continuous circle produced by a whirling firebrand, and in our life also by a metaphorical *alātaśānti* (or extinction of the firebrand), we may discover that all ordinary experience is unreal as the circle of light produced by children at play in the gathering twilight. Soon all will be dark, and in the darkness the truth lies hidden, and in the sense of unreality the real.[1]

Negation could hardly go farther than this, and it was left for Śaṅkara to take up the development of thought, and show how negation might reasonably go almost as far as this, and yet not lead to utter futility but form the way of approach to a reality positive in the very highest degree.

[1] Cf. Prof. P. D. Shastri, *Doctrine of Māyā*, 84.

III

ŚAṄKARA AND RĀMĀNUJA: THEIR LIVES, THEIR COMMENTARIES, AND THEIR TRADITIONAL PHILOSOPHICAL SIGNIFICANCE

IT has been already pointed out that the peculiar character of the *Sūtras* with which we are specially concerned has led to the general necessity of commentaries. Whilst other *Sūtras* might possibly be understood without assistance, the case was altogether different with the two supreme *Sūtras* (of which the *Vedānta Sūtras* is one). Their mnemonic character and technical language made commentaries indispensable, and they could be made intelligible only if elucidated by those who were qualified to reproduce their original setting and proceed consistently from it. A recent Indian writer says, 'As for the Sūtras, it is in their nature to be easily elastic; and when unsupported by tradition, nothing indeed can be made out of them.'[1] The commentators, of whom Śaṅkara and Rāmānuja are the chief, set themselves to restate the thoughts suggested or suggestible by the *Sūtras*.

The indefiniteness and vagueness of the Upanishads also provided an additional necessity for Commentaries. Seeing that the *Sūtras*, although they purported to give the essence of the Upanishad teaching, had yet failed, by reason of their obscurity, to present this teaching in any authoritative form, it still remained open to, and, indeed, obligatory upon, succeeding scholars to establish what they regarded as the true doctrine of the sacred literary deposit. Their function, as they conceived it, was not to initiate new speculation, except perhaps in comparatively insignificant details, but to make clear the exact meaning of the authorities whom they professed to revere.

We have already referred to the esotericism of previous literature and to Deussen's suggestion that this esotericism was deliberate. While we cannot subscribe altogether to the view that the esotericism was intentional, yet it is undoubted that such an attitude must have formed the background of thought, and it is exceedingly natural that the commentators should be influenced by the same spirit. This would almost inevitably

[1] Aiyar, 73.

express itself in the endeavour to enhance the value of their esoteric possession. They would proceed to do this by elaborating it as much as possible, by developing suggestions into systems and intuitions into arguments, so that the initiates might feel that they had not been led on by false hopes, but had really been made to share in an inheritance of the greatest significance. And seeing that the commentators had bestowed so much labour upon it, they might quite justifiably feel that they were conferring a boon which was very much worth giving. The greater the elaboration the greater the value of what they had to impart. But we must not think of them as influenced exclusively by an esoteric spirit. While cherishing this and making as much of it as possible, they at the same time wished to give interpretations which would be more widely intelligible and acceptable. For their own reputation they would wish to do this; and motives also of a higher and benevolent character would enter in. While Śaṅkara always preserved an esoteric kernel of his thought, which he declared to be only for the few, yet he was frequently also animated by a genuinely missionary spirit, under the influence of which he felt himself called upon to dilute his thought for the benefit of the multitude.

It should be noted that a Bhāshya—the name often given to a commentary—is not properly a commentary in the usually accepted sense of the word. Its primary aim is not to elucidate a text (although it may do this with considerable thoroughness), but rather to construct a philosophy on the basis of the authoritative text selected. A comparison may again be made with the procedure in Indian music according to which the *rag*, or fixed form, while dominating any new composition, at the same time permits of very considerable variation.

Life of Śaṅkara

Śaṅkara is the earliest of the commentators on the *Sūtras* whose work is extant, and he is still regarded as the most important in the whole succession. He has been described in glowing terms as 'the greatest intellect of the world' and 'the most towering personality of Hinduism in its renaissance period'.[1] He is said to have been born at Kaladi in North

[1] Cf. Pal, 1 and 16.

Travancore about the year A.D. 788. There is considerable unanimity about the year of his birth, but whether he died at the comparatively early age of thirty-two, or lived to a good old age, perhaps until about the year 850, seems to be a matter of great uncertainty. To those who argue that 820 was the date of his death the reply is made that this was merely the date of his final renunciation of all ties which bound him to ordinary life; and, generally speaking, biographers seem to be undecided whether the greater honour will accrue to Śaṅkara if he is regarded as an example of youthful precocity or found to be a depositary of the garnered wisdom of a lengthy life.

His biographers are numerous, but it cannot be said that they supply us with a very trustworthy record. Indeed some of them frankly disavow any direct dependence on historical fact. 'What have we to do with the minor incidents of Śaṅkara's life?' says Mr. D. N. Pal.[1] 'We have his philosophy, we have his religion, we have his personality, we have his Ethics. All Hindus . . . breathe in Śaṅkara's spirit.' The poverty of biographical material may indeed be taken as simply an illustration of the self-effacing spirit of all India's great religious teachers; it is but fitting that their outer life should be a blank and that the details of it should not remain in the memory of man. Consequently it is argued that, if there are not facts available by the interpretation of which we may arrive at an appreciation of the spirit of a man, it is quite permissible, after having obtained from his teaching some indication of his character, to construct a body of 'facts' suitable for expressing the spirit of this character. We may argue that 'if this is not true, then something like it is true', or we may apply the very elastic measurement which seems to be suggested by Mr. Pal in such words as 'It is a very probable story, and assuredly a true story'.[2]

The way is thus opened for the expression of enthusiastic admiration under the guise of the forms of biography. It must not, however, be thought that Indian writers are all liable to this tendency. Mr. C. N. Krishnaswami Aiyar, e.g., takes up a much more critical attitude, and speaks very severely of 'the misguided enthusiasm of later admirers from whom every great person has reason to pray to be saved'.

[1] Pal, 96. [2] Ib. 57.

But it would on the whole be true to say that in considering the lives of Śaṅkara we have for the most part to deal with facts which are under the governance of ideas, or with facts which have burst through the limitations of history and are on the way to becoming transparent expressions of spiritual truths. And, after all, there is not much reason to complain, for there is abundant justification in the frequent contention of Indian biographers that Śaṅkara's teaching is of much more importance than his life, and we need not be too anxious to distinguish rigidly between history and drama, or be too critical of attempts to give this teaching an appropriate setting in concrete circumstance if this setting helps us to understand the teaching more adequately. Even if, on occasion, the alleged facts are merely the product of 'misguided enthusiasm', the statement of them is useful as a proof of the existence of the enthusiasm and an indication of its extent, and we may safeguard ourselves by valuing the enthusiasm according to our estimate of the intrinsic excellence of the teaching rather than on the basis of the facts which are supposed to have evoked it.

With this proviso—that the enthusiasm should be related to the ideas rather than to the facts—we may proceed to give a brief account of the details of his life which are fairly generally agreed upon. Considerable mystery surrounds his birth, and an instance of retrospective narrative, wise after the event, is immediately forthcoming in the story that Śaṅkara's mother, having been offered the choice of having a number of dunces or only one short-lived but clever son, decided in favour of the latter. His steadfastness of purpose, even in his early years, is indicated by the stress which his biographers lay upon the degree of family opposition which he had to overcome in order to carry out his desire of becoming a *sannyāsī*.

One event of his early life is well authenticated and of considerable importance. His search for a Guru led him to become a pupil of Govinda, who, as we have already seen, was himself a pupil of Gauḍapāda. This shows that Śaṅkara was at the beginning of his career brought under the influence of the rigorously monistic doctrine which was the prevailing doctrine of Gauḍapāda's *Kārikās*; and here there is also indicated a channel of Buddhistic influence. An entirely apocryphal story, chronologically of course impossible, tells how, after Śaṅkara had settled at Benares, he was visited by Vyāsa, the reputed author of the *Vedānta-sūtras*, and had many long and learned conversations with him. This story might be taken as indicating allegorically Śaṅkara's early interest in the meaning of the *Sūtras*, and might also suggest the beginning of controversy as to whether he was properly interpreting them, the visit of Vyāsa being cited of course in order to show that Śaṅkara had opportunities of first-hand knowledge such as almost made mistake impossible. Of more importance are his disputations with Maṇḍana Miśra, the favourite pupil of Kumārila Bhaṭṭa, who was famous as a reactionary from Buddhism, and a staunch defender of the ritual and sacrificial practices which had been handed down from Vedic times—the way of works, or the *karma-mārga*. In Śaṅkara's victorious disputation with Maṇḍana we have a presentation of the former's fundamental preference for the way of knowledge over the way of works. At the same time the contrast between the vigorous persecution which Maṇḍana, as well as his predecessor Kumārila Bhaṭṭa, directed against the Buddhists, and the more tolerant attitude of Śaṅkara towards his vanquished opponents is an expression of Śaṅkara's catholicity, and also a parallel in the practical sphere to that theoretical method which allowed him unconcernedly to place side by side esoteric and exoteric truth and permit continued adherence to the latter until such time as the former should prevail. In passing, also, we may allude to the pathetic but beautiful story of Śaṅkara's interview with his dying mother. She had asked him to discourse on matters which would bring peace to her soul, but he began to expound the abstruse doctrines of his philosophy. On finding that these gave her no comfort, he fell back upon hymns of devotion which he himself had composed in honour of Śiva. The inclusion of this story—whatever its historicity—indicates an impression in the minds of his biographers that Śaṅkara's doctrines were too abstruse for the ordinary mind and needed to be accompanied by some accommodation to the simpler understanding.

Also the story of his interview with one of the Kāpālikas (or skull-men), who asked Śaṅkara for the gift of his head as a sacrifice to Kālī, urging that, according to the principles of the

Advaita philosophy, Śaṅkara ought to be completely indifferent to the loss of such an appurtenance of individuality, reads almost like a satire designed to bring out the unpractical nature of Śaṅkara's teaching.

Śaṅkara spent several years at Benares, and it was probably there that he made a beginning with the chief works with which his name is associated. But his life was essentially that of a peripatetic philosopher, and tradition has it that he travelled all over India. He seems to have had considerable gifts of organization, and several Mutts, or houses of monastic learning, which continue to this day, owe their origin to him. He is said to have ended his life at Kedarnāth, in the far north of India, but whether his death took place in 820 or thirty years later is still a matter of uncertainty.

Provisional summary of Śaṅkara's teaching.

We may give here a preliminary indication of the main points in Śaṅkara's doctrine. By representative Indian writers Śaṅkara is described as a 'rigorous monist',[1] and perhaps such a phrase gives us most concisely the key-note of his teaching. He asserts one reality, and only one, for there is no such thing as plurality or difference anywhere, and, therefore, no beginning and no ending, nothing but that nearest experience which comes to each one of us, the consciousness of the self, intelligent just because it is conscious, but essentially universal rather than individual. If we can merge all things in our consciousness, and merge ourselves as individuals in the universal consciousness, we shall reach the goal of all our striving, the solution of all our difficulties. If we can negate the world we shall find that the world is well lost, for there is really no world, no individuality to lose, nothing but the all-pervading, eternal, infinite Reality, the fundamental, self-luminous Being.

And yet even in the shortest summary, it is necessary to express the doubt whether the mood which lies behind this attitude is really so negative as might at first sight appear. Can we go so far as to call it altogether negative? May it not be rather that simpler but more fundamental feeling of the stupendousness of the universe which overwhelms mankind at the first

[1] Cf. Kirtikar, 2.

dawning of the religious consciousness? The burden of awareness seems almost too great for us to bear, and would crush us were not some means found of lessening its weight. And may not the human mind under such conditions find refuge in the thought that much of the burden is unreal—in fact that it is all unreal, except in so far as we find ourselves again in it and discover that the seeming oppression is but the insistence upon us of the universal in which we live and move and have our being?

Śaṅkara's thought may be followed along the usual lines made familiar to us by idealist philosophy. Being is essentially relative to thought. No object can exist except as known—'Where there is no knowledge, there is no knowable.' [1] And carrying forward with him the ideal of knowledge suggested even in the days of Vedic sacrifice in India—the ideal of the merging of the knower and the known, of the mystic communion of subject and object following upon the destruction of the separateness of the worshipper and the worshipped—Śaṅkara proceeds to sublate all the distinctions which divide the subject and the object, and the variety of particular objects from each other. Space, time, causality, and other categories both definite and vague, even the thought of difference itself, are all swept out of the way until the soul is left only with the sense of the unity of individual experience. And the differences disappear in pure being with which consciousness also is found to be at one.

Our consciousness is not really individual, for it is beginningless, and no individual can be without a beginning. It has moreover no lurking plurality within itself, no distinction of a knower behind his knowledge which may form the basis of a quasi-material separateness. Śaṅkara warns us against attributing objective qualities to the subject, by which warning he means that we should not attempt to view the self in an external way, as if it were merely an ordinary object, popularily and particularly conceived. Consciousness is not possessed by some entity beyond consciousness, but is *pure* consciousness, ultimate being, transparent through and through. There can be no distinction between the individual and the universal, any more than between the individual subject and the object known. Pure undifferenced unity is all that can be established.

[1] Cf. Śaṅkara's Commentary on *Praśna U.* VI. 2.

But whence then came the world with all the details of our ordinary experience? We cannot avoid its recognition, but we should regard it as only phenomenal, as having merely *vyāvahārika* or practical existence. Even this amount of existence is due to ignorance, and not to our ignorance only but to a cosmic ignorance. This cosmic ignorance when combined with power becomes a principle of illusion or *Māyā*. This cosmic, phantasm-creating energy is beginningless, and, although the ultimate Being or Brahman is without qualities or without plurality, somehow or other it becomes attached to him. It is both *sat* and *asat*, the first as not being due only to our invention, and the second as being, after all, only phenomenal. It is an eternal power producing unreal appearances.

It is difficult to unfold all that is contained in this double mode of conceiving the principle as at once real and unreal. But it might be a step forward in interpretation to say that the principle is an absolute expression of the idea of the inexplicable—according to Prof. Radhakrishnan, a statement of a metaphysical position which might thus be described: 'As for the metaphysical ramifications which also exist, the non-dualist says, well, they are there, and there is an end of it. We do not know and cannot know why. It is all a contradiction and yet it is actual.'[1] Now, from the point of view of a completely rounded philosophy, the idea of the inexplicable carries with it a slightly depreciatory significance, and perhaps this idea of subjective disapproval is intended to be conveyed in some of the interpretations of the term *Māyā*, which, notwithstanding many rehabilitations, never quite detaches itself from the idea of illusion, deepening occasionally into the ideas of delusion and deception. In any case it tends always to suggest something of the idea of a lower reality, what *should not be* from the point of view of true knowledge. At the same time this conception of *Māyā* does afford us some relief from the burden of the inexplicable, just as on awaking from a troublesome and perplexing dream we are comforted by discovering that it is nothing but a dream.

In association with the power of *Māyā*, Brahman becomes Īśvara, the Absolute with qualities, the Creator, the Preserver,

[1] Radhakrishnan, I. 35.

and Destroyer of the world. In this way the phenomenal world may, in contradiction to the Buddhists, be provisionally accepted, and the variety of nature, as well as the existence of individual souls may be to a certain extent explained, all materialistic and purely naturalistic theories being, as a consequence, ruled out of court. But yet, however perfect the systematization may be, it has to be confessed in the end that the universe thus constructed is not real in the fullest sense, and our salvation will consist in attaining this knowledge. Such knowledge will not be an active force destroying error, but simply a recognition that the content of error does not exist.

Our liberation will proceed by various stages, as we gradually get rid of the limiting adjuncts or 'sheaths' of our personality. We rise from the life of pure impulse to that of ritual observance, which will lead us by the 'way of the fathers'—the *pitriyāna*—to an existence of considerable, though temporary, enjoyment. The next stage is marked by a worship of the highest qualitative Brahman, and 'by way of the gods'—the *Devayāna*—will bring us to the divine regions where we shall live in communion with this Brahman of qualities. But when this qualitative Brahman is merged in the Brahman without qualities, we ourselves may share in this identification, and reach, or rather discover, a state in which we are united with the Para-Brahman, without the slightest difference remaining.

Life and Teaching of Rāmānuja

After this purely provisional account of the *Advaitavāda* of Śaṅkara we may turn to a short treatment of the life and teaching of Rāmānuja, in order that we may set the two great teachers in relation to each other, and be in a position to decide which of them we ought chiefly to follow in our further exposition of the Vedānta. That some sort of choice has to be made between them will be evident from the vigorous way in which Rāmānuja himself states his opposition to the doctrines of Śaṅkara. Adverse judgement could hardly be more uncompromisingly expressed than in the following passage: 'This entire theory rests on a fictitious foundation of altogether hollow and vicious arguments, incapable of being stated in definite logical alternatives, and devised by men who are destitute of those particular qualities which cause individuals to be chosen by the Supreme Person revealed in the Upanishads; whose intellects are darkened by the impression of beginningless evil; and who thus have no insight into the meaning of words and sentences, into the real purport conveyed by them, and into the procedure of sound argumentation, with all its methods depending on perception and other instruments of right knowledge. The theory therefore must needs be rejected by all those who, through texts, perception, and the other means of knowledge—assisted by sound reasoning—have an insight into the true nature of things.'[1] This quotation not only indicates vehemence of opposition, but is also a guide to the points upon which criticism was to be specially directed. It shows, amongst other things, that Rāmānuja disapproved of the idea of a beginningless power of *Māyā* and did not share the distrust of human faculties therein implied; and also that, in his opinion, Śaṅkara was not a reliable interpreter of the Upanishads, which pointed to the existence rather of a Supreme Person than of a characterless Absolute.[2]

Rāmānuja is important both on his own account and on account of the tradition which he represents. His Commentary is the next oldest to that of Śaṅkara, and is itself a brilliant piece of exposition and criticism, described by a recent competent writer as one of the most influential works that India has produced.[3] And the same writer seems disposed to regard him, in relation to Śaṅkara, as a typical representative of one of the fundamental metaphysical tendencies in the history of human thought: 'For two Magnitudes of the highest rank struggle here with each other in Śaṅkara and Rāmānuja, who are only their representatives. The almost altogether mysterious and overwhelming, world-destroying, ultimately irrational, inconceivable, undefinable Absolute Unity is in conflict with the Lord, the feeling, willing, personal, rational, loving, and beloved God of the heart and conscience.'[4]

[1] Cf. *S. B. E.* XLVIII. 8.

[2] The vigour of language in the passage just cited almost justifies the comment of Prof. Otto, 'And now begins the struggle of proposition against proposition, assertion against assertion—a struggle in the truest sense, breast to breast, and knee to knee, a struggle of the utmost intensity, without pause to draw breath or take, until limb by limb the opponent is overcome and crushed to the earth' (Otto, *Siddhānta des Rāmānuja*, 2).

[3] Cf. Otto, *op. cit.*, p. 1.

[4] *Op. cit.*, p. 2.

From the point of view of history rather than of metaphysics, Rāmānuja might be described as one who has carried further the more purely theistic teaching of the *Vedānta Sūtras*. He was not at all distressed by the slightly dualistic and realistic tendency which had set in before the time of Śaṅkara, and from which the latter represented a reaction. Rather was he inclined to welcome such a tendency. He would have ranged himself alongside of Kumārila Bhaṭṭa in opposition to the Buddhists, and, while he would also have sympathized with much of the anti-ritualistic fervour which placed Śaṅkara in opposition to Kumārila Bhaṭṭa, he was by no means disposed to go all the way with Śaṅkara in the direction of abstraction. He had much more regard for the ordinary religious needs of humanity, and was unwilling to patronize the populace by allowing them graciously to occupy a lower station while a higher one was reserved for the true philosopher. He held that religious satisfaction and metaphysical validity might coincide, and that the air of the highest heights to which the philosopher might aspire was not too rarified for common men to breathe. If the common man still had to be selected from a somewhat restricted class, this disability might be put down to traditional caste-necessity and not to intrinsic intellectual or spiritual inferiority.

Rāmānuja's period was the end of the eleventh century and the beginning of the twelfth. He was born at Śrī-perumbūdūr, near Madras, and, after a youth of extraordinary precocity, he became the Āchārya, or spiritual leader connected with the temple at Śrīraṅgam, near Trichinopoly, and at the same time occupied the position of *Āchārya* of the Śri-Vaishṇava sect, the greatest of all the Vaishṇava sects. It is said that his domestic life was not particularly happy, and he suffered much from sectarian persecution. He seems from the first to have adopted a more liberal attitude towards non-Brāhman castes than did some of his predecessors. He indeed restricted the reading of the Vedas to the 'twice-born', but he was willing to communicate his religious teaching even to Śūdras and outcastes. The story is told of him that with great difficulty he persuaded a certain guru to unlock for him the secrets of the esoteric mysteries, under promise that these secrets would not be published except to a worthy disciple who had been properly tested.

Rāmānuja, however, found that the doctrines were so important and so vital for salvation, that for the sake of the general good he preferred himself to become a castaway if by any means —even by the breaking of a promise—he could save some. When the Guru in the vehemence of wrath threatened him with eternal punishment hereafter, Rāmānuja replied that he would gladly suffer hell himself if he could bring a message of salvation to the suffering people.

He represented to a considerable extent the tendency of thought manifested in the Purāṇas. He was an adherent further of the Vaishṇava religion in which great stress was laid on the *bhakti* attitude to the divine. Within the confines of this sect Rāmānuja entered into a kind of apostolical succession. Amongst its leaders at an earlier period was a special group of devotees called Ālvārs, who were renowned for their religious hymns and honoured as saints almost on the threshold of divinity. They laid special stress on the central tenet of *bhakti*, and, while holding no official place in the sect, were exceedingly influential by reason of the nobility and purity of their lives. These were succeeded by a group called Āchāryas, regarded as perhaps less fully inspired, but still greatly venerated. They exercised a considerable amount of authority over the sect, and performed certain priestly functions. Of these Rāmānuja was said to be the fifth in succession.

But, notwithstanding the strength of traditional influence, Rāmānuja's acceptance of the views he ultimately held was the result of conscious choice following upon controversy, and was not merely mechanical. At Conjeeveram he studied for some time under Yādavaprakāśa, a teacher of the school of Śaṅkara, and Rāmānuja's adherence to a modified form of monism was the result of repeated study of the pure monism of his guru. Much travelling in search of instruction had the effect of strengthening him in his views, and finally he felt himself qualified to succeed Alavandar, his immediate predecessor in the list of Āchāryas—at the famous temple of Śrīraṅgam. This place continued to be his head-quarters, except when driven into exile by reason of Saiva persecution, and during one long journey which he undertook for the spreading of his doctrines. His long life came to an end in 1137.

By his energy he consolidated the sect to which he belonged and left a powerful organization behind him. But his theoretical consolidation was of much greater importance than his institutional, for in his *Śrībhāshya* he gave to his sect a supporting philosophy, and at the same time, seeing that he commented on such important documents as the *Vedānta Sūtras*, traced that philosophy back to the traditional Vedānta sources. The twin principles of *bhakti* and *vidyā* which Rāmānuja followed strikingly indicate his close connexion both with the popular polytheistic and theistic religion on the one hand and also with central philosophical tendencies on the other. These principles, moreover, interact with each other in his system to their mutual advantage. The intensely emotional fervour associated with *bhakti*, as, e.g., in the *Bhāgavata Purāṇa*, was never adopted by Rāmānuja, and his *bhakti* is of a much more moderate type. On the other hand the coldly philosophical meditations of thinkers such as Śaṅkara are humanized and diverted from the abstract to the concrete.

With such a tradition and in such an environment it was to be expected that Rāmānuja would not be able to approve of Śaṅkara's doctrine of two orders of knowledge which compelled the seeker to go beyond a Divine Being who could attract the human heart and fill it with devotion, and search for an abstract unqualified Absolute. For Rāmānuja there was not a higher and a lower Brahman, but the so-called 'lower' Brahman was himself the ultimate, compact of auspicious qualities. The favourite assertion of the monists that here there 'was no diversity' was simply meant, according to Rāmānuja, to imply the unification of the attributes (which were incapable of ultimately detached existence) and the denial of any source of power other than Brahman. Creation is real and not a merely illusory activity. To three entities reality must always be allowed—to God, the individual souls, and non-intelligent matter. To God two stages of existence must be assigned. In the *pralaya* state of absolute quiescence souls and matter exist in Him in subtle form. At creation, again, they come forth into visible expression, and creation is the result of a positive volitional effort on the part of Brahman, who pervades the universe in which he expresses himself and in relation to whom all living creatures exist as modes (*prakāra*). The individual soul is not essentially one with Brahman in the sense that it has no present freedom and is bound eventually to lose its individuality. Rather does it become one with Brahman merely in the sense of acquiring the divine qualities, and its destiny, when it is released, through steady devotion and contemplation and by the gift of the grace of God, from the trammels of transmigration, is to enjoy communion in paradise with the personal Lord of all. The general character of Rāmānuja's conception of God was such that it was possible for him, without intellectual contradiction, to identify Brahman with Vishṇu, the God of the Vaishṇavas, and at the same time to claim that the worship of Vishṇu was a direct fulfilment of the teaching of the Vedānta texts, and the religious counterpart of the only tenable philosophical position. Rāmānuja's work had considerable influence upon subsequent religious development and gavc to the faith of the Vaishṇavas a stability and dignity which it did not previously possess.[1]

Śaṅkara's philosophy is known as Advaita (non-dualism), and Rāmānuja's as Viśishṭādvaita (modified non-dualism), and it will be obvious from the short account we have given of the tenets of the two philosophers that the qualifying adjective indicates a very vital difference. That the second of the protagonists was himself vividly conscious of the difference is evident from the quotation we have already given from Rāmānuja's own polemical writings. The intensity of opposition has not diminished in the course of the centuries, as is indicated by a saying recently attributed to a leader of one of the schools of thought in southern India, which is dominated by the Viśishṭādvaita doctrine He is represented as declaring that he had rather see all India abandoning Hinduism altogether than that 'it should fall a prey to the Vedānta of Śaṅkara'.[2] It will therefore be readily understood how difficult it is in any exposition of the Vedānta to include as equally important data the teachings of both Śaṅkara and Rāmānuja. As Max Müller says, 'It must be admitted that in India, instead of one Vedānta philo-

[1] We may note especially his influence on the doctrines of the Sātwata school, as these are set forth by Prof. Bhagavat Kumar Shastri in his book upon *The Bhakti Cult in Ancient India*. Cf. pp. 173 ff.

[2] Quoted in Frazer's *Indian Thought*, 72.

sophy, we have really two, springing from the same root but extending its branches in two very different directions, that of Śaṅkara being kept for unflinching reasoners who, supported by an unwavering faith in Monism, do not shrink from any of its consequences, . . . another, that of Rāmānuja, trying hard to reconcile their Monism with the demands of the human heart that required, and always will require, a personal God, as the last cause of all that is, and an eternal soul that yearns for an approach to or a reunion with that Being.' [1]

It is therefore necessary to inquire which of the two philosophers is accepted as the typical Vedantist by Indian thinkers, and to what extent the popular verdict reflects a recognition of continuity between the favoured teaching on the one hand and the teaching of the Upanishads and the *Vedānta Sūtras* on the other. If we can prove that one of the two rival commentators is clearly outstanding, the simplest procedure in our subsequent exposition will be to adopt as a basis the teaching accepted by the majority, and use the other as a starting-point for lines of criticism.

There can be little doubt that pre-eminence must be assigned to Śaṅkara. So far as counting of heads goes, it has been estimated even by a follower of Rāmānuja that out of the total number of Vedantins 75 per cent. are adherents of Śaṅkara, and only 15 per cent. of Rāmānuja, while the remaining 10 per cent. may be distributed amongst minor sects also laying claim to the name of Vedantins. And that this popularity is not merely accidental, but is based upon and justified by a considered estimate of the significance of Śaṅkara's teaching, is evidenced by the opinion of leading scholars, even down to the present day. In their opinion the triumph of Vedantic ideas is due fundamentally to the work of Śaṅkara. 'It was given to Śaṅkara', says Mr. C. N. Krishnaswami Aiyar, 'to make Vedānta the basis of every religious sect that India has known, so as to satisfy the needs of men of all shades of intelligence and bias.' [2] And Mr. D. N. Pal, after citing a long list of appreciations of Vedantism to be found in the writings of European scholars, exclaims, 'All this is due to Śaṅkara. Without his master mind, this grand thing remained inconceivable.' [3] Mr. P. N. Sen

[1] Müller, *S. S.* 192. [2] Aiyar, 9. [3] Pal, 141.

holds that 'the philosophy of Śaṅkara has now been unalterably identified with the Vedānta philosophy'.[1] Prof. S. N. Das Gupta writes in much the same strain, 'Whenever we speak of the Vedānta philosophy, we mean the philosophy that was expounded by Śaṅkara,'[2] and he claims also that the popularity of the philosophy is based on the intrinsic merit of 'the subtle and deep ideas it contains'. Dr. Thibaut takes the *Śaṅkara-bhāshya* to represent the orthodox side of Brahmanical theology and describes the doctrine advocated by Śaṅkara as 'the most important and interesting which has arisen on Indian soil; neither those forms of the Vedānta which diverge from the view represented by Śaṅkara nor any of the non-Vedantic systems can be compared with the so-called orthodox Vedānta in boldness, depth, and subtlety of speculation'.[3]

Having established the centrality of Śaṅkara himself in popular and scholarly estimation, it now remains for us to ask whether he can serve himself heir to the fundamental ideas of his authorities, i.e. whether he can by right of succession be called orthodox. To what extent is he a reliable interpreter of the Upanishads and of the *Sūtras*? Although both he and Rāmānuja represent philosophical tendencies divergent alike from the Upanishads and the *Sūtras*, and although—to borrow a metaphor from Max Müller—they both are citizens of philosophical colonies which have detached themselves to some extent from the mother-country, yet on the whole neither of them is so individualistic as to neglect the obvious strengthening of their respective positions which would come from a properly established connexion with the ancient authorities. They shared the universally accepted view that no system could be regarded as having sufficient standing if it could be shown to be in opposition to the tradition of ancient thought. It has already been shown, however, that we cannot assert any simple identification between the doctrines of the Upanishads and of the *Sūtras*, and therefore we cannot expect that the attitude of Śaṅkara and Rāmānuja, whether divergent from each other or not, will be exactly the same in regard to the *Sūtras* as in regard to the Upanishads. It may turn out that Śaṅkara is the more

[1] Sen, 5. [2] Das Gupta, I. 429.
[3] *S. B. E.* XXXIV, p. xiv.

faithful interpreter of the Upanishads and Rāmānuja of the *Sūtras*, or vice versa.

There are one or two *a priori* considerations which may throw some light upon the problem. Śaṅkara, e.g., is disposed to treat the *Sūtras* as of much less importance than the Upanishads. He assigns, as we have seen, to the former merely 'the purpose of stringing together the flowers of the Vedānta passages'.[1] Consequently, if any conflict should arise between the *Sūtras* and the Upanishads, Śaṅkara will feel bound to accept the teaching of the latter rather than of the former, and will, on the other hand, feel more at liberty to transform the primary meaning of the *Sūtras*. Moreover, Śaṅkara took a much stricter view than Rāmānuja of the authority of the Upanishads. His attitude is predominantly one of submission leaving little room for freedom. In his comment on I. 1. 2 he indeed allows that, while supreme reverence is to be paid to the Vedānta texts, yet the knowledge derived from them may be supplemented by intuition which 'may be had recourse to according to the occasion'. Inference also may be regarded as 'an instrument of right knowledge in so far as it does not contradict the Vedānta texts'. But in reference to I. 1. 11 he takes up the more uncompromising position that 'Reasoning which disregards the holy texts and rests on individual opinion only, has no proper foundation. . . . The true nature of the cause of the world cannot . . . even be thought of without the help of the holy texts.'

We shall return a little later to Śaṅkara's general conception of the place of authority, but in the meantime it may be noted that in relation especially to the Upanishads his attitude will lead us to expect an exceedingly careful rendering of what he takes to be their meaning. On the other hand, we may note that Rāmānuja adopts a much freer attitude to the Upanishads, and lays down the general principle that, when perception and Scripture come into conflict, Scripture is not necessarily to be regarded as the more authoritative.[2] As a consequence of this we may very naturally form the expectation that in any cases of variance between the Upanishads and the *Sūtras*, Rāmānuja will feel more at liberty to follow the plain meaning of the *Sūtras*.

[1] Cf. Commentary on Sūtra I. 1. 2, *S. B. E.* XXXIV. 17.
[2] Cf. *S. B. E.* XLVIII. 73.

Another *a priori* consideration has reference to the distribution of the contents of the *Sūtras*. By far the larger portion of them deals with topics which, according to Śaṅkara's principles, are of secondary importance. He will therefore be compelled to concentrate his attention upon what in respect of bulk is a minor portion, and, contrariwise, will be disposed to treat the major portion with considerable freedom and subject it to a method of interpretation which will detract from the importance it might have had on a plain rendering. He will have to expend a good deal of effort in order to extract from it a secondary meaning more in accordance with the import of the minor portion. It is, of course, possible that this secondary meaning will be the essential meaning, but the probabilities are the other way, and *a priori* we shall be disposed to attribute the greater accuracy to the simpler interpretation. The right to adopt an esoteric point of view must always be somewhat reluctantly conceded unless on other grounds it can be shown that the Scriptures in question were intended to have a double meaning.

The question of the affiliation of Śaṅkara's doctrine to the *Sūtras* and the Upanishads respectively cannot, however, be decided on *a priori* grounds merely, but must depend for settlement on an investigation of the sources of some of Śaṅkara's leading doctrines. Dr. Thibaut has made an elaborate study of this question, and has selected as points for discussion the problems of two orders of knowledge, the distinction between a higher and a lower Brahman, the doctrine of Māyā, and the relation of the individual souls to Brahman.[1] As our main purpose is expository rather than historical, a brief discussion of Śaṅkara's relations to the *Sūtras* and the Upanishads as revealed in his treatment of these topics is all that is necessary here.

We have seen that the distinction between ordinary and real knowledge is at the basis of much of Śaṅkara's teaching. The assumption is that statements may be true from the *vyāvahārika* or ordinary point of view, but not true from the *pāramārthika* or transcendental point of view. If this distinction is recognized

[1] The same topics, though not in the same order, have been discussed at considerable length in the present writer's *Pantheism and the Value of Life*, 193–230.

as fundamental in the Sūtra teaching, we should naturally expect that only he would be regarded as having attained the highest stage of emancipation who had also attained to the highest knowledge. But, as a matter of fact, in the fourth division of the *Sūtras*, a description is given at considerable length of one who knows Brahman, and yet this description is declared by Śaṅkara to apply to one who only has the lower knowledge, and therefore cannot have risen to the level of the highest attainment possible. If, however, the *Sūtras* had agreed with his view, it is difficult to understand how they could have placed such a description in such a setting where we should naturally have expected a reference to the highest conceivable state. The *Īśā Upanishad* I. 9 may seem to be a passage favourable to Śaṅkara's view. Here it is said that 'those who delight in knowledge enter, as it were, into greater darkness', and Śaṅkara interprets it as indicating a depreciation of those who possess only the lower knowledge. But its true significance seems to be that it gives a decision on the point that when a choice has to be made between knowledge and works, the alternative of knowledge alone is more dangerous than the alternative of works alone. About all that can be said in reference to Upanishad support of Śaṅkara's general distinction is that it affords a convenient method of arranging the different strata in their teaching and of dealing with *higher and lower material*.

It is also difficult to prove that support can be found in the *Sūtras* for the negative procedure which results in the identification of the individual soul with Brahman. Śaṅkara indeed argues that individuality is entirely due to nescience, and that the 'joining' which is spoken of in *Sūtras* I. 1. 19 can mean only identity and nothing else. It is, however, to be noticed that this interpretation is so far from being regarded as the only possible one, that Rāmānuja, in reference to the same passage, makes the vigorous comment that 'To say that any one is identical with that by which he obtains bliss, would be madness indeed'.[1] A passage having great significance for this question is to be found in *Sūtras* II. 3. 43, 'The soul is a part of the Lord, on account of the declaration of difference.' In order to bring this into agreement with his system, Śaṅkara has to insert the

[1] Cf. *S. B. E.* XLVIII. 236.

qualification, 'a part, *as it were*,' whereas Rāmānuja can take the statement far more simply. Moreover, a slightly earlier *Sūtra* of the same Pada [1] speaks of the soul as an 'agent', thus seeming to convey an impression of individuality. It would not be difficult, however, to show that the Upanishads give far greater support than the *Sūtras* to Śaṅkara's denial of individuality. The *Kaushītaki Upanishad* [2] is favourable to the maintenance of individuality, but such passages as *Bṛihadāraṇyaka Upanishad* I. 4. 19, 'From death to death goes he who sees plurality anywhere,' tell strongly in the opposite direction. Still more convincing is the consideration that the prevailing tendency of the Upanishads is in the direction of regarding the association of Brahman with plurality simply as a concession to the weakness of the empirical consciousness, and of insisting that the final state is one of complete identification of the individual soul with Brahman.

The situation is very much the same in regard to Śaṅkara's distinction between the *saguṇam* and *nirguṇam* Brahman. This distinction does not seem to be supported by the *Sūtras*. They persist in ascribing one quality after another to Brahman, and they put the inquiry into Brahman as 'an ocean of auspicious qualities' in the very forefront of their endeavour. This, to say the least of it, would be a slightly curious and futile proceeding, if the Sūtrakara indeed considered that the Brahman of qualities was not the highest from his point of view, even though it might not be the highest in the sense of the word 'highest' accepted by Śaṅkara. But Śaṅkara argues that, though it must be admitted that there are passages in the Upanishads which might very naturally be construed as referring to a qualitative Brahman, yet these very passages are contradicted by passages which come later; and, as a contradiction must always follow that which is contradicted, these later passages must be taken as more authoritative than the earlier. A criterion based upon the order of the passages is, however, of doubtful validity, and, in any case, if rigorously applied, the criterion would not always tell in favour of Śaṅkara.[3] At the same time Śaṅkara is in the main justified in regard to the Upanishads. Although they do not

[1] II. 3. 33. [2] Cf. especially II. 15.
[3] Cf. the present writer's *Pantheism and the Value of Life*, p. 198.

make any formal and explicit distinction between the qualitative and non-qualitative Brahman, yet their general tendency is in a negative direction and towards a Brahman of abstract character, in regard to which they can make use of only the vaguest predicates or of none at all. On the whole it would be correct to say that they show a distrust of any categories drawn from ordinary experience.

In regard to the relation of God to the world, we have to ask whether the *Sūtras* support Śaṅkara's view of Māyā as a purely negative illusion. This question is bound up with the one we have just been considering, as, if a qualitative Brahman is to be regarded as the ultimate object of belief in the *Sūtras*, obviously Śaṅkara's position which degrades such a qualitative Brahman to the level of the first product of Māyā is attacked at the very foundation. We are the more inclined to believe that Śaṅkara has difficulty in deriving support for his doctrine from the *Sūtras*, because of the frequency with which he begs the question. He puts his opponents out of court and brushes their arguments aside on the ground that these are statements regarding a merely *supposed* reality and therefore worthless. Now when a man consistently refuses to take the statements of his opponents at their face value in their intention, the probability is that this face value is not very favourable to him. And a study of the *Sūtras* would seem to bear out the view that Śaṅkara is wise in not making any very direct appeal to them. One of their fundamental positions is that God is not only the originating but also the material cause of the world, in which case it is obvious that the effect would partake of the reality of the cause. A minor consideration is that Śaṅkara himself seems sometimes, and especially in the heat of his conflict with the Buddhists, to accept the distinction made in the *Sūtras*, without seeking to minimize it or explain it away. In reference to *Sūtra* III. 2. 3 he emphasizes the distinction between the dream-world and the waking world, and the contention that the dream-world, as being Māyā, is different from the actual waking world—from which it would surely follow that the actual world is *not* Māyā. Śaṅkara, as has been said, temporarily accepts this conclusion.

As regards the Upanishads, it may be said that the Māyā doctrine certainly does not appear in any explicit form in the earlier Upanishads, and there is a good deal to support the position that on the whole they favour a realistic interpretation of the universe. But at the same time it must be admitted that the Māyā doctrine is present in germ and that its further development is thoroughly natural and almost inevitable. It is really the result of a desire—pressed indeed to its uttermost—for a philosophical unity of the most rigorous kind. If the contention has been accepted that nothing *is apart* from Brahman, and, if it is found difficult to reconcile the plurality with the unity, rigorous logic would seem to demand the denial of the plurality. It probably would not be too much to say that the general teaching of the Upanishads was in favour of such a demand.

Thus we seem to have reached the position that, in respect of the chief parts of his doctrine, Śaṅkara is not a very faithful interpreter of the *Sūtras*, but that on the whole he reproduces and carries farther the main tendencies of the Upanishads. This is very much the position taken up by Thibaut, who has devoted much careful consideration to the problem; and he is supported on both counts by the majority of scholars. Gough, e.g., says that 'the teaching of Śaṅkara is the natural and legitimate interpretation of the philosophy of the Upanishads',[1] and in reference to the *Sūṭras* Max Müller says that 'Śaṅkara's philosophy, with its unflinching monism, is his own rather than Bādarāyaṇa's'.[2] Jacobi [3] says that Śaṅkara does violence to the sense of the *Sūtras* but is nearer to the Upanishads. Garbe [4] takes the opposite view and holds that it is Rāmānuja who 'introduces into Bādarāyaṇa's treatise views which are alien to the true Vedantic doctrine'; and he asserts that of the Indian adherents of the Vedānta, 'three-fourths accept Śaṅkara's interpretation of the *Brahmasūtras*.' Facts hardly bear out this statement. Garbe seems almost to regard the *Brahma Sūtras* and the Upanishads as agreeing on all important points, which is very far from being the case. The truer position would seem to be that while three-fourths of the Vedantists would agree in regarding Śaṅkara as a typical Vedantist, they are not in the

[1] Gough, *Philosophy of the Upanishads*, p. vii.
[2] Müller, *S. S.* 117.
[3] *Das Licht vom Osten*, 50.
[4] *E. R. E.* XII. 597.

majority of cases willing to allow that he is a faithful interpreter of the *Sūtras*.

Indeed, Indian writers are not quite so ready as Deussen and Gough to agree even that Śaṅkara is altogether reliable as an interpreter of the Upanishads. Prof. Radhakrishnan, e.g., takes up an exceedingly cautious attitude on this point; [1] but on the whole in this reference they accept him as a pillar of orthodoxy, and their general attitude would, as we have seen, justify us in regarding him as the main source of material for the exposition and estimation of the Vedānta philosophy. But in regard to the *Sūtras* they are almost all (*pace* Prof. Garbe) in agreement that he does not faithfully interpret the *Sūtras*. One notable exception, however, is Prof. P. D. Shastri, who calls Śaṅkara 'the best and most satisfactory exponent of Bādarāyaṇa's views on the Vedānta problems'.[2] Sir R. G. Bhandarkar, on the other hand, and more representatively, says, 'There are two doctrines indicative of the relation of God to the world, the so-called Pariṇāmavāda and the Vivartavāda. The last is the doctrine of Śaṅkarāchārya . . .; while the first is that clearly held by the author of the *Sūtras*.' [3] He is supported by Prof. S. N. Das Gupta, who is 'inclined to believe that the dualistic interpretations of the *Brahmasūtras* were more faithful to the *Sūtras* than the interpretations of Śaṅkara'.[4]

We may then take up generally the position that Śaṅkara represents a reaction in the direction of the Upanishads and away from the slightly dualistic tendency manifest in the *Sūtras*; and, on this understanding, may proceed to our fuller investigation of Śaṅkara's views as typical of the Vedānta philosophy. History to a very considerable extent places him in the position of *the* orthodox exponent, although it does not rule out the consideration of opposing views. And after all, whatever his affiliations may be, it is with Śaṅkara's own unfolding of his philosophy that we have mainly to do; for, as Prof. Das Gupta says, 'a system in the *Sūtras* is weak and helpless as a new born babe'; and the Upanishads themselves awaited through the centuries the coherence of doctrine which only a systematizer could give.

[1] Cf. Radhakrishnan, I. 141.
[2] P. D. Shastri, 96.
[3] *Vaishṇavism*, p. 160.
[4] Das Gupta, I. 421.

IV

THE APPROACH TO ŚAṄKARA'S CENTRAL TEACHING: PRELIMINARY CONDITIONS; HIS CONCEPTION OF AUTHORITY; THE IDEALISTIC ATTITUDE; HIS RELATION TO BUDDHISM

ACCORDING to Śaṅkara, certain preliminary conditions of philosophic study have to be observed. These are broadly similar to those we have already noted in connexion with the Upanishads. For Śaṅkara also the conditions are both external and internal, i.e. they are either largely beyond our control or largely within our control. We find that the spirit of esotericism has persisted even to Śaṅkara's day, and that of the external conditions one of the most important is that the aspirant should belong to the proper class or caste. The Vedānta is essentially aristocratic. Although its ultimate doctrine is the unity of the Self with Brahman and the denial of the diversity of things, and we might suppose that this denial would apply also to the diverse conditions of human beings, yet from the first this knowledge is jealously guarded as a privilege of only certain sections of the population. The rebirth of the soul which the enlightenment makes possible must have as its counterpart the external ceremony of rebirth, the *upanāyana* ceremony, the investiture of the youth with the sacred thread, for which only the three highest castes are eligible. The Śūdras, or lower caste, are rigorously excluded. The Śūdra may need this knowledge as much as other men, and he may also be capable of it, but still he must not be allowed the opportunity of acquiring it.[1]

This exclusiveness was bound up, as we shall see, with other external conditions such as the Vedantist dependence on the authority of the Veda and upon instruction by a teacher, and we shall discuss these further in connexion with the general question of the place of authority in the Vedānta. In the meantime it may be noted that this limitation of the reading of the

[1] Cf. Śaṅkara's Commentary on *Sūtra* I. 3. 25 ff., where he discusses the question as to who are eligible, and lays down the rule that 'men only of the three higher castes are . . . not excluded by prohibitions', and are qualified by being 'subject to the precepts about the *upanāyana* ceremony and so on'. Cf. *S. B. E.* XXXIV. 197, and Colebrooke's *Miscellaneous Essays*, I. 223.

Vedas was supposed to have been broken only in one or two legendary cases, which were in themselves of doubtful historicity, and which, in any case were of the nature of exceptions proving the rule rather than contradicting it. Śaṅkara himself explicitly accepts the injunction that the Vedas were never to be read in the presence of a Śūdra, with the consequence that the knowledge derivable only from the Vedas was a privilege to which the lowest class could not aspire. He states that 'the mere circumstance of being in a condition of desire does not furnish a reason for qualification if capability is absent. Mere temporal capability again does not constitute a reason for qualification, spiritual qualification being required in spiritual matters.'[1] And spiritual qualification he defines in the same paragraph as meaning simply not being excluded from the reading of the Vedas. Further he quotes with seeming acceptance the stern Vedic prescription that 'the ears of him who hears the Veda are to be filled with molten lead and lac, "For the Śūdra is (like) a cemetery, therefore (the Veda) is not to be read in the vicinity of a Śūdra" '.[2]

It is more pleasant and more just, however, to turn from these external restrictions to the internal conditions which Śaṅkara lays down. The importance of these is indicated in the very first *Sūtra*, 'Then, therefore the enquiry into Brahman', especially by the word 'Then'. According to Śaṅkara, 'then' does not at all refer to a preliminary acquaintance with, or performance of, religious works. These, as we shall see later, have only ascetic or propaedeutic value, and do not of themselves bring about any abiding result. The true conditions are purely spiritual, and are enumerated by Śaṅkara as follows: (1) discrimination of what is eternal and what is non-eternal; (2) renunciation of desire for reward both here and hereafter; (3) the attainment of the six means—tranquillity, restraint, renunciation of religious ceremonies, patience, concentration, belief; (4) the longing for liberation.

A study of these conditions reveals a very pure and elevated conception of the philosophic spirit. There must be as a preliminary a generally philosophical attitude, a readiness to distinguish between the changing and the permanent. There must

[1] Cf. *S. B. E.* XXXIV. 224. [2] Ib. 228.

be a singleness of aim and no mingling of material ambitions with the pure pursuit after truth. There must be an abandonment of the sceptical spirit, not to the extent of being the victim of obstructive dogmatism or being unwilling to investigate all problems, but to the extent of being willing to believe that investigation can bring about a result, which result must be viewed in an other-worldly, ascetic rather than humanistic, spirit, properly described by the phrase, 'longing for liberation'. The 'six means' indicate the prevailing state of the mind of the true philosopher. He must be entirely independent of external ceremonies, and patient—to a greater extent even than Aristotle would demand—of the vicissitudes of fortune. He must have his senses wholly under control, and have acquired a Stoic calm. Above all he must be capable of, and practise, concentration—passive to the extent of a recognition that the knowledge of Brahman 'does not depend on human energy', but active in the sense that for him concentration means the gathering up of the highest human powers and requires a persistent holding of the divine unity before the mind. Concentration must be carefully distinguished from mere sluggishness of mind. This mixture of the passive and the active attitude is strikingly anticipative of Spinoza, and it may be noted in passing that Rāmānuja in a similar spirit defines meditation as 'steady remembrance'.[1]

Given, then, this spiritual attitude of mind, how does the inquirer proceed? Is there any assistance from human—or, perhaps from Divine—sources available for him in his quest after God? Will he have to depend on his own resources entirely, or are there authorities which may, nay *must*, help him? This brings us to the general question of the importance ascribed in the Vedānta to *authority*.

The Place of Authority in the Vedānta

We have seen that Śaṅkara took up a fairly submissive attitude in regard to the authority of the Upanishad texts. He considered that he was bound to show the agreement of his main doctrines with these texts. It might turn out that there was agreement also with experience and reason, but such

[1] Cf. *S. B. E.* XLVIII. 11.

subordinate agreement would be only a consequence of the truth of the doctrine, and neither experience nor reason could be regarded as in any important sense the sources of the doctrine. The ultimate source must lie in authority, reason being given a merely supplementary place and allowed to have validity only 'in so far as it does not contradict the Vedānta texts',[1] and in so far as it deals with comparatively minor considerations.[2] According to Śaṅkara, only perfect knowledge can give release; and perfect knowledge, just because it deals with permanent things and wins universal acceptance, cannot be dependent on mere reasoning. He says in his Commentary on *Sūtra* I. 1–11, 'As the thoughts of men are altogether unfettered, reasoning which disregards the holy texts, and rests on individual opinion only, has no proper foundation.' And again, 'On account of the diversity of men's opinions, it is impossible to accept mere reasoning as having a sure foundation.'[3]

Now there has been a tendency both in ancient and modern times for searchers after truth to turn away in disgust from the conflict of opinions and the jarring noises of controversy, and to seek for the region where 'beyond these voices there is peace'; but Śaṅkara goes farther than most, and asserts in a positive manner that from the nature of the case the highest truth *must* rest upon authority. In his Commentary on I. 8. 4 we read, 'The fact of everything having its Self in Brahman cannot be grasped without the aid of the Scriptural passage, "That art Thou".'[4] And in I. 8. 11 we read further, 'The true nature of the cause of the world upon which final emancipation depends, cannot, on account of its abstruseness, even be thought of without the help of the holy texts; for . . . it cannot become the object of perception because it does not possess qualities such as form and the like, and, as it is devoid of characteristic signs, it does not lend itself to inference and the other means of right knowledge.'[5] He quotes with approval *Kāṭhaka Upanishad* I. 2. 9, 'That doctrine is not to be obtained by argument, but when it is declared by another, then it is easy to understand'.[6] We must reject the ordinary means of proof which rest on

[1] Cf. *Sūtra* I. 1. 2.
[2] Cf. Deussen, 95.
[3] Cf. *S. B. E.* XXXIV. 315.
[4] Cf. Ib. 23.
[5] Ib. 316.
[6] Ib. 307.

perception and inference; or, if we still retain these psychological terms, we must sublimate them. Perception may be transformed into a kind of mystical intuition, similar to sense-perception in its directness; or the two terms may be used in conjunction as indicating the two divisions of the sacred canon, viz. *śruti* and *smṛiti*, 'hearing' and 'remembrance'. According to Śaṅkara's most usual practice, the first division is equivalent to the older Upanishads, and the second to the *Bhagavadgītā.*

The sacred texts not only serve the central purpose of religious enlightenment, but have also a more comprehensive usefulness. Even what we should now regard as details of scientific knowledge may be believed on the basis of Scripture.[1] Practical guidance also may be derived from them. In connexion with III. 1. 26 it is stated that 'the knowledge of an action being right is based on Scripture only'.

Finally, it should be noticed that Śaṅkara does not indulge in any elaborate argument in order to establish the authoritativeness of the Scriptures; he simply accepts this as something which cannot be gainsaid. 'Nor can the authoritativeness of the texts', he says, 'be proved by inferential reasoning; so that it would be dependent on instances observed elsewhere.'[2]

It has long been the practice of older writers on the Vedānta to lay almost excessive emphasis upon Śaṅkara's implicit reliance upon authority. They compare him with the scholastics of Europe, and visit him with the contempt which is frequently meted out to such dim-minded medievalists as some of them were. Muir, e.g., speaks of Śaṅkara's method in a rather lofty manner: 'These arguments are not likely to seem convincing to any persons but the adherents of the schools from which they have severally emanated. The European student can only look upon these opinions as matters of historical interest, as illustrations of the course of religious thought among a highly acute and speculative people.'[3] A more modern writer to a certain extent redresses the balance by drawing the parallel with the scholastics simply and without depreciation: 'As Śaṅkara argues with his opponents, his position resembles that of a Scholastic

[1] Cf. Commentary on II. 3. 10, *S. B. E.* XXXVIII. 22, where we are told about the production of water from fire.

[2] *S. B. E.* XXXIV. 23.

[3] *Sanskrit Texts*, III. 209.

philosopher in medieval Europe. Each believed that he had an infallible authority behind him with which the results of speculative inquiry must be harmonized. The Christian teacher might start from Aristotle, but he must end with Scripture and the Church. The Hindu might use the methods of reasoning as freely as the Greek, but he must bring their issue into accord with the Veda.'[1]

At the same time it must be admitted that Śaṅkara's apparent abdication of private judgement, his reliance on instruction imparted by another, and his abhorrence of unfettered thought, are disconcertingly suggestive of the narrowness of European medieval philosophy, and seem to place a deep chasm between Vedantic and modern speculation. It would seem at first sight almost impossible to treat as serious philosophy a system which submitted thus tamely to bondage, and it is therefore a matter of considerable importance to inquire whether the bondage is really so complete as might appear on the surface. This is all the more necessary because modern Indian writers are perfectly well aware of the requirements of the philosophic spirit; and, unless we are irresistibly compelled by facts, it would be unfair to bind upon them an inheritance which would limit their speculative freedom. Prof. Radhakrishnan, e.g., in the course of his treatment of the philosophy of the *Bhagavadgītā*, is responsible for the dictum that 'a half-truth won for ourselves is worth more than a whole truth learned from others'.[2] And in general it may be said that his fellow countrymen are also more or less conscious of the contradiction between the exercise of the philosophic spirit and implicit obedience to authority. Because of loyalty to the spirit of investigation they desire to be free; and yet, if they continue to be loyal also to the tradition of reliance upon Scripture, they would appear to be in bondage. What then can be said of the tradition itself, so far as Śaṅkara is concerned? Was he with his followers merely a scholastic adherent of philosophic maxims handed down to them by teachers, or did their adherence to Scriptural authority arise from a deeper motive and one less embarrassing to the freedom of speculative inquiry?

It is, of course, impossible anywhere to get away entirely from

[1] Carpenter, 310. [2] Radhakrishnan, I. 553.

authority, just as impossible as it is to cut oneself altogether loose from one's own past, and there is much truth in what was said of Edward Caird, 'The more original a man, the more heavy the tribute he exacts from the world and the more intimate his dependence. He cannot go before it; he can only set free its significance.' Further, if the reality of the universe is revealing itself to men through the growing knowledge of humanity, we are always at liberty to ask the question whether this revelation is direct or indirect; is it made to each individual afresh or may we not also rely upon the accumulated knowledge handed down by tradition? And the indirect, massed knowledge may come to us in the form of authority. The general consideration may also be premised that nominal or formal submission to authority has often coexisted with actual speculative freedom, which is left unhindered in practice so long as the authority is not challenged. A recent writer in the *Hibbert Journal*,[1] e.g., has pointed out—with what justification we shall not presume to say—that the official prescription of doctrinal uniformity in the Roman Catholic Church became obviously restrictive only on the emergence of Modernist doctrines. It is probably true that the demand for credal uniformity became more stringent in India as the result of a reaction from Buddhism, and therefore did not represent a permanently paralysing limitation of thought.

Further, in attempting to estimate the fettering effect of authority we have always to keep in mind the degree of accustomedness or naturalness which has been induced. Fetters which have been worn for a long time do not interfere with freedom to the same extent as when they were first imposed; and, further, the liberty of the individual does not seem to be, and is actually not so severely circumscribed when the imposition of restrictions arises gradually and naturally from a particular kind of environment. Under such circumstances the irksomeness and feeling of restraint—which subjective effects are all-important in connexion with philosophic independence—seem appreciably lessened, although, of course, we would not go so far as to say that a man who has been a long time in prison, or who is surrounded by others similarly confined, is in the same condition objectively as one who is free.

[1] October 1925.

It has been already pointed out[1] that the course of philosophic development in India was different from that of Western philosophy; that in the West one system succeeded another or was built on destructive criticism of the former, whereas in India the same system persisted through the centuries; the main lines of thought were prescribed by tradition; and development could consist only in the interpretation and re-interpretation of existing authorities. The Sūtra literature was taken to be typical of the whole. Because of their succinctness, they were unintelligible except to the initiated, and were thus esoteric in their effect and marked the power of authority, while, just because of their unintelligibility, they left room for considerable variety of interpretation and freedom of manipulation. In India it was perhaps truer than of any other land that a great philosopher could not go before the thought-tradition which he had inherited but could only set free its significance.

It might also be useful to draw further attention at this point to the great emphasis which, in the development of Indian thought, is placed upon instruction by a Guru or teacher. We have already noticed Śaṅkara's approving quotation from the *Kāṭhaka Upanishad* I. 2. 9,[2] and the same thought reappears in the *Chhāndogya Upanishad* VII. 25, 'One who does not attend on a teacher, does not believe'. There is a considerable development in the degree of importance assigned to the teacher, and the growing insistence upon the necessity of such assistance may have been due to Brahmanic influence. But whether this latter cause was operative or not, it is the case that long before Śaṅkara's day the presence of a teacher had become the recognized background of Indian thought. The dramatic setting of the Upanishads is largely constituted by the search for a teacher who will reveal the deepest mysteries; and, when he has been found, unbounded devotion and the most minute practical service is demanded of the pupil. The persistence of the attitude may be traced even to the present day. A recent Indian writer thus speaks in reference to the highest knowledge, 'The sole source of this knowledge is a clear and accurate understanding of the Vedic text, "Tḥat thou art"; but, however much one may analyse its meaning by means of his own reason or with

[1] p. 9. [2] p. 76.

the aid of commentaries, the direct realization of the self cannot take place unless the Vedic text in question reaches the student through the mouth of a spiritual teacher.'[1] And in the course of the development and as a result of it, devotion to truth and devotion to the Guru become almost synonymous. The latter comes to be regarded as well advanced on the way to deification; his personal authority is thus enhanced, and the principle of authority becomes more and more deeply engrained in the mental attitude of the Indian seeker after truth.

Whether this is altogether advantageous or not has been very seriously questioned. One writer speaks thus of the reverence for the Guru : 'It is a training not in self-reliance and independence of judgement, but in subservience to authority and reverence for what is established, just because it is established.'[2] An Indian writer is even more emphatic as regards the effect upon the consciousness of the people. Mr. D. N. Pal says, 'They had lost the power of independent judgement long ago—they had left it in the hands of the Brāhman from time immemorial; and the result we all know to our cost'.[3]

But whether desirable or not, the attitude spread to the whole environment. We have already noted Śaṅkara's acceptance of the principle that morality may be a matter of prescription, and this idea is deeply rooted in the life of the people. It is implied in their conception of *dharma*. A recent writer says, 'The idea of dharma is, like the Roman *pietas*, very closely bound up with the details as well as with the general spirit of a man's daily life and conduct as a member of the family or caste group. As a rule his duty is so clearly indicated by custom that he can be in no doubt about it.' And again, 'Actions are not right or wrong in their nature but only as they conform, or fail to conform, to a standard of propriety set up by general consent.'[4]

We thus see that authority is not something abruptly and obtrusively imposed upon a man from without, but something which almost imperceptibly emerges from, and gathers up, the spirit of the whole environment. The pressure of it upon the individual is thus softened by its exceeding naturalness. In

[1] Veṅkatarāmanan, 'Śaṅkara's Philosophy of Saṁsāra', in *Three Great Acharyas*, p. 111.

[2] McKenzie, *Hindu Ethics*, 50.

[3] Pal, 65.

[4] Margaret M. Urquhart, *Women of Bengal*, 33 and 57.

addition to this it is modified by certain tendencies towards valuation which save it from being merely a blind submission to detailed prescriptions having authority just because they were traditional. The ancient seers were considered to be worthy of respect, not simply because they were old but because of their pre-eminent merits, and for the reason that it was at least conceivable that men of former ages might have been capable of more direct intuition of God than was possible for their descendants of a later day. Śaṅkara explicitly takes this view, 'What is for us imperceptible was perceptible for the ancients: thus it is recorded that Vyāsa and others used to meet the Gods and Ṛishis face to face. . . . We must therefore believe that the ancients, in consequence of pre-eminent merits, held visible converse with Gods and Ṛishis.'[1] There is here at least a suggestion of a transition from the conception of the authority of age to that of the authority of the specialist in religion. There is further a recognition of an inherent satisfactoriness in the contents of the texts. They shine by their own light and have independent authority by reason of the character of their contents. They are convincing by their intrinsic value.[2]

Now it is but a short step from subjective satisfaction to evaluation on a metaphysical and more objective basis. The Vedānta passages come to have value, not merely as authorities, but because they have for their objects 'firmly established things'. Their fundamental aim is 'not to alter existing things but to make them appear as they are'.[3] But the real is the permanent, and the next very closely connected movement of thought is to the idea that the Scriptures, just because they deal with reality and therefore with the eternal, must themselves be eternal. They cannot be the work of a personal author; and their validity must be recognized by raising them above any phenomenal changes and placing them on the level of the noumenal which is independent of change. This conception of the eternity of the Vedas is supported by repeated discussions of the eternity of the words of which they are composed and even

[1] Quoted by Deussen, *S. V.* 38.

[2] Cf. 'The passages of Scripture about the negation of all difference have a meaning which leaves nothing more to be wished for.' *S.B.E.* XXXVIII. 395.

[3] Cf. Commentary on *Praśna U.* VI. 2,

of the sounds which the words indicate. There is alleged to be a natural and not merely conventional relation between words and that which they signify; words have an intrinsic denotation which is the essence of their authority.[1]

Further, words themselves acquire deeper metaphysical significance when, on the ground that they are injunctive (i.e. commanding things to be done) or that they are purposive (indicating plans of action), they are allied with the idea of creativeness. Prof. Paterson in his recent book refers to the early association of word with creative energy, 'The oral rite was felt to be highly charged with mysterious energy.' 'The uttered "must",' as Marett observes, 'is the very type of spiritual projectile, for nothing indicates an imperative more clearly, cutting it away from the formative matrix of thought and launching it on its free career, than the spoken word, and nothing finds its way home to another mind more sharply.'[2]

When this idea is associated with divine power, we are on the edge of a conception very similar to that which permits the ascription of cosmological significance to the syllable *Om*, and also to the less symbolic, but much deeper, concept embodied in the *Logos* doctrine of St. John's Gospel, 'In the beginning was the Word, and the Word was with God, and the Word was God.'[3] The earlier *Mīmāṁsā Sūtras* were content to prove the eternity of the Word, but the *Vedānta Sūtras* definitely connect with this the idea of the Word as an emanation from God, and as indicating divine activity. God revealed himself in the sound forms and sent forth his activity into the planning and accomplishment of the world.

Now if we think in this way, we can readily conceive of the process by which reverence for the Scriptures became reverence for the Word in general, and reverence for the Word became reverence for the Divine energy behind it. The Scriptures are invested with an almost metaphysical reality of their own, and respect for authority becomes, in idea at least, reverence for God. The Word heard by man is the plan followed by God, as

[1] Cf. Farquhar, 125, 'The absolute authority of the Veda requires for its establishment the doctrine of its eternity, and that leads in turn to the doctrine of the eternity of sound, and the indefeasible connexion between the sound of a word and its meaning.'

[2] Paterson, *Nature of Religion*, 390.

[3] John i. 1.

well as the energy through which the plan is realized. We pass from the region of blind submission to authority to that of religious devotion to a supreme Reality.

When, further, we remember what was regarded by Śaṅkara as the central doctrine of the tradition handed down to him, viz. the assertion of the essential unity of the Divine and the human, we may trace a further step in the direction of the substantializing and internalizing of authority. After all, Śaṅkara did not go to the sacred texts for anything in the nature of detailed instructions, but just for support of this central doctrine, and it was the assertion of this truth which, above everything else, he found in the texts. These served as a framework to this truth, and when the truth was discovered it was even possible that the framework might be discarded. The contents, the supreme contents of the Scriptures, were all that mattered, and their purpose was just the encouraging of an apprehension of the One Reality, in the apprehension of which the seeker submitted to no external authority but realized the essence of his own Self. Śaṅkara himself gives explicit permission for this transcending of scriptural authority, although it must be admitted that in one particular case he does so under circumstances which are slightly suggestive of a desire to escape from a logical contradiction.[1] It may be noted that in this connexion Rāmānuja pertinently observes that such a concession weakens Śaṅkara's whole position, inasmuch as, if Scripture is itself founded upon nescience and disappears when nescience disappears, it cannot be used to correct the errors of ordinary perception.[2]

In all this discussion we have been concerned simply to establish what we consider to be a position of some importance, viz. that it is necessary to take a broader view than in some quarters is customary of Śaṅkara's conception of authority, and that in the last resort his subjection to authority is not necessarily inimical to the philosophical spirit. There is much truth in the contention of Prof. S. N. Tattvabhushan that Śaṅkara's 'appeal to Scripture is not as to an external authority to be blindly re-

[1] Cf. Commentary on *Sūtras*, IV. 1. 3, 'Nor do we mind your objecting that, if perception &c., cease to be valid, scripture itself ceases to be so, for this conclusion is just what we assume. . . . We ourselves assume that, when knowledge springs up, scripture ceases to be valid.' *S. B. E.* XXXVIII. 340.

[2] Cf. *S. B. E.* XLVIII. 73.

ceived, but as to a valuable help to the attainment of true wisdom—wisdom which is attainable by every true seeker after truth'.[1] As we try to understand the attitude of Śaṅkara we shall find that we are frequently not far distant from the idea that religion cannot be merely a subjective product of individual imagination, but must be a response of the best within us to the best without, this 'best without us' being discovered to be of the same spiritual quality and essence as the 'best within'.[2]

We must next inquire as to the influence which Śaṅkara's views of authority had upon his method. Although, as we have seen, his speculative freedom may not have been greatly restricted, yet it cannot be denied that he did not always live up to the ideal we have suggested as associable with his attitude, and that his acceptance of authority had to a certain extent a hampering effect. It seems to lead, e.g., to a slight unfairness in his treatment of his opponents. He assumes at the outset that he has the monopoly of authority, and that, therefore, while he may appeal from perception to authority, it is not permissible for his opponents to do so. The latter must rely wholly on experience and can find no escape from its contradictions. He alone occupies the privileged position.

Further, because of his respect for his authorities, Śaṅkara feels himself constrained to follow the order of the *Sūtras*. Instead of constructing his arguments on lines of his own and arranging them so that they may lead most naturally to his main conclusions, he has to follow a somewhat tortuous course, winding in and out amongst the topics suggested by the *Sūtras*, and the main doctrines have to be established, as it were, by the way. Moreover, seeing that the main object formally was to show agreement of the doctrines with the Vedānta texts, the internal consistency of the arguments fell to a position of secondary importance, and the necessity of so arranging them as to bring out their coherence and completeness was not so keenly felt as it might otherwise have been.[3] Also, as Deussen points out in the same connexion, that fondness for dialectical disputation which so often arises in association with minute

[1] *Three Great Acharyas*, 76.
[2] Cf. Prof. J. Arthur Thomson in *Religions of the Empire*, p. 300.
[3] Cf. Deussen, *S. V.* 220.

textual interest and desire to prove a scriptural basis led to a certain want of proportion. Arguments for or against particular positions were bandied to and fro without sufficient regard to the importance of the disputed point relatively to the whole.

But the chief difficulty for Śaṅkara in the application of his doctrine of authority was caused by the want of harmony amongst the Upanishad texts themselves. It was easy when Scripture was in conflict with sense perception to decide dogmatically in favour of the former, but when Scripture conflicted with Scripture, what was to be done? Under such circumstances it was clearly not to be hoped that all the texts should support directly Śaṅkara's philosophical position. Yet if his authority was to remain unimpaired, it was necessary that they should at least appear to do so; and if their own intrinsic reliability was to remain undamaged, it was necessary that discrepancies should be removed. Śaṅkara was ready with two devices—both of which have been popular with writers throughout the ages, when their canonical authorities have caused them searchings of heart. The one is the principle of earlier and later, to which we have already briefly referred in discussing Śaṅkara's affiliation to the *Sūtras*. He applies it with great vigour to the question of the distinction between the qualitative and non-qualitative Brahman, on the basis of the principle which he lays down as follows: 'There being a conflict between the two passages, we . . . decide that the texts referring to Brahman as devoid of qualities are of greater force, because they are later in order than those which speak of Brahman as having qualities. Thus everything is settled.'[1] The man of straw has to be set up before he can be satisfactorily knocked down. In application of the principle we find, e.g., that a passage such as *Muṇḍaka Upanishad* I. 1. 9, 'From him who perceives all and knows all, whose brooding consists of knowledge, from him is born Hiraṇyagarbha, names, form and matter', seems to favour the qualitative view; whereas *Bṛihadāraṇyaka Upanishad* III. 4. 2, 'Thou couldst not see the true seer of sight', &c., seems to favour the non-qualitative. Unfortunately, as we have also seen, the application of the principle does not always work

[1] *S. B. E.* XLVIII. 26.

out in favour of Śaṅkara, for we find that, even in the same Upanishad, passages with a negative tendency precede those with a positive tendency.[1]

Śaṅkara's method of reconciliation becomes more interesting, and at the same time more elusive, when he adopts the second device. We have already referred to it as one of the *a priori* considerations affecting our estimate of his reliability as an interpreter of the *Sūtras* and the Upanishads. It is based on the relation between the literal and the figurative, and ultimately on the distinction which he draws between the exoteric and the esoteric and between lower and higher orders of knowledge. He makes great use of these distinctions and finds them very convenient for the purpose of removing discrepancies. We are here concerned with his use of the distinction between lower and higher knowledge only in connexion with the reconciliation of isolated and apparently contradictory texts; and it would be unfair at this stage to prejudge the question whether the distinction is in general ultimately defensible. As a method of adjusting differences it may be said to proceed on the principle that, if a passage contradicts his main doctrine, it will have to be interpreted figuratively, whereas, if it is in agreement with his central views, it may be taken literally; and in passing we may repeat the observation that, on the whole, Śaṅkara finds himself compelled to make much fuller use of figurative interpretation than does Rāmānuja. As an illustration of Śaṅkara's method we may take his refutation of the Sāṅkhya doctrine of the origin of the world in a non-intelligent *pradhāna*. He points out in his Commentary on *Sūtra* I. 1. 6 that we must not make use of metaphor in order to attribute the term 'self' to the *pradhāna* or non-intelligent principle. But in connexion with another *Sūtra*, viz. II. 4. 2, he claims the right to interpret a *Sūtra* figuratively if it occurs in the *pūrvapaksha*, or in relation to a doctrine which has to be refuted, while on the other hand if it occurs in a *siddhānta Sūtra*, or in relation to a doctrine which has to be established, he retains the right to interpret literally.[2] And in general, if difficulties occur in connexion with the created world, he is inclined to have recourse to the idea that the world

[1] Cf. *Muṇḍaka U.* I. 1. 6 and I. 1. 9.
[2] Cf. *S. B. E.* XXXVIII. 77.

has been created only in a figurative sense and that, therefore, any difficulties which may arise are difficulties only from an exoteric point of view.

Śaṅkara's Idealistic Attitude

Having considered Śaṅkara's statement of preliminary conditions and his attitude to, and application of, the principle of authority, we may now turn to his method of approach to his main problem. His procedure might be described as an expression of the idealistic spirit in philosophy, in so far as this implies a turning away from the immediate and naïvely realistic pronouncements of common sense. Deussen finds in him an exemplification of the fundamental attitude of metaphysics—that attitude without which metaphysics cannot exist, arising out of dissatisfaction with the immediate data of the senses, discontent with merely empirical and narrowly scientific investigation, and an earnest desire to penetrate beyond the appearances of things to the innermost secret of real being. In the fleeting experiences of ordinary perception, in the changing contents of space and time, in the unending succession of causes and effects, there can be no rest for the human spirit. Śaṅkara has embarked on that unchanging quest in which philosophy and religion are united, driven onwards by that insistent consciousness the very essence of which, as Hegel tells us, is 'the parting from and forsaking of what is immediate, what is finite', and the seeking for that home-country of the soul which, again in Hegel's words, is 'the region of eternal truth, of eternal rest, of eternal peace'.[1]

And yet, in our fully justified endeavour to place Śaṅkara in the main line of philosophical succession, we must not allow our description of the general philosophical attitude to be coloured by an anticipation of what we conceive Śaṅkara's particular philosophy to be. Because we may have a preliminary consciousness that Śaṅkara teaches a doctrine of empirical illusionism, we must not take it for granted that all philosophy is rooted in a similar belief. Neither, on the other hand, should we allow ourselves to take the most negative possible view of Śaṅkara's concept of illusion, under the influence of any general

[1] Hegel, *Philosophy of Religion*, 1 and 106.

reflection that in this matter he is in agreement with all philosophers of consequence. It *may* not be true that all philosophers of consequence start with a theory of illusion, and it may also turn out to be doubtful whether Śaṅkara's own doctrine in this respect is so extreme as it is often supposed to be. We cannot help thinking that Deussen has been neglectful of cautionary considerations of this kind, and that his conception of what philosophy has been, is, and always ought to be may have influenced unduly his particular interpretation of the Vedānta philosophy. He describes, e.g., the disposition to metaphysics as 'a more or less clear consciousness that all empirical investigation and knowledge amounts in the end only to a great deception, grounded in the nature of our knowing faculties, to open our eyes to which is the task of metaphysics'.[1] On the same page he asserts dogmatically that this 'more or less clear consciousness "became" a conviction' in the teaching of Kant. And with this view of philosophy as a basis he proceeds to erect his System of the Vedānta.

Now it may be true that, e.g., Descartes, the father of modern Western philosophy, began with the supposition that all the things he saw around him might be fictitious, and that he advocated a preliminary universal scepticism.[2] But surely a preliminary supposition is very different from a dogmatic conclusion, and to say that our senses may deceive us is very different from asserting that they actually lead us astray, or that all empirical data are illusory. Neither is it legitimate, as we shall afterwards have occasion to point out more fully, to describe Kant's position as dogmatically negative rather than as provisionally agnostic. But what we wish specially to protest against at the present juncture is the deduction which Deussen draws from his general philosophical position, and his resulting inclination to prejudice the issue by suggesting that, if Śaṅkara is to be placed alongside of the greatest philosophers of all ages, it must be expected at the outset that he will reach purely negative conclusions, according to which the whole empirical world will be swept away as altogether illusory.

Śaṅkara's general idealistic position is clearly stated in the summary of his doctrines given by Rāmānuja, 'Therefore know

[1] Deussen, *S. V.* 48. [2] Cf. Meditation, II.

that all particular things like rocks, oceans, hills, and so on, have proceeded from intelligence. . . . Nothing whatever, at any place or any time, exists apart from intelligence.'[1] This dependence of so-called objective reality upon mind is a fundamental assumption. Idealism, in almost all systems associated with the term, has both an objective and a subjective phase, sometimes the one and sometimes the other receiving the greater emphasis. In connexion with the Vedānta it may be easier to get a clear-cut statement of the objective than of the subjective phase, but we believe that subjective idealism is the natural way of approach to idealism of a negative and cosmical character, and that the Vedānta, as interpretated by Śaṅkara, is no exception to this rule. If the world of experience is made up of unsubstantial things such as dreams are made of, it would seem necessary, in order to fill out the conception, to view this world both as a projection of the individual self and as the outcome of cosmic imagining. The first point of view, giving centrality to the consciousness of the ordinary perceiver, would seem to have temporal priority in the thought of the individual philosopher.

This idea of the centrality of consciousness is emphasized by Śaṅkara, in the summary of his doctrines given by Rāmānuja. He has been attacking the realists for having failed to give due consideration to the power of consciousness and he proceeds: 'The fact is, that in perceiving colour and other qualities of things, we are not aware of a "shining forth" as an attribute of these things, and as something different from consciousness; nor can the assumption of an attribute of things called "light", or "shining forth" be proved in any way, since the entire empirical world itself can be proved only through consciousness. . . . Consciousness is independent of any other thing, because, through its connexion with other things, it is the cause of their attributes and of the empirical judgements concerning them. . . . Consciousness is itself the cause of its own "shining forth" as well as of the empirically observed shining forth of objects such as jars and the like.'[2]

It may seem strange that we should quote from Rāmānuja this statement of Śaṅkara's position, but the *Great Pūrvapaksha*,

[1] *S. B. E.* XLVIII. 23.

[2] *S. B. E.* XLVIII. 35.

as set forth by Rāmānuja, seems to us as clear a presentation of Śaṅkara's view as can be obtained; and it is admitted to be such by competent scholars. Dr. Otto, e.g., says: 'This Pūrvapaksha is almost in every detail the standpoint of Śaṅkara. Clearly, essentially, and also incisively is his position consecutively and gradually developed. And the presentation not only goes to the root of the matter but is also fair. It is really the opponent who here speaks, speaks well, and often with such brilliant and illuminating treatment of his reasons that one becomes concerned as to how Rāmānuja can possibly maintain his ground against him. It would not be easy to find a clearer, and, one might add, a more impressive setting forth of the Māyā-vāda than is offered in the Pūrvapaksha.'[1] But even if we still remain slightly suspicious of a statement of Śaṅkara's position which emanates from Rāmānuja, we find the centrality of consciousness set forth unequivocally by Śaṅkara himself, though admittedly in close anticipation of a universalistic or more objective point of view, in the following: 'And if the doctrine of the independent existence of the individual soul has to be set aside, then the opinion of the entire phenomenal world—*which is based on the individual soul*—having an independent existence is likewise to be set aside.'[2] The words which we have italicized are relevant to our purpose.

A broader foundation for our study may perhaps be found in the introductory pages to Śaṅkara's Commentary on the *Vedānta Sūtras*. In connexion with *Sūtra* I. 8. 1 he lays down very emphatically the distinction between subject and object, and warns us against superimposing the qualities of the object upon the subject or the qualities of the subject upon the object. They are as different as darkness and light, and the mixture of them is due to ignorance. From this coupling and confusion of the Real and Unreal arise all our difficulties. We must clearly recognize that the intelligent Self is alone real and that all objects are the product of wrong knowledge. In the passage referred to, Śaṅkara is more immediately concerned with showing how mistaken we are in regard to the Self, if we treat it as an Object and identify it with the body and the experiences of the body which come from sense-perception. But we may turn

[1] Otto, *Siddhānta des Rāmānuja*, 3. [2] *S. B. E.* XXXIV. 320.

his principle the other way about, and develop his warning in the other direction, taking it as a caution against superimposing the Self—or reality-value—upon ordinary objects. In this way we shall understand his intense opposition to the idea that the data of our ordinary experience have objective reality. Only the Self is real in the truest sense, and to treat the objects of experience also as real is to confuse them with the Self—a procedure altogether illegitimate. In Śaṅkara's terminology 'qualities of the object' mean qualities of unreality.

We thus arrive at the point of view from which all the diversities of our experience are regarded as only names and forms. The forms of space and time, the categories of causality, &c., are but our ways of viewing the world. So-called objects are subjective merely—in the modern use of the term 'subjective' as indicating creation by the individual consciousness. The Self is the only reality and everything else is relative to it. In his Commentary on the *Praśna Upanishad* VI. 2, Śaṅkara says, 'It cannot be said that there exists an object, but it cannot be known. It is like saying that a visible object is seen but there is no eye.... When there is no knowledge, there is no knowable.' [1] Space, time, and causality are not characteristics of things in themselves, but merely subjective determinations, and thus the particular diversified appearances of things, in their unceasing change and their interaction with one another, are seen to be without any standing except that which is given to them as projections of our inner experience.

Śaṅkara's Relation to Buddhism

But in thus emphasizing the subjective aspect of the matter we might seem to be assigning to Śaṅkara an almost purely Buddhistic position, and to be reckoning him as a follower of the doctrine which asserts the momentariness of all things, denies the reality of the self and the external world, and holds that for completeness of view there is no need to go beyond our own ideas and that vague principle of continuity which binds them together in an endless chain. And indeed there have been many, both in his own day and in ours, who have not hesitated to regard Śaṅkara as almost entirely under Buddhistic

[1] Quoted by Pundit S. N. Tattvabhushan, *Three Great Acharyas*, 82.

influence. Some have gone so far as to describe him as a crypto-Buddhist, or a Buddhist in disguise. Prof. Das Gupta thus concludes the first volume of his *History of Indian Philosophy*: 'Śaṅkara and his followers borrowed much of their dialectic form of criticism from the Buddhists. His Brahman is very much like the *śūnya* of Nāgārjuna. It is difficult to distinguish between pure being and pure non-being as a category. The debts of Śaṅkara to the self-luminosity of the Vijñānavāda Buddhism can hardly be overestimated. . . . I am led to think that Śaṅkara's philosophy is largely a compound of Vijñānavāda and Śūnyavāda Buddhism with the Upanishad notion of the permanence of self superadded.'[1] Prof. Poussin says that the two systems bear *un air de famille* which has been taken into account more than once and from both sides.[2]

And indeed it would not be surprising if there were many close points of contact between Śaṅkara and Buddhism. The upholders of the tradition which he inherited were engaged in constant controversy with the followers of Buddhistic thought. Kumārila Bhaṭṭa, with whom Śaṅkara had much serious controversy not unmingled with sympathy, was himself in early days a student of Buddhism, and his reinstitution of Vedic Hinduism was largely inspired by reaction from Buddhism. It would be but natural, therefore, that when Śaṅkara came to the conclusion that Kumārila Bhaṭṭa had gone too far in his restoration of external ritual practice, he should have recourse to the teachings of the school to which his opponent was also opposed. Moreover, we have already noticed the close connexion between Śaṅkara and Gauḍapāda[3] through Govinda, and the possibility that Gauḍapāda may have been himself a Buddhist. It seems indeed probable that Gauḍapāda, even if not actually a Buddhist, at least regarded the Buddhist doctrine of the void as a possible interpretation of the Upanishads. Prof. Poussin calls him 'the spiritual grandfather of Śaṅkara', and points out that it is not without significance for the latter's philosophy that Gauḍapāda 'seems to have used Buddhistic works or sayings, and to have adjusted them to his Vedantic design'.[4]

[1] Das Gupta, I. 494.
[2] Art. 'Vedānta and Buddhism', *J. R. A. S.*, 1910. [3] *Supra*, p. 53.
[4] Cf. Art. 'Vedānta and Buddhism', *J. R. A. S.*, 1910.

But this leads to the further consideration that, in tracing the influence of Buddhism upon Śaṅkara, we have not to deal with an alien system but with one which had fundamental natural affiliations to that type of thought in the Upanishads of which Śaṅkara was the sworn defender. The depreciation of ordinary experience, of the usual sources of pleasure and of external ritualistic practices, was to be found equally in Buddhism and the Upanishads; and there is a good deal in favour of the view that Buddha, without explicitly stating his attitude, implicitly admitted an ultimate reality. The difficulty of distinguishing between pure Being and pure non-Being is one that is constantly reappearing in Indian thought, and it is not easy to say dogmatically that a teacher who asserts pure non-Being is not at the same time affirming his belief in an absolute but indescribable reality. Prof. Das Gupta asserts roundly that Aśvaghoṣa, an early Buddhistic teacher of the first century A.D., 'plainly admitted an unspeakable reality as the ultimate truth'.[1] Prof. Radhakrishnan is equally emphatic. He regards early Buddhism as 'only a restatement of the Upanishads from a new standpoint'.[2] and holds that 'the spirit of the Upanishads is the life-spring of Buddhism'. The difference between them is, according to such views, only a difference of emphasis. Buddhism finds a foundation in the law of causation, and the Upanishads in a permanent substratum, and it may be argued that, unless causation is to become meaningless, it must imply a permanent basis of change. Both Buddhism and the Upanishads refuse to ascribe reality to any sections of the process of becoming, but it cannot be said that Buddhism altogether denied ultimate reality. At most, the school adopted an agnostic attitude, and although the agnosticism often came dangerously near to denial, or at least to the suggestion that any admission of reality was to be taken only as a provisional compromise, it would be perhaps unwarranted to assert that the Buddhistic teachers ever abandoned altogether the position indicated in the early verses of the *Udana* VIII. 3: 'There is an unborn, an unoriginated, an uncompounded; were there not, O mendicants, there would be no escape from the world of the born, the originated, the made, and the compounded.'[3]

[1] Das Gupta, I. 138. [2] Radhakrishnan, I. 361.
[3] Cf. also Radhakrishnan, I. 379.

The similarity with Upanishad teaching in this connexion is so striking that the *Laṅkāvatāra* is at pains to explain it away as a piece of deliberate deception, 'This explanation is given in order to attract to our creed those heretics who are superstitiously inclined to believe in the *ātman* doctrine.'[1]

Thus it does not seem so passing strange that there should be striking similarities between Buddhism and Śaṅkara, seeing that the sources of their thought lie so near together, and they have certain fundamental conceptions in common. But in view of all this, what are we to say of the vehement opposition to Buddhism which we find in Śaṅkara's own writings, and particularly in the second section of the second chapter of his Commentary on the *Vedānta Sūtras*? Here he passes in review the various schools of Buddhism, and shows uncompromising opposition. His language is that of the full-blooded controversialist rather than of the abstractly intellectual reasoner, and he states his final opinion in these vigorous terms: 'From whatever new points of view the Buddha system is tested with reference to its probability, it gives way on all sides, like the walls of a well dug in sandy soil. It has in fact no foundation to rest upon, and hence the attempt to use it as a guide in the practical concerns of life is mere folly. Moreover, Buddha, by propounding these mutually contradictory systems, teaching respectively the reality of the external world, the reality of ideas only, and general nothingness, has himself made it clear that he was a man given to make incoherent assertions, or else that hatred of all beings induced him to propound absurd doctrines by accepting which they would become thoroughly confused. So that . . . Buddha's doctrine has to be entirely disregarded by those who have a regard for their own happiness.'[2]

The first of these theories mentioned in this quotation, i.e. that of realists (or Sarvāstivādins), need not detain us. As an atomic theory in a crudely realistic form, Śaṅkara has already disposed of it in his refutation of the Vaiśeshikas, and he is concerned now only with that aspect which is peculiarly Buddhistic, viz. the doctrine of momentariness. If the atoms are momentary, he argues, aggregates are much less possible

[1] Quoted in Das Gupta, I. 147.
[2] *S. B. E.* XXXIV. 428.

than they were on the basis of the Vaiśeshika philosophy.[1] Further, the causal relation is impossible, if the cause (as momentary) has entirely passed out of existence before the effect begins to be.[2] Again, the phenomena of memory are inexplicable on the basis of momentariness: 'The consciousness of recognition takes place only in the case of the observing and remembering subject being one.'[3] Finally, the doctrine of momentariness leads to the principle that entity may spring from non-entity, and this doctrine contradicts experience, for, as non-entity is always the same, the variety of effects would be unintelligible. From a practical point of view, also, as Śaṅkara humorously points out, such a view would be an encouragement to laziness, for, 'if it were admitted that entity comes from non-entity, lazy inactive people would also obtain their purposes, since non-existence is a thing to be had without much trouble. Rice would grow for the husbandman even if he did not cultivate his field; and the weaver, too lazy to weave the threads into a whole, would nevertheless have in the end finished pieces of cloth, just as if he had been weaving.'[4]

But Śaṅkara's criticism of the other Buddhistic doctrines is of much greater importance, and he expressly regards these as representing the true views of Buddha, any concession to a belief in the reality of the external world being merely a compromise through which Buddha conformed himself to the mental state of some of his disciples.[5] Supposing we admit that there are no entities, that it does not matter whether or not existence can come from non-existence for the simple reason that there is no existence at all, then also there is neither positive nor negative, and everything partakes of the character of dreams. We may take the first step towards this nothingness by regarding all the qualities of the so-called external world as imaginary projections, set a-going by certain tendencies of an instinctive character, and held together by a vague principle of mental unity, called *alayavijñāna*. The process by which we acquire knowledge of the supposed external things is really altogether internal, and the hypothesis of the existence of ex-

[1] Cf. *Sūtra* II. 2. 19. [2] Ib. II. 2. 20. [3] Ib. II. 2. 25.
[4] Ib. II. 2. 27, *S. B. E.* XXXIV. 417.
[5] Cf. *S. B. E.* XXXIV. 418.

ternal things is altogether superfluous.[1] Buddha would not even leave us that remnant of abstraction which Marvell would allow when he speaks of

> annihilating all that 's made
> To a green thought in a green shade.

The act of knowledge and the object of knowledge are identical, and waking states are constituted of ideas only in the same manner as dreams. The variety amongst our experiences is to be explained by impressions left by previous ideas, and, if we ask for an explanation of the beginning of these previous ideas, the reply given will be that there is no such beginning.

It was against this doctrine of Vijñānavāda, or mentalism, that Śaṅkara specially directed his polemic. He appeals first of all to the testimony of consciousness and the absurdity of denying it, an absurdity equal to that of a man who, in the very act of eating, should deny that he was eating. If the Buddhists admit that the internal object of cognition is *like* something external, then Śaṅkara further points out that this is an implicit admission that something external exists. Again—and here Śaṅkara provides us with an illustration of the popular tendency which Hume afterwards found so useful to analyse—we cannot explain varying perception except by reference to permanent and distinct, and therefore external, realities. In short, according to Śaṅkara, when he gets fully under way in this particular discussion, ideas are not self-contained; they imply external things, and their variety cannot be explained apart from the assumption of an external variety. To take refuge from this difficulty in the idea of a beginningless process is an absurdity. They imply also an apprehending Self, which 'is self-proved and cannot be denied'.[2] If, Śaṅkara further urges, the apprehending Self is momentary, as the Buddhists allege—and here in turn Śaṅkara is criticizing Hume by anticipation—where can we find a mental sphere for the impressions which are supposed to be self-explanatory? Finally, our ideas of waking life cannot be compared to those of dreams, because the latter are, and the former are not, negated by our waking experience. Śaṅkara emphasizes this distinction still further in *Sūtra* III. 2. 3, where

[1] Cf. *S. B. E.* XXXIV. 419. [2] Cf. Ib. XXXIV. 424.

he says, 'It is not true that the world of dreams is true; it is mere illusion and there is not a particle of reality in it.'[1] Thus Śaṅkara goes on with his relentless destructive criticism of the Buddhistic positions until in the end he reaches the vigorous conclusion to which we have already referred, that 'Buddha's doctrine has to be entirely disregarded by all those who have a regard for their own happiness'.

And yet, after having completely overthrown Buddhism in this manner, Śaṅkara in his main doctrines seems to return to the very position which he has just been demolishing. After having re-established the external world in great scorn of Buddhism, he apparently sweeps it out of existence again when the main principles of his philosophy are brought into operation, and his negation seems as complete as that of Buddhism. He retracts into the Self all the distinctions of phenomenal things; he dismisses the categories as dealing with unrealities; and he quotes with approval the Upanishad saying that 'from death to death goes he who sees plurality anywhere'. He tells us explicitly that 'modifications or effects are names only, while in reality there exists no such thing as a modification'.[2] In short he seems by anticipation to have made impossible the distinction which has just been drawn between dreams and waking experiences and to leave us unprotected from the conclusion that waking experience is also only a dream. To adapt an Indian metaphor, the fire which has been riding upon the piece of wood has burned the whole city and also the original piece of wood itself. And Kirtikar would seem to be justified when he says that, according to the strictest Advaita, 'the correct position is . . . that the Universe has no reality'.[3]

Is there indeed a contradiction here which cannot be explained? It is easy enough to dismiss it as simply an inconsistency, but that would be a rather crude procedure. It seems at least necessary to relate it to Śaṅkara's broad distinction between higher and lower knowledge, and between the esoteric and the exoteric; and, while reserving judgement for a little on the validity of the distinction in general, to admit in the present connexion that Śaṅkara's criticism of the Buddhists was wholly

[1] *S.B.E.* XXXVIII. 135. [2] Ib. XXXIV. 320.
[3] Kirtikar, 194.

justified from the exoteric point of view, and to suggest that, if he otherwise departed from this point of view, the departure was intentional and not merely an instance of logical inconsistency.

It is further necessary to point out that Śaṅkara's polemic against the Buddhists was largely due to his feeling that they had insufficiently grasped the idea of the reality of the Self, and from his emphasis on this idea he never departed. This is the underlying motive of his objection to the doctrine of momentariness. In this connexion we may refer to the contention of Prof. S. N. Tattvabhushan, who argues that the positions of Śaṅkara and the Buddhists are quite distinct, and that therefore he was at liberty to refute the Buddhists without abandoning his own central doctrine.[1] The truth is that Śaṅkara agreed with the Buddhists in a universal mental reference, but by 'mind' the Buddhists were thinking primarily of transient acts of perception, whereas Śaṅkara had a much more permanent entity in view. He may therefore quite well object to the position that all that exists is those acts of the mind out of reference to the minds that perform them, while holding still to the idea that all acts of perception are dependent on a knowing subject. In fact the confusion of Śaṅkara's position with that of the Buddhists (it may further be pointed out) connects itself very closely with the identification of the illusory with the phenomenal. We are not yet prepared to accept this identification, and until it is established, it is at least possible to conceive that Śaṅkara might have objected to the Buddhist doctrine of illusoriness, while still clinging to a doctrine of phenomenal reference as his own central theme.

One or two other considerations may help to an understanding of Śaṅkara's position in reference to the Buddhists. While he was certainly opposed to the crude ritualistic realism of Kumārila Bhaṭṭa, he was far more vehemently opposed to the wide-sweeping negations of Buddhism. Therefore, in accordance with his generally tolerant attitude to the popular religion of his times, he may quite well have tried to establish a position which, by emphasis upon the legitimacy of the exoteric, would indicate his partial approval of popular practices as contrasted with his wholesale denunciation of Buddhistic

[1] Cf. *Three Great Acharyas*, 91.

V

THE ULTIMATE UNITY: THE TWO ORDERS OF KNOWLEDGE: THE PLACE OF WORKS

IN our last chapter we left Śaṅkara uncertainly poised between the subjective idealism of the Buddhists and a kind of common-sense realism, which realism, however, ought to be treated as provisional. Its admission might be taken as a training of the mind in the right direction, with the reasonable hope of a further advance. If the mind can be accustomed to the transition from the flux of ideas to something which is more permanent than they are, it will not be so difficult to go on to recognize the more general impermanence of the so-called external things of experience, to regard them as the products of our ignorance and to turn from them to a more constant reality. We shall learn that to trust ourselves to them in their particularity is a mistake—whose mistake, it may be unnecessary to say. It may be our mistake, or it may be a cosmic mistake, but in any case it is a mistake, at least in the sense that it is a position in which we cannot rest. As we saw in the short summary already given, we must, in order to reach a position ultimately satisfactory to the philosophical mind, retract our concession of the reality of particulars, we must get rid of the diversifying influence of space and time, and wind up the stretched-out chain of causes and effects into the One Being in which, in general, cause and effect are indistinguishable. Whatever may be our doubts about the reality of particulars in the Vedānta and about the closeness of Śaṅkara's affiliation with Buddhism, there can be no uncertainty whatsoever about his assertion of the reality of the One. For him 'the One remains, the many change and pass', and under his guidance we are expected to reach the abiding One, passing through a vivid consciousness of the transiency of the many, and a recognition of them as merely names and form, the suppositions of our ignorance—and yet, perhaps, not of *our* ignorance alone.

Space has been used to aid us to distinguish one particular thing from another, and all particular things from our own selves, as when we say, 'This is here', and 'This is there', and 'This is not myself'. But may we not, it is suggested, abolish these distinctions and find rather in the unbroken continuity of space a symbol of the underlying unity in which all differences between 'things', all differences between them and us, disappear? As Dr. Carpenter puts it, 'The knowledge of Brahman is embarrassed with no space relations.'[1] Similarly the unbroken continuity of time may become suggestive of that which time cannot affect—the permanent and the unchanging. And where there are no changes, there can be no causal relations, for, if we mean anything by cause and effect at all, we mean an event or an occurrence. So one after another, the categories may be retracted into the unbroken unity of the self, and perhaps it may turn out that the illusion of diversity in which they have encouraged us is a mistake also as regards the self of the individual, and that there is but one Infinite Self, the distinction between ourselves and the infinite disappearing in company with all other diversities. 'The One remains.'

This would certainly seem to be a 'rigorous monism', as Kirtikar describes it,[2] though for the time being we may leave open the question whether, in its rigour, it is monism or non-dualism, the difference between the two seeming to be that in non-dualism the distinctions are actual but not ultimate, whereas in monism they are neither actual (from the proper point of view) nor ultimate. Non-dualism suggests the ultimate transcendence of distinctions, whereas monism suggests rather their ultimate negation. The textual basis for this view of reality is to be found mainly in the Commentary on *Sūtra* II. 1. 14. In connexion with this, as well as with the earlier, I. 1. 4, Śaṅkara relies to a considerable extent on the Sixth Prapāṭhaka of the *Chhāndogya Upanishad*, and quotes with approval the passages, 'as by one clod of clay all that is made of clay is known, the difference being only a name, arising from speech, but the truth being that all is clay', and, 'Thus vanishes what we call fire, as a mere variety, being a name, arising from speech.'[3] He quotes also, with special reference to the idea of unity with the Universal Self, 'In that all this has its Self; it is the True, it is the Self, thou art That.'[4] His expository comment on these and other passages from the Upanishads is: 'These modifications or

[1] Carpenter, 339.
[2] Kirtikar, 3.
[3] *Chhāndogya U.* VI. 1. 4 and VI. 4. 1.
[4] Ib. VI. 8. 7.

effects are names only, exist through or originate from speech only, while in reality there exists no such thing as a modification.' And, again, 'This manifold world with its objects of enjoyment, enjoyers, and so on, has no existence apart from Brahman.'[1] He is apparently at the same time conscious that such passages might be susceptible of a less rigorously monistic interpretation and used to support the doctrine that both unity and the manifold are true. So he goes on to make his meaning explicit as against the upholders of the relative reality of the manifold. 'The phrase', he says, 'having its origin in speech,' declares the 'unreality of all effects'. And he removes all possible doubt by the further statement, 'Unity is the one true existence, while manifoldness is evolved out of wrong knowledge.'[2] Over and over again he reiterates the opinion that 'the Self is altogether without qualities and is absolutely changeless'. Nothing can be real, according to him, which has only non-continuous existence. The temporal is the denial of reality, and the real can be found only in the eternal.[3] In similar vein Max Müller says that the general principle of the Vedānta is 'that nothing that is real can ever be annihilated, so that nothing which is liable to annihilation has a right to be called real.'[4] Śaṅkara's underlying thought, translated into more modern language, seems to be this. Our categories are thrown out in order to grasp the objects of the world, and are more or less adequate in so far as these objects are considered in their particularity and from the ordinary empirical point of view. But for the ultimate reality they are inadequate, and the world they have helped us to construct dissolves into nothingnesses when we recognize the nominalistic and subjective character of its contents. And yet in its very dissolution are we not left with a consciousness, not of absolute nonentity, but of fundamental reality? These categories and forms of knowledge, together with the world they give us, are indeed a construction of our self. But what is this self? Is it a lonely existence? It has sent out the categories, as it were, and taken them back again into itself, but does it thereby contract into a mere pin-point of existence? Surely there must be some significance in this con-

[1] *S. B. E.* XXXIV. 320, 321.
[2] *S. B. E.* XXXIV. 322, 323.
[3] Cf. *S. B. E.* XLVIII. 33. 37.
[4] Müller, *S. S.* 154.

stant striving beyond the self; surely it indicates some connexion between the self and a further existence. From philosophic motive we may have cancelled or denied the outgoing expansive movement, but this does not necessarily mean that it is altogether wrong. The truer attitude would be to say rather that it has taken a wrong direction. And we may correct this error of direction, while preserving the significance of the expansive movement. Not by going outwards but by penetrating inwards shall we find the reality we are in search of. Our self is not a shadowy and vanishing point of existence, but a focusing of the universal Self, a coming into concentrated luminousness of that vast ultimate Being with which we are essentially one. In this new direction the reality which our categories have failed to grasp may be found. That art Thou—*tat tvaṁ asi.*

Śaṅkara tells us that this great truth, which Max Müller describes as the 'boldest and truest synthesis in the whole history of philosophy',[1] can be established only by the Scriptures. We remember that in his Commentary on *Sūtra* I. 1. 4 he says: 'Nor again can Brahman . . . be the object of perception and the other means of knowledge; for the fact of everything having its self in Brahman cannot be grasped without the aid of the Scriptural passage, 'That art thou.'[2] We were not, however, disposed fully to accept Śaṅkara's statement or to accuse him of being so unphilosophical as to rely implicitly on authority. We are inclined rather to regard this identity consciousness as welling up from the depths of experience and as corroborated by rather than founded upon the appeal to authority. As Prof. B. K. Shastri puts it, 'Life trained upon itself cannot but reveal its own potentialities.'[3] We are disposed to think that Śaṅkara discovered his ultimate unity by training life or experience upon itself, and not merely through the Scriptures. But however this may be, it was in any case a bold synthesis, and would carry more conviction if individual conviction was linked up with communal intellectual tradition.

The direction of thought is mainly negative and may seem to be wholly abstract, the result of simply thinking away differentiations until nothing is left. It may be due, as we shall

[1] Müller, *S. S.* 123. [2] *S. B. E.* XXXIV. 23. [3] B. K. Shastri, 220.

later have to suggest, to a too exclusively intellectual attitude over against the ultimate reality, or, within the range of this attitude, it may arise from a wrong conception of how thought should work towards a completed form of knowledge. The underlying principle may be taken to be that perfect knowledge involves identity with its object, and authority for this may be found in *Muṇḍaka Upanishad* III. 2. 9, 'He who knows Brahman becomes Brahman.' It is urged that in all cognitions approaching perfection the perceiving subject unites itself with the principle of the essential self of the object perceived. Even in popular language to know a thing is to enter into the spirit of the thing; and the philosophical interpretation of this is that to know a thing you must become that thing; or, as Kirtikar puts it, 'When the cognition is complete, the subject and object must become identical.'[1]

In regard to its direction this intellectualistic endeavour after identity may be profitably contrasted with the position set forth by Mr. Bertrand Russell, 'Philosophical contemplation, when it is unalloyed, does not aim at proving that the rest of the universe is akin to man. All acquisition of knowledge is an enlargement of the Self, but this enlargement is best attained when it is not directly sought. It is obtained when the desire for knowledge is alone operative, by a study which does not wish in advance that its objects should have this or that character, but adapts the Self to the characters which it finds in its objects. This enlargement of the Self is not obtained when, taking the Self as it is, we try to show that the world is so similar to this Self that knowledge of it is possible without any admission of what seems alien. The desire to prove this is a form of self-assertion, it is an obstacle to the growth of the Self which it desires and of which the Self knows itself capable.'[2]

The tendency which Mr. Russell is here criticizing is of course slightly different from that found in Śaṅkara, inasmuch as the latter did not consider the external world as of such importance that any knowledge of it whatsoever would lead to an expansion of the Self; and in emphasizing the necessity of directing thought towards the Self, Śaṅkara had certainly not in view the idea of obtaining thereby a fuller knowledge of the

[1] Kirtikar, 59.

[2] *Problems of Philosophy*, 246.

external world. An effort so directed would have been for Śaṅkara a contravention of his fundamental caution that we should not apply the qualities of the Subject to the Object. But the passage seems to be worth quoting in order to show the vivid contrast between the spirit of realism, whether new or old, and the spirit of such idealistic monism as Śaṅkara represents. For the latter the expansion of the Self is essentially to be found, not by looking outwards but by looking inwards, not by affirmation and construction, but by negation and retraction; and this metaphysical introspection, so far from being an obstacle, is the only true method of knowledge.

But while we have spoken of the narrowly intellectualistic character of this attitude, and of its negative and abstract tendency, we must on no account dismiss it as if this were a complete characterization of it. We must never forget that it is an expression of the yearning of the mystic throughout the ages, and that Śaṅkara is also striving to satisfy a desire which is innate in human nature. Positively it belongs to the 'Type of the wise who soar but never roam';[1] negatively it is the result of

> those obstinate questionings
> Of Sense and outward things,
> Fallings from us, vanishings,
> Blank misgivings of a creature
> Moving about in worlds not realized.[2]

Amongst the mystics, Juliana of Norwich says that it is her aim to 'noughten all else that is made, for to love and to have God that is unmade', and, in the same strain, Jacob Boehmen says, 'When thou canst throw thyself for a moment into that where no creature dwelleth, then thou hearest what God speaketh.' And when we go farther back in history we find an almost exact anticipation of the spirit of Śaṅkara's quest in the thought and practice connected with the Eleusinian mysteries. A recent writer has beautifully expressed the essence of the religious movement in words which might so easily be taken as a description of Śaṅkara's main teaching that it is worth while quoting them at length. 'This yearning to embrace and become the All, to lose and dissolve himself and the separate natures

[1] Wordsworth, *To a Skylark*.
[2] Wordsworth, *Intimations of Immortality*.

of all other things in the absolute simplicity of some deeper form of being, reveals the secret of man's sin and imperfection and the way of his salvation. It is the homing instinct of the soul, guiding her unerringly through the trackless variety of the manifold world with all its swirling confusion of phantom forms and things, back to the undivided unity and calm of God, there to yield up her distraught and restless individuality and forget her separate self and the separate selves of all other things in him. The existence of many natures and things in their difference and isolation. . . . is evidence of a metaphysical catastrophe. . . . Or it is at least the sign of some monstrous deformity of our vision which makes us see what is really One as if it were many, and what is really perfect as if it were imperfect.'[1]

Coming back again to more modern times, we may trace the same line of thought in one who could hardly claim to be enrolled amongst religious mystics, but who, nevertheless, has some points of affinity with them. Schopenhauer was greatly influenced by the Upanishads, and he makes use of their central idea in his analysis of aesthetic contemplation in language which is strikingly suggestive of Śaṅkara: 'If, raised by the power of the mind, a man relinquishes the common way of looking at things, . . . if he thus ceases to consider the where and the when, the why and the whither of things, and looks solely at the what ; if further he does not allow abstract thought, the concepts of the reason to take possession of his consciousness, but instead of all this gives the whole power of his mind to perception, sinks himself entirely in this; . . . if thus the object has passed out of all relation to something outside it, and the subject out of all relation to the will, then that which is known is no longer the particular thing as such; and therefore he who is sunk in this perception is no longer individual, for in such perception the individual has lost himself; but he is pure, will-less, painless, timeless subject of knowledge . . . whoever now has, after the manner referred to, become so absorbed and lost in the perception of nature that he only continues to exist as the pure knowing subject, becomes in this way directly conscious that, as such, he is the condition, that is, the supporter of the world and all objective existence. . . . Thus he draws nature

[1] Art. by B. A. G. Fullar in *Hibbert Journal*, Oct. 1922.

into himself, so that he sees it to be merely an accident of his own being.'[1]

We have quoted these parallels from the mystics and quasi-mystics in order to support the view that Śaṅkara's position exemplifies a very natural tendency of the human soul. Sometimes we wonder, however, whether he has reached in all its fullness the faith of the true mystic who desires 'the expansion of the Self to become the Self of all',[2] and whether the negative and restrictive attitude which sometimes appears as a slightly unattractive element in his teaching may not be due to the fact that he did not surrender himself wholeheartedly to the implications of his own assertion of identity. We are led to refer here again to his excessively intellectual point of view and its hampering influence. In his attempt to gain a *knowledge* of the Self is he not tempted to forget his own rule that the Subject must never be treated as an Object? We are far from objecting—as will be pointed out hereafter—to the subject-object relation even in respect of the Divine reality, provided that this kind of relationship is associated with the necessary safeguards, but our contention at this stage is that for Śaṅkara, so long as he retains an almost purely intellectualistic attitude, this is a dangerous procedure. It leads him to embark upon an impossible quest. Whilst he remains within the sphere of knowledge merely, he must perforce use the categories, but yet, just as he has discovered in other respects, he finds them inadequate, and is thus forced into successive abstractions and negations. Despite his own principle, the Self, because of his intellectualism, remains an object, and because he has provided no other than purely intellectual means for overcoming the separateness of the object, he is, as it were, hoist with his own petard.

Thus Śaṅkara is forced to share with Bradley and Ward the experience that in our quest for the real self we cannot turn the self into an object without its ceasing to be a subject, i.e. without its ceasing to be the very kind of reality of which we are in search. Through two whole chapters Bradley pursues the search for the Self, and remains discouraged. He comes in the end to the conclusion that the self is unintelligible, that 'in whatever way the

[1] Schopenhauer, *World as Will and Idea*, Bk. III. 231 and 234.
[2] Cf. Kirtikar, 129.

self is taken, it will prove to be appearance'.[1] It does not provide a principle of explanation, but 'so far from supplying such a principle, . . . seems, where not hiding itself in obscurity, a mere bundle of discrepancies'.[2] And Śaṅkara's warning against transferring objective qualities to the subject leads him to a line of thought almost exactly similar to that of Ward. Śaṅkara points out with justice that, if we make the self the object of psychological inquiry, it constantly eludes us. If we attempt to put into form our knowledge of the Self, another self has constantly to be posited to carry through this formulation. We discover that as soon as the self acquires content as the result of our investigations, this content has immediately to be transferred from the 'I' to the 'me', from the pure to the empirical ego. The 'I' still remains which refuses to become an object. It acquires content only to surrender it again. It enters into knowledge only as it becomes the empirical self and therefore ceases to be that which we want to know. In more modern terminology, such as Ward would favour, we can never get beyond the eternal distinction between subject and object, and we find that the subject persistently resists any attempt to treat it as an object.[3]

Can this constant subject, then, never be known? Both Śaṅkara and Ward would answer this question in the negative as far as ordinary knowledge is concerned, but both would make a distinction between ordinary knowledge and a higher kind of experience or intuition, and would so far qualify their denial. But in making this concession there is an important difference between the two philosophers. For Ward experience yields up a fuller result than is possible for Śaṅkara by reason of the latter's more purely intellectual point of view. We are sure of the pure ego, according to Ward, just because of its *activity*, which is persistent so long as we have experience. Śaṅkara, on the other hand, refuses to allow that the Self is an agent. In his Commentary on *Sūtra* II. 3. 40 he says, 'The Self's being an agent cannot be founded on its real nature, because (if it were so) the impossibility of final release would follow. For if being

[1] *Appearance and Reality*, 101 and 118. [2] Ib. 120.

[3] Cf. Ward, *Principles of Psychology*, 376 ff, and the present writer's article on 'Śaṅkara and James Ward' in the *Sir Asutosh Mukherjea Jubilee Volumes*, I. 331 ff.

an agent belongs to the soul's nature, it can never free itself from it; and, as long as man has not freed himself from activity, he cannot obtain his highest end, since activity is essentially painful.'[1] And again he says, 'The result of all this is that the agentship of the Self is due to limiting adjuncts only.'[2] If Śaṅkara had not made this refusal of activity to the Self, he would have found that experience would have given him fuller results. And he would have been able to overcome more adequately the externality of the Self treated as an object. For, if the idea of intelligence is dissociated from activity, the Self tends to remain an object of contemplation, or at least to pass from the subjective to the objective sphere, in which sphere the categories turn out to be insufficient; and we can get beyond appearances only if we are content to allow the pure ego to be a characterless universal. So, on this procedure we seem to be shut up to negation. As Prof. Radhakrishnan puts it, 'We cannot find the self in any corner of the field of consciousness. Not finding it there, we rush to the conclusion that it is nothing.'[3] The Self, still treated as an object, becomes unknowable and indefinable, and the identification aimed at in the Vedānta has to be arrived at by way of negation. Thus we argue that if Śaṅkara had made more use of the concept of activity, he would have been more consistent with his own principles and would have reached fuller results through the application of his ideal of mystical identification with the universal. It was no doubt hard for him to modify his intellectualism, for it was upon intellectual procedure that fundamentally he relied; and he once went so far as to suggest that a man who adopted an erroneous argument might compromise his salvation. Yet some advance in this direction would have had useful consequences. As Prof. Alexander says, 'The world is not what it is merely for intellect alone; its nisus towards what is higher enters into its constitution, and as impregnated with this tendency, it affects the mind by ways other than cognition, though interpretable in the ways of cognition.'[4] If greater stress had been laid on the principle of activity, Śaṅkara might have approached more nearly to the position that union with the divine may be accomplished, not so

[1] *S.B.E.* XXXVIII. 53. [2] Ib. XXXVIII. 57. [3] Radhakrishnan, I. 163.
[4] Alexander, *Space, Time, and Deity*, II. 377.

much by abstraction from, or thinning down of, experience as by emphasis on the idea that the human mind in its activity is reproducing the orderly and manifold activities of the Divine mind.

Now the idea of identity, when associated with the idea of activity, is on the point of passing over into the idea of communion, in which the subject-object relation, while not abolished, does not remain poverty-stricken as with Śaṅkara, but finds its poverty transformed into riches. Activity carries with it an interpretative power which the purely intellectual attitude does not possess. The latter is always more or less helpless before the problem of deriving plurality from unity, and can deal with the unity satisfactorily only by denying the plurality in its distribution and in its changes. When further, this unity is given a narrowly religious application and used to satisfy a desire for salvation by means of deliverance or release, this further association increases the naturally unproductive character of a purely intellectual solution. There is greater readiness to acquiesce in the conception of a pure undifferenced unity from which there is no return to particularity, if no such return is desired. Dissatisfaction with such a characterless negation can come only from a desire to explain the world or to operate within it; but when all connexion with the world is felt as a disturbance of religious ecstasy, the desire to explain it vanishes away, and acquiescence in a non-explanatory and intrinsically unintelligible principle is complete. When practical relationships with the world are ignored at the bidding of religious requirements narrowly conceived, the use of the concept of activity for the purposes of the interpretation of the ultimate is not likely to be either popular or effective.

In the further treatment of his supreme principle Śaṅkara's general position is that predicates which may be applied are to be taken not as implying actual differences in the Ultimate, but simply as refuting contrary predicates obviously unsuitable.[1] When, e.g., we say that Brahman is knowledge we are concerned rather with affirming that Brahman is not not-knowledge than with ascribing any positive characteristic to him. Properly we can apply to Brahman only the reiterated statement 'neti, neti', 'it is not, it is not'. We may call him Being (*sat*), if we please, but

[1] Cf. *S. B. E.* XLVIII. 28.

we must also remember that he is non-Being in respect of any empirical conception of existence. We may call him thought (*cit*), but we must use this in accordance with the general principle just stated, to signify that Brahman is nothing lower than thought, and we must refrain from ascribing to him any consciousness with which we are familiar in our experience. Especially must we be careful not to think of him as the subject of cognition, because this would imply a differentiated object, and, on the other side of the relation, would also imply a distinction between the knower and the consciousness which he possesses. Brahman is consciousness pure and simple, not a conscious subject *plus* his consciousness. Any difference between consciousness and the conscious subject would have to be ascribed to an unreal principle of egoity. Similarly, we may ascribe to him the predicate of bliss (*ānanda*), but we must remember that it is bliss 'without the fruition of happiness'. It is not the awareness of satisfied endeavour, it is rather the assured calm of absolute self-absorption, the conscious gradual sinking into Being, the oncoming sense of infinity, without disturbance of particular thought or particular interest.

But having discovered to some extent what Śaṅkara intends by identity with this pure Being, whom for the present we must leave in such a state of purity and vagueness that it is difficult, though not impossible, to distinguish it from Nothing, we must next ask how this identification is to be accomplished. This leads us to consider that fundamental distinction between *lower and higher knowledge*, through which Śaṅkara arrives at the consummation of his endeavour. The point which we have specially to keep in view is the degree of abruptness of the distinction. If the goal is negative, it is probable that the approach to it will be by means of abrupt negation, but we have also to keep in mind the other possibility that the negation of the lower may be its fulfilment and that the negative may be the cutting edge of a positive.

Śaṅkara's view would seem to be that the differences between the ordinary and the truly philosophical points of view are so striking that the processes and results with which we are concerned in the two spheres cannot be put into the same class. In the one class we have a body of knowledge which is altogether exoteric, a lower doctrine (*aparā vidyā*), and in the other an illuminating, momentary, and yet eternal, flash of combined intuition and revelation, yielding—if ever it can be fixated—the higher doctrine (*parā vidyā*) which alone attains to truth. In the first group we may put all our ordinary experiences, our search after location and date, causes and effects, with all the practical consequences which flow from this conglomeration of information, all the gropings of our reasoning faculty, and all the speculative problems which remain unsolved so long as we try to lighten the darkness by the flickering candle of our own powers of intellect. Within this lower knowledge we are helpless prisoners, and cannot by any means save our souls. We may pass restlessly from one phase of experience to another, but cannot shake ourselves free from the degradation of the ordinary. We may by strenuousness rise painfully and slowly upwards towards God, but at the end it is not the Absolute or the Ultimate into whose presence we come. We have reached only what might be described as a 'service' God, who may be suitable as an object of worship and with whom we may desire indefinitely continued communion. But he will not be the goal of our soul's endeavour, because we shall still be ascribing qualities to him, and these qualities will hang like veils between us and the ultimate reality. And whilst the God to whom we attain, and whom we think we know, continues in misleading distinctness before us as an object, we shall yet remain in separation from him, and shall not reach that consummation of unity which constitutes our release and our salvation.

And on the other side we may place that higher wisdom through which God and man are so closely brought together that we can hardly decide whether we ought to speak of revelation or of intuition—so inevitably does the descending of the Divine come to meet the uprising of the human heart, the best without us mingling with the best within. The product of this commingling is a knowledge of that Reality which lies hidden beneath all the experiences of man, that God without qualities hidden behind that fullness of divine quality which we take as the object of our worship. In this knowledge is our peace, for we are delivered from all that perplexes us in our outward gazing upon the world, and the God whom we are in search of no longer stands over against us in a separating distinctness, but, through that vagueness in which all outlines are blurred, passes from the outward to the inward and welcomes us to a unity which we discover has always been the truth of things, even though at this critical point of transition it may be presented with the abruptness of a new discovery. As has been said, in such knowledge intuition and revelation become merged in one; and so the position of Śaṅkara recalls the old texts of the *Muṇḍaka Upanishad*, where it is said that 'when a man's nature has become purified by the serene light of knowledge, then he sees him, meditating upon him as without parts', and, again, 'the wise, having reached Him who is omnipresent everywhere, devoted to the Self, enter into him wholly'.[1] And to those who are familiar with the New Testament it suggests that wisdom which is both pure and peaceable, which is from above,—a gift which 'cometh down from the Father of lights, with whom is no variableness, neither shadow of turning'.[2]

The contrast between the two divisions is made so definite by Śaṅkara that the points of view become almost exclusive of one another. We reach the unity only by passing very resolutely from the one kind of experience to the other, and when we escape from the land of bondage we carry nothing with us. We are led to ask the question whether this abrupt distinction and definitive transition is either natural or necessary? Is it even possible, or, if it is possible, is it desirable? Must we have separation as well as distinction?

The distinction certainly gathers up within itself and continues two common differentiations, viz. between the ordinary and the scientific point of view, and between the scientific and the purely philosophical. With the first distinction we are but little concerned, as the necessity for it would be a matter of agreement amongst all who have ceased to be the slaves of custom and convention and prudential maxims. It is with the second distinction that we have to do, and here also there is considerable agreement about its necessity, and controversy has reference only to the degree of abruptness with which the distinction ought to be made.

[1] *Muṇḍaka U.* III. 1. 8 and III. 2. 5.

[2] James I. 17

In these days no one would contend that merely scientific categories are adequate to reality, but all down through the ages also—from the Upanishads, through Śaṅkara, right down to modern Western thinkers—we find a continuous depreciation of mere knowledge of a purely scientific character. In the *Bṛihadāraṇyaka Upanishad* III. 5. 1 we read, 'Therefore let a Brāhmaṇa, after he has done with learning, wish to stand by a childlike state.' It is true that Max Müller, mainly because of a suspicion that 'knowledge of babes' may be 'a Christian rather than an Indian idea',[1] translates the passage 'Therefore let a Brāhmaṇa, after he has done with learning, wish to stand by real strength'. But even Max Müller interprets 'real strength' as meaning 'knowledge . . . which enables us to dispense with all other knowledge', and the translation which implies 'childlikeness' is supported by such authorities as Gough and Deussen. Still more striking is the support which is given to this interpretation by Śaṅkara himself, who takes for granted the meaning of 'childlikeness', refutes certain mistaken deductions from it, and expounds the passage as follows, 'The meaning of the clause under discussion thus is, Let him be free from guile, pride and so on, not manifesting himself by a display of knowledge, learning and virtuousness, just as a child . . . does not strive to make a display of himself before others.'[2] Thus in both ancient and medieval Indian thought there is testimony to the idea that he who would enter the kingdom of the knowledge of God must become as a little child. And if we wish to bring the testimony down to modern times we may unite in relation to this attitude both East and West, and find the lesson of humility in respect of knowledge impressively taught by one of the foremost scientists of modern times. 'Science', says Prof. J. Arthur Thomson, 'gives us no more than descriptive formulations, and we strain at the limitations of our faculties when, as Sir Thomas Browne said, "we think of things that thoughts do but tenderly touch". Even when the minor mysteries disappear before Science, the fundamental mysteriousness of nature remains, unless we are content or positivistically compelled to sink the big questions altogether. Even when we reduce everything

[1] Cf. *S.B.E.* XV. 130 and Radhakrishnan, I. 177.
[2] *S.B.E.* XXXVIII. 326.

measurable and ponderable to the lowest common denominators—the irreducibles of the day, like electrons and protons—our experience is not thereby rationalized. We seek for a synoptic vision, in the light of the Greatest Common Measure. When the half-gods go, the God arrives.'[1]

But as we probe farther into the matter and attempt to represent more definitely the central teaching of Śaṅkara, we find that he reaches conclusions in regard to which it would be difficult to claim general agreement. We have hints not merely of the necessity of a higher point of view but of its *total separation* from the lower. The particular character of the difficulty may be set forth by a phrase which Deussen uses when introducing this very topic of Śaṅkara's distinction between the exoteric and the esoteric. The German philosopher says that metaphysics must 'in many cases renounce results that can be clearly represented', and adds, 'All this demands great power and habit of abstraction, *attainable only by a few*.'[2] Now this may be quite true, but the way in which the statement is put suggests an excessive emphasis upon the abstraction and negation, and implies an abrupt cutting off of the higher from the lower. Deussen thus prepares our minds for the acceptance of the definite separation which is to be found in Śaṅkara himself, and for which, it may be noted in passing, the latter derives little support either from the Upanishads or the *Sūtras*. Further, the words we have italicized seem to suggest an aristocratic exclusiveness—perhaps not altogether unconnected with traditional caste-divisions—which results in placing the two kinds of knowledge side by side, stressing their opposition rather than their relationship, and assigning possession of them to different classes of people rather than to different stages in the same mental development. The idea of privilege thus creeps in, an idea similar to that which Lotze so severely criticizes in the

[1] In *Religions of the Empire*, 413. We may compare also the attitude of Schopenhauer, expressive, however, of a very different mood: 'This is the state which I have described above as necessary for the knowledge of the Idea, as pure contemplation, as sinking oneself in perception, losing oneself in the object, forgetting all individuality, succeeding that kind of knowledge which follows only the principle of sufficient reason and comprehends only relations.' We perhaps find something of the same tendency in the abhorrence of the merely moralistic point of view which is expressed by such writers as Bosanquet.

[2] Deussen, 97 [italics mine].

concluding chapter of his *Philosophy of Religion*, where he contrasts the attitude of the man who attempts to make a symbolic creed yield up its meaning to intellectual inquiry with that of the man who considers the creed as it stands sufficient for the needs of the crowd while he himself occupies somewhat disdainfully the vantage ground of the higher point of view. We are here concerned, however, not with the social but with the intellectual aspect of the matter, and it is difficult not to connect the distinction with a certain intellectual pride and a contempt for the lower—a looking on it as unworthy in itself or as susceptible only of negation rather than of elevation or transformation. In this way, in the sphere of the intellect renunciation or negation takes the place of sublimation or transcendence. There is no natural point of contact between the two kinds of knowledge, and the higher is slightly patronizing in reference to the lower.

Śaṅkara himself finds it impossible to conceive of co-operation between the two orders. They are mutually exclusive. 'How can the cognition of unity', he asks, 'remove the manifold if both are true?'[1] They are as separate as dream and waking reality; and just as when we awake we do not take the trouble to modify a dream, but entirely sublate it, so, when the true knowledge arises, 'the world of effects with the means and objects of right knowledge and its results of action is untrue'.[2] In the same way, just as we look upon the crises of a dream as harmless, so may we look upon the world of the ordinary in the same kindly but intellectually lethargic way. 'As long as true knowledge does not present itself, there is no reason why the ordinary course of secular and religious activity should not hold on undisturbed.'[3] No reason! And yet we are told that it is a far country where the soul exists as an alien and a 'wanderer', and it seems a pity that the soul should be so lightly permitted to continue its wanderings.

Further, this abrupt separation leads to consequences which are not all of them desirable. If there are two sharply distinguished points of view, we shall very likely be tempted to think that difficulties which arise from one point of view may be disregarded while we flee unconcernedly to the other. Mr. D. N. Pal

[1] *S. B. E.* XXXIV. 323. [2] Ib. 324. [3] Ib. 324.

unconsciously suggests a danger of this kind when he tells us that 'Śaṅkara has found a wonderful way out'. Of course to deny the validity of certain groups of disconcerting conclusions by pointing out that the procedure by which we arrive at these conclusions is unnecessary or mistaken, is simply another way of saying that the conclusions are not ultimately satisfactory. But, all the same, an effort to deal directly with the particular difficulties which the empirical conclusions leave unresolved would give an impression of greater philosophical courage, whilst, on the other hand, the method of escape, with slightly contemptuous backward glance, is apt to encourage a certain *laissez-faire* attitude to the difficulties left behind. The higher point of view becomes so detached from the lower that it is unable by its insistent truthfulness to force the latter to yield up a solution of its contradictions. If the lower knowledge is despised as being on the level of dream-experiences, we become disposed to leave it alone in its confusions. If we dream of a man with two heads, we do not trouble when we awake to point out that such a monstrosity is impossible on physiological grounds. We simply dismiss it as a dream, and leave it alone with the truth which it had as an actual element in the dream experience. In this way the standard is lowered, and we are compelled to admit an element of truth in Puroshottama Misra's rather cynical remark, 'in this system, which maintains that everything transcends explanation, unreasonableness is no objection'.[1] Things may be accepted as true up to a certain point and left there. Although we have a vague feeling that they are not wholly true, we do not trouble to challenge the half-truth we have already got and compel it to yield up the fuller truth. In the language of logic we might say that the separation we are considering forces us to use a hypothesis which is continually changing its ground, and thus failing to conform to the rules of a good hypothesis. A hypothesis, if it is to be considered legitimate, should not be employed on one level and then, because of the greater difficulties in which it involves us, altogether abandoned on a higher level while still permitted to be valid on the lower. It should be carried through and tested by its adequacy in dealing with the whole situation. Yet Śaṅkara's

[1] Quoted in Goreh's *Rational Refutation*, 355.

argument against the Buddhists, while to a large extent its logical consistency may be upheld, is not wholly free from objections of this sort. And for the same reason we may also have to view somewhat critically certain implications of his doctrine of *Māyā*, and also the argument by which he seeks to prove that God is not responsible for the disconcerting evil of the world.

There is another unfortunate consequence. The conception of the negative and indescribable character of ultimate reality is often the outcome of that desperate search for a mysterious and elusive substance beyond qualities of which Prof. Pringle-Pattison has so well shown the futility in his *Idea of God*. Śaṅkara is right in his contention that scientific knowledge must fail in such a quest, but his method conceals both from himself and from others the true conclusion that the quest is really a hopeless one. He rather suggests that, though such a reality cannot be reached on the empirical level, it may be reached by the higher knowledge. The empirical investigator is practically told that he has failed because he has been searching in the wrong place and not because he has been searching for the wrong thing. He is prevented from discovering for himself the barrenness of the mystical substance for which he is searching by having it suggested to him that he should leave the inquiry to that higher knowledge to which he has not yet attained. And, in addition to this, the higher knowledge also encourages him in his abstract view, for there is associated with it the idea of vagueness rather than of definiteness, and even he who has attained to it has to be content with the abstract and the negative and the undefined. He is not encouraged to press onwards in the quest for an ultimate unity which will provide an explanation of the empirical variety of the world. He is apt to fall into the error of those who, as Prof. Laird puts it, 'mistake a useless spectre for the last word in profundity, and often advance the extraordinary doctrine that truth is an incomprehensible reality, while the thing that we know is a comprehensible unreality'.[1]

Although it may be true, as Prof. K. Shastri so frequently points out in his book upon the *Adwaita Philosophy*, that Śaṅkara's aim was to show that the details of the world are

[1] *Idea of the Soul*, 60.

nothing *apart* from Brahman, the separation between the two orders of knowledge compels Śaṅkara to run the serious risk of coming to the conclusion that they are nothing at all. And the vagueness of the apprehension of unity with the undifferenced Brahman which the higher knowledge affords, is apt to make us forget that the goal of philosophy is to discover the infinitely transcendent source of all things which will at once give them reality and explain them. The procedure we have been studying is rather a temptation to turn the true ideas of the 'infinite' and the 'inexhaustible' into the 'inaccessible'. Vagueness has received a benediction through being connected with a higher order of knowledge.

Further, when we are thus left in presence of the merely characterless and abstract, we find it difficult to maintain spiritual conceptions in their requisite purity. Physical conceptions, which, in general, philosophy has to make constant efforts to transcend, reassert themselves. We become less aware of and less appreciative of the importance of the activity of consciousness. Our desire indeed is—if at this level we can still have desires—to rise to something higher than consciousness, but the danger is that, in presence of this vague ultimate which we have detached from experience, we may fall below, instead of rise above, the level of consciousness and reach unity by way of the unconscious. Intense and concentrated contemplation is no doubt the ideal which Śaṅkara has in view, but we cannot help feeling that, in common with all mystics, as Prof. Pringle-Pattison has pointed out, he is to some extent inclined first of all to treat contemplation as very nearly equivalent to absorption, and then to give to the latter term a meaning derived from observation of the mixture of physical substances and fluids.

There are evidences even within the bounds of the Vedānta philosophy that this abrupt separation between the two orders of knowledge did not always satisfy. Śaṅkara himself, as we shall immediately see, did not persistently maintain what Prof. Radhakrishnan has described as his 'ultra-philosophical moods'. Ever and again he turned his thoughts back again to the consideration of the multiplicity of the world. The philosophy of Rāmānuja is, of course, based upon a denial of this separation.

And surely it remains true that we can best preserve what is valuable in the doctrine of higher knowledge by showing that such knowledge is the completion and not the negation of lower knowledge. It ought to signify simply the wider conclusions in which the contradictions of the empirical are resolved. Intuition is the supplement of intellect and fills up what is lacking in the somewhat unsatisfactory conclusions of the latter. Reality is reached, not by turning away from experience, but by fuller and more reverent study of the facts with which it supplies us, just as in ethical endeavour the ideal is approached through the fulfilment of ordinary duties. There is much truth in Prof. Bertrand Russell's saying that 'in contemplation we start from the not-Self, and through its greatness the boundaries of the Self are enlarged' (*Problems of Philosophy*, 246). Even the symbols of imagination and worship are not to be taken as pure fiction or as meaningless, but rather as more or less valuable hints of truth. The distinction which we have been considering serves us best if we allow it to deepen our reverence, but not to increase our distrust of our own powers. We should like to take it as ultimately expressive of the spirit of the beautiful passage in which Coleridge tells us that all knowledge begins and ends with wonder, but we have to replace the first wonder, which is the child of ignorance, by the larger wonder which is the parent of adoration.[1]

In our next chapter we shall have to deal with some of the mediating conceptions by means of which Śaṅkara and other Vedantins strive to soften the rigours of their negations and introduce some definiteness into the vagueness of their abstractions. But this chapter may appropriately close with some further reference to Śaṅkara's views as to the efficacy of works in introducing us to the higher knowledge. We have touched slightly upon this topic in connexion with the preliminary conditions of philosophic study, but something may be gained by bringing it into relation with the nature of the knowledge in which deliverance consists, and especially its detachment from the lower kind of knowledge. Śaṅkara's position is that, by the very nature of the case, works, seeing that they belong to that

[1] Quoted in *Religions of the Empire*, 412.

sphere of experience which has to be transcended, can have very little direct efficacy in the securing of our salvation. As he puts it in his Commentary on the first of the *Sūtras*: 'The knowledge of active religious duty has for its fruit transitory felicity, and that again depends on the performance of religious acts. The inquiry into Brahman on the other hand, has for its fruit eternal bliss, and does not depend on the performance of any act.'[1] The whole conception of activity, as ordinarily understood, is alien to the sphere of the higher knowledge. Action has to do with what has not yet come into existence, whereas knowledge, and especially the knowledge of Brahman, has to do with something already existent. It is concerned, not with that which is to be, but with that which eternally *is*. Works have their relation to the transmigratory sphere, where the category of cause and effect is applicable. Further, on the subjective side, it is exceedingly difficult to dissociate from ritual works, and indeed from works of any kind, the idea of merit, which moves through the degrees of more or less, tending now in the direction of pleasure and now in that of pain, and alternating between the moods of hope and fear. But there is no place for such degrees in association with the kind of knowledge which brings release. Inasmuch as it is the knowledge of that which in itself is not susceptible of increase of decrease, the knowledge also is either there or not there. It is immediate, and it is wholly inappropriate to regard it as the gradual acquisition of repeated endeavour. Moreover, every action is a finite cause which can have only a finite and, therefore, temporary, effect; but, on the other hand, 'that release is something eternal, is acknowledged by whoever admits it at all, and the teaching concerning Brahman can therefore not be merely supplementary to actions.'[2]

Nor is the case for action improved, according to Śaṅkara, if we take it in its purely intellectual aspect, and argue that, because release is the result of action, therefore it must involve mental activity. To such a contention Śaṅkara would reply that the knowledge which is active belongs to that lower order in which the object is still distinguished from the subject. We are active in knowledge, according to Śaṅkara, only when we disregard his fundamental warning and attempt to treat the Self

[1] *S.B.E.* XXXIV. 11. [2] *S.B.E.* XXXIV. 29.

as an Object. We should rather fall back upon that form of realization which is deeper than active knowledge, and which follows the spirit of the *Kena Upanishad* II. 3, where it is said, 'By whom it is not thought, by him it is thought, by whom it is thought, he does not know it; unknown by those who know it, it is known by those who do not know it.' Such contemplation as is here indicated, is certainly not active in the ordinary sense, although we must not rule out the possibility of its implying a transcendental activity in the form of intense concentration, aliveness, or awareness.

But even if, returning to the practical sphere, we confine our attention to action of the highest moral character, we cannot say, according to Śaṅkara, that releasing knowledge results from this. The Self which even the most elevated action serves to purify, is only the empirical Self, whereas the Self which we wish to attain in the consummation of salvation, is the unchangeable Self, which can only be realized, and cannot be improved by the addition of good qualities or the removal of defects. Action of even the highest kind is meant to alter the soul, and the Self cannot be altered. Further, although we may be aware of the binding and individualizing effect of many actions, and, because of this awareness, may seek deliverance by emphasizing actions of social tendency, even this will not be sufficient. Actions of service and sacrifice certainly loosen the bonds of the merely selfish Self, and may derive their inspiration from a consciousness of the identity of the Self in us with the Self in other men, but they will lead to deliverance only by extension of the Self, whereas what we seek is that deliverance which depends on greater intensiveness—on deepening rather than broadening. We may unite ourselves more closely with our fellows, we may perfect our relations with them in every respect, and as a result may go far towards founding a kingdom of God upon earth, but such a kingdom will still be only earthly, and our connexion with it will still be a bondage of the spirit. We may become perfect instruments for the good of the community, but we shall be instruments still. And we as children of the eternal cannot work with whole-hearted enthusiasm for ends which are constituted even by ideal social relationship. Such conceptions of a perfect society, it must be remembered, vary from age to age and are different in every nation, and therefore, even a complete identification with the ideals of a particular age or a particular society cannot give us eternal release, based upon absolutely universal conditions.

Such, in general, is Śaṅkara's position as regards the fruit of works. 'Knowledge, having once sprung up, requires no help towards the accomplishment of its fruit.' But we should be doing an injustice to his school of thought if we did not point out that he assigns at least a subordinate value to works. Indeed the very sentence from which we have just quoted concludes with the words, 'but it does stand in need of something else with a view to its own origination.'[1] It is only selfish works which are entirely useless; all other works may be regarded as indirectly, though not directly, serviceable for salvation. They purify the mind, they strengthen our control of the passions, they induce that calmness and collectedness which are the necessary conditions of the vision of the true Self. They are, in short, as has been pointed out, ascetic rather than meritorious in their effect. They may remove the hindrances which stand in the way of perfect knowledge, that knowledge which is alone efficacious. Even if they cannot secure the origination of this knowledge in any one particular life, they may so assemble conditions that it will of necessity arise in an immediately subsequent life. But, notwithstanding all these concessions, it must be clearly understood, according to Śaṅkara, that, whatever may be the subordinate value of works, they are never to be regarded as ends in themselves. If they are so regarded, bondage either for the individual or the community will be the inevitable result.

In his Commentaries on some of the Upanishads, Śaṅkara speaks of four stages in the life of man. With the first, which is under the rule of lawless impulse, and with the second, which is constituted by unintelligent observance of ritual, he concerns himself little. The third stage, however, unites knowledge and works of a higher order, and it may be said that Śaṅkara's chief endeavour is to show that the combination is not absolutely necessary, and that knowledge alone may be sufficient. When works have been performed so as to secure the purification of the soul, there is no further need of them. As he says in his

[1] *S.B.E.* XXXVIII. 317.

Commentary on *Sūtra* III. 4. 14, 'To a man who knows, no work will cling, should he perform works during his whole life even, owing to the power of knowledge. And this clearly glorifies knowledge.'[1] Co-operation between *jñāna* and *karma* is necessary only as a preparatory discipline, and the enlightened man will be free from the fetters of both good and evil works. The moralistic standpoint will be altogether transcended. The point of view is in striking contrast to that which, e.g., is expressed by Solovyof, who says, 'Asceticism in itself is not necessarily good, and cannot therefore be the supreme or absolute principle of morality. The true (the moral) ascetic acquires control over the flesh, not simply for the sake of increasing the power of the spirit, but for furthering the realization of the good.'[2]

But with Śaṅkara both good and evil works disappear when the true knowledge arises. He would have been content with the first statement of the *Bṛihadāraṇyaka Upanishad* that 'all who worship what is not knowledge enter into blind darkness', and if his attention had been directed to the succeeding phrase, 'Those who delight in knowledge enter, as it were, into greater darkness,' he would have immediately replied, as we have seen above, that the knowledge which is here referred to, is the lower knowledge only, and that the passage taken as a whole gives no suggestion of disparagement of the true knowledge which is all-sufficient in itself. Salvation is of faith through knowledge, or is the result of that knowledge whose similarity to faith we indicate by calling it intuition. With St. Paul he would have held that the doing of the works of the law cannot bring salvation, but, as Deussen points out, Śaṅkara did not hold that the law could not be fulfilled, but rather that, granted its fulfilment, it would even then be fulfilled only from egoistic motives and would therefore be void of effect in the direction of release. He would hardly have agreed with Prof. B. K. Shastri that 'a *simultaneous* training in duties and devotion qualifies a man for absolute concentration on the Supreme Soul which leads directly to eternal self-realization or liberation'.[3]

The question whether this lands us in an antinomian position

[1] *S. B. E.* XXXVII. 294.

[2] Solovyof, *The Justification of the Good*, 57.

[3] B. K. Shastri, 77.

will be further considered when we come to treat of the ethical effect of the Vedānta, but in the meantime it may be sufficient to point out that an unqualified imputation of antinomianism would be unjust. In the first place, while Śaṅkara indeed deprecates activity, it must be recognized that his ultimate knowledge is of such a character as to contain within itself an activity of a higher order, not the progressive activity of ordinary works or even of ordinary knowledge, but of intense concentration and awareness. It has, moreover, to be repeated again and again, as Śaṅkara brings out very explicitly in his Commentary on *Sūtra* IV. I. I.[1]

In the second place, while the enlightened sage may 'live as he pleases', and good and evil works are theoretically equally indifferent to him, there may be in this a suggestion that he is above the moral law, not in the sense that he may despise it, but in the sense that he has absorbed it into himself, has overcome its externality, and fulfils it in that spirit of artistic carelessness which is really the highest carefulness. But whether this interpretation of the sage's attitude is admitted or not, it is hardly to be thought that one who has realized the value of good works as a necessary propaedeutic, will not continue practically a preference for them over evil works. He will surely still feel, at least in his less stringently philosophical moods, that the health of his soul in its highest spiritual realization is not altogether dissociated from the continuing performance of these good works.

From an ethical point of view, as we shall see more fully later, the most serious consequence of Śaṅkara's position is connected with his depreciation of the enduring value of works of social service and self-sacrifice. A certain want of enthusiasm at least for such works would seem to be inseparable from his general theoretical position. Ultimately, he regards them as forging new fetters, and he seems to be unable to accept the view that while not ends in themselves, they may be ends for the Kingdom of God. Because he has so completely detached earth from God, he cannot make use of a conception of the kingdom of God upon earth. Deussen seems to think that this is a matter of little consequence. He says, 'Whether this meta-

[1] Cf. *S. B. E.* XXXVIII. 332.

physical consciousness, which lifts us above the world . . . leads over into Quietism . . . or is realized in deeds of love, touches only its form of appearance and establishes no difference in the value of what appears here.'[1]

There does seem to us to be a most important difference in value, and in place of accepting this transcendental equalization and indifference, we prefer to draw attention, as Prof. Tattvabhushan does, to a concession which Śaṅkara himself is inclined to make. In his Commentary on the eleventh verse of the second chapter of the *Gita*, he allows that the performance of duties for the good of the world by Śri Kṛishṇa and others was not incompatible with even the highest knowledge.[2] We are inclined to think that such an admission may be symbolic of a feeling that the world of ordinary duties and service, temporal though it may be, is not ultimately to be completely detached from the eternal reality. We shall find that such a feeling finds fuller expression in Śaṅkara's doctrine of Māyā to which we must now turn.

[1] Deussen, *S. V.* 424.

[2] Cf. Tattvabhushan in *Three Great Acharyas*, 101.

VI

THE DOCTRINE OF *MĀYĀ* AND *AVIDYĀ*. RELATION TO KANT. THE GOD OF QUALITIES

'THE eye reaches it not, speech reaches it not, thought reaches it not'—from the dim and mysterious distance which this verse suggests how can we return to a realistic interpretation of that world of ordinary experience with which after all we have to concern ourselves? This is the difficulty which constantly presents itself to all students of the Vedānta and indeed of Indian philosophy generally, and it was a difficulty of which Śaṅkara himself was ever and again poignantly aware. Under his guidance we may have floated upwards from the lower knowledge to the higher, we may have reached that mystical union with the characterless Absolute which he indicates as the goal of all our philosophical and religious searching, and which constitutes our salvation, but under the pressure of experience we have to come back again to that world from which we have so painfully detached ourselves and which we still find cannot be left out of consideration. As Deussen says, 'We demand from the philosopher as from the empiric investigator, a full interest in the visible world and its wonderful phenomena, only that he must see them with other eyes than the empiric.'[1] That Śaṅkara himself is aware of the insistence of such a demand is obvious from his placing the two orders of knowledge side by side and from his giving at least subordinate recognition to the lower; and, though his interest in the wonderful phenomena of nature and humanity cannot be called 'full', he is at least not prepared to leave the empirical world suspended uncertainly in the philosophic void.

He relies for connexion and explanation on the term *Māyā* with all the implications of this elusive conception. *Māyā* is the mysterious power which, through undefinable association with the Absolute, turns the non-qualitative Brahman into the qualitative, so that the Unmanifested becomes manifested, is transformed into an 'ocean of auspicious qualities'. From one point of view these qualities are 'limiting adjuncts' (*upādhis*), but from another point of view they are the seminal forces of

[1] Deussen, *S. V.* 81.

the universe. Brahman, as qualitative, is the sum-total of the *upādhis*, and the world of nature and human spirits is their manifestation, and constitutes the body of Brahman and the concrete revelation of his being. *Māyā* is the principle of individuation and the fullest explanation we can give of the visible universe in all the variety of its 'names and forms' and the opportunities it presents for the existence and responsible activities of mankind.

We may notice two particular directions of the activity of *Māyā*. Through the power of envelopment (*āvaraṇa*) it produces the idea of individualized Self-hood, and through the power of projection (*vikṣepa*) it produces all the phenomena of the external world. Or, as it has been put, ignorance has both 'the power of obstruction by which it hides from our view the real nature of things, and the power of development by which it gives to airy nothing a habitation and a name'.[1] Another Indian writer avails himself usefully of the conception of 'polarization'. '*Māyā* is the divine power which manifests itself in various ways, but the nature of its operation has this constant characteristic that it brings about diversity (*bheda*) out of unity (*abheda*); the opposition which it sets up between the subject and the object may be compared to the action of a magnetic force which lets off opposite kinds of magnetism at the two poles of a magnet.'[2]

And yet, even if we are to admit the existence of *māyā*, we must, according to Śaṅkara, hold firmly to the contrast between it and the absolute Source from which it springs—to the contrast between the non-qualitative and the qualitative, the infinite and the finite, the changeless and the changing, the imperishable and the perishable, the invisible and the visible, the unity and the manifold. If we indeed permit ourselves to turn towards the world of experience, we must always remember that our steps are leading us downwards. We may seek to know the world in which we live; but after all, for the sake of this knowledge, we have to leave behind—and sacrifice—the incognizable Reality; and that which cannot be known through the ordinary forms of cognition remains the ultimate foundation of

[1] Pundit K. N. Tarkabagisa.
[2] P. N. Sen, *Philosophy of the Vedānta*, 116.

all things. Thus a sense of depreciation attends us even as we set out upon our quest for a solution of the problems of the world.

This sense may lie hidden in that interpretation which is so often given to the conception of *māyā*, by which it is taken to be the equivalent of 'illusion'. We consider that it is entirely wrong to accept this interpretation in a crude and literal sense, and without some kind of qualification. There is a wealth of significance in the conception of *māyā* which the English word 'illusion' does not by any means fully express, and the precise degree of suitability which attaches to the translation requires considerable investigation. But before we undertake any critical analysis we may trace the growth of the *māyā* conception itself and indicate generally Śaṅkara's own use of the term.

In the earliest usage, as far back as the *Ṛigveda*, the root idea associated with the term would seem to be the wonderful power of the gods, through the operation of which they display a wisdom far transcending our ordinary experience or faculties of comprehension. But with the idea of the wonderful the idea of the mysterious is combined, and by a further not unnatural transition of thought, the idea of the mysterious may be transformed into the idea of the deceptive. In our attempts to grasp what is beyond the reach of our faculties, we inevitably make mistakes; but mistakes for which we are not willing to shoulder the responsibility, come to be regarded as attempts on the part of others to deceive us. Our inability to apprehend the gods adequately has as its natural counterpart an intention on the part of the gods to mislead us. And we entertain this slightly malign idea of deception all the more easily if, as was the case in Ṛigvedic times, religious belief attaches itself to two sets of gods, one of which is benevolent and the other malevolent. A mysterious supernatural power the exercise of which is conceivably beneficent is ascribed to the good gods, whereas the mistakes which we make and the practical blunders which work our misery are ascribed to the evil gods, and appear as maleficent powers belonging to the latter. A firm association thus grows up between the idea of divine power and the idea of deception, and when once the association is formed it is not easily broken.[1]

[1] Cf. P. D. Shastri, 10 and Happel, *Grundanschauung der Inder*, 88.

In fact as the idea of mystery deepens and terror darkens the originally familiar relations between men and gods in Ṛigvedic times, new scope is found for the working of the idea of deception, inasmuch as what a man fears he hates, and what he hates he is inclined to interpret malevolently. Hence, when the idea of the supernatural is so strongly emphasized as it is in the latest of the Vedas—the *Atharvaveda*—it is not by any means surprising that the idea of magic or deceptive illusion should become increasingly prevalent.

We shall find that all attempts to describe the character of *māyā* have to face the difficulty of deciding whether it is to be regarded as Being or non-Being, *sat* or *asat*. The implications of this alternative will require later treatment, but in the meantime we may use the contrast as an indication of the course of historical development. From the ordinary naïve point of view the actual is the real—everything else is *asat*, mysterious, unreal, uncanny. But as the sense of mystery deepens, and philosophical interest develops and becomes more penetrating, the supersensible acquires greater importance than the sensible. The former becomes the real—the truly real—and the facts and events of ordinary experience become attenuated into the veils which hide reality from us. They in turn are now the *asat*, the dreamlike, the fictitious, constituting the world of appearance, almost the realm of illusion. The philosopher has indeed come to 'see with other eyes than the empiric', and what the latter calls *sat*, he calls *asat*. The fluidity of the distinction between the real and the unreal, and the interchange of characters, recalls the definition in the Platonic philosophy of opinion, which has been described as 'something lying between the purely existent and the absolutely non-existent—something more dusky than knowledge, but more luminous than ignorance'.[1]

Our present purpose does not require us to trace the historical process in further detail. Śaṅkara, it has been pointed out, does not obtain much support for a rigorous doctrine of *māyā* from the *Vedānta Sūtras*, and, in reference to their sources in the Upanishads, there is a good deal to be said for the contention of Colebrooke, Cowell, and Dr. Barnett, that these favour

[1] For an excellent description of the relation between *sat and asat*, cf. Kirtikar, *Studies in Vedānta*, 191.

a realistic interpretation of the universe and that the *māyā* doctrine is not to be found explicitly in them. Yet, on the other hand, it cannot be gainsaid that there are implicit suggestions of the doctrine from the very beginning of the Upanishad development. Deussen regards the conception as being the necessary complement of the doctrine of the sole reality of the Ātman, which, according to him, is the fundamental teaching of even the oldest Upanishads; and it may be argued that Śaṅkara gives on the whole the true interpretation of the ultimate position taken up by the Upanishads in face of the difficulties of reconciling the manifold unity and the finite with the infinite. To Śaṅkara's own position we must now turn.

He certainly does not, in his language at least, guard with any great care against an extreme illusory interpretation. In his Commentary on *Sūtra* I. 3. 19 he tells us that the one highest Lord 'manifests himself in various ways, just as a thaumaturge appears in different shapes by means of his magical power'.[1] In I. 4. 3 he asserts plainly that the causal potentiality 'is of the nature of an illusion'.[2] And the entire effect of this potentiality is 'a figment of nescience', and the 'germs of the entire expanse of the phenomenal world are the result of illusion'.[3] Still more emphatic is he in his Commentary on II. 1. 23, 'This entire apparent world, in which good and evil actions are done, is a mere illusion, and does in reality exist not at all'.[4] Also in the retractation of the world which he has evolved, the supreme Lord preserves the detachment and indifference of the magician. All effects, according to the Vedantic view, are but illusory appearances of the cause. The changes which attract our notice are but *vivartavāda* changes, and not *pariṇāmavāda*, the former term indicating a less degree of actual effectuation than the latter. According to Sir R. G. Bhandarkar, 'the former implies an illusive development and the latter real development.'[5] Śaṅkara combines this idea of *vivartavāda* changes with the doctrine, repeatedly stated by him, that cause and effect are identical, and, when confronted with the objection that, if this is so, the cause will be affected by the evils and defects of the world, he cites first of all the analogy of the clay remaining

[1] *S. B. E.* XXXIV. 190. [2] Ib. 243. [3] Cf. *Sūtra* II. 1. 14.
[4] *S. B. E.* XXXIV. 345. [5] *Vaishṇavism*, 160.

unaffected finally by the form of the particular vessels made out of it, but bases his main defence upon the contention that the evolution has not after all been real. His conclusion upon the question is that just 'as the magician is not affected at any time by the magical illusion produced by himself, because it is unreal, so the highest Self is not affected by the world-illusion'.[1] Such passages would certainly seem to support very strongly the interpretation of illusion, and many writers accept this meaning unhesitatingly and without qualification. Usually it is against non-Indian writers that the charge of precipitancy in this respect is brought, but some Indian writers are equally ready to accept this view. Prof. Prabhu Dutt Shastri, e.g., says, 'It is true beyond doubt that Śaṅkara means by Māyā nothing but illusion.'[2] And Prof. S. N. Das Gupta is of much the same opinion, 'In Śaṅkara the word *Māyā* is used in the sense of illusion, both as a principle of creation, as a *śakti* (power) or accessory cause, and as the phenomenal creation itself, as the illusion of world-appearance.'[3]

The impression of detachment from all effects of the magical power is strengthened when we take into consideration the motive which is ascribed to the highest Lord in the creation of the cosmic illusion. This is a corollary of the accepted doctrine of salvation; for if salvation is to consist in a realization of the ephemeral character of the world rather than in submission to a rigid system of inexorable laws, then it is obvious that a similar freedom and light-heartedness must be attributed to the Lord who exercises the magical power. There must be, as Max Müller points out, a considerable degree of self-forgetfulness.[4] The Creator cannot be conceived of as labouring from a sense of need or for the accomplishment of any serious purpose. He needs nothing, he aims at nothing. Rather is he like the child of sportive impulse, blowing bubbles lovely as the rainbow but no more lasting. Or he is like a mighty prince of satiated desire, who yet must find some amusement to relieve the tedium of the passing hour.[5]

Now at first sight this might seem to be a wholly frivolous conception, and it has, as such, been subjected to much hostile

[1] *S.B.E.* XXXIV. 312.
[2] P. D. Shastri, 26.
[3] Das Gupta, I. 470.
[4] Cf. Müller, *S.S.* 185.

criticism. But we venture to think that a good deal of this criticism is undeserved. The conception may be wanting in depth, and it may be allowed that it would only be possible for one in whom the tendency to depreciate the world system was already strongly marked. But at the same time it at least hints at ideas of considerable philosophical importance. It may be an attempt to deal in a symbolic way with the difficulty of connecting the idea of purpose with the Absolute, a problem which occupies much space in the writings of Lotze and is one of the most important topics in Prof. Pringle-Pattison's *Idea of God.* Further, the thought of play is not far removed from the idea of the exercise of energy without strain, as in the healthful rhythm of breathing, or from the idea of effortless growth towards perfection. 'Consider the lilies of the field, how they grow; they toil not, neither do they spin: and yet I say unto you, that even Solomon in all his glory was not arrayed like one of these.'[1] A recent writer in the *Hibbert Journal* emphasizes the idea that play is as important as work in the evolutionary process, and urges us to realize the kinship of recreation to creation.[2] An allied idea appears very frequently in the writings of Dr. Rabindranath Tagore, who holds that joy is of the essence of the divine nature and that we should approach more nearly to the secrets of the origin of the world if we would assign greater importance to the idea of creative imagination.

In any case, whatever general philosophic import we may assign to it, the idea of *līlā*, or 'sport', can be rightly estimated only if we take it in connexion with the anti-realistic tendency of Śaṅkara's whole system. If the conception seems sometimes to work out into a cold indifference to the sufferings of humanity, yet our sense of fitness is not offended to the same extent as in a more realistic system. We might conceive of Śaṅkara as saying in reference to suffering, 'It *is not*, and therefore does not matter,' whereas a more realistic thinker would have to say, 'It *is*, and yet it does not matter.' A statement such as the following from the more realistically inclined Vedantist, Rāmānuja, is much more disconcerting than if it had emanated from a

[1] Matthew vi. 28.

[2] Art. 'The Spirit of Play', by Greville Macdonald, *Hibbert Journal*, Jan. 1923.

thoroughgoing anti-realist like Śaṅkara: 'To the soul, therefore, which is subject to karman, the connexion with different things is a source of imperfection and suffering; while to the highest Brahman, which is subject to itself only, the same connexion is the source of playful sport.'[1]

But, in order to gain a more complete understanding of the conception of *māyā*, it is necessary to proceed to an analysis of a term which has been left too long out of account, viz. *avidyā*, or Nescience. For the purposes of his refutation of Buddhistic subjectivism Śaṅkara adopted provisionally the ordinary empirical belief in an external world, but later discarded such a belief, in order to prepare the way for an assertion of the one and only reality. He objected to the Buddhistic view that our experience is independent of external data; but he adopts also the position that the external data are themselves untrustworthy and that unity alone exists. Psychologically, the motive for this procedure of Śaṅkara's may have been a sense of the inadequacy of our ordinary categories, and in respect of the agnosticism which is implied in the word *avidyā*, Śaṅkara may be legitimately regarded as a precursor of Kant, to whom he is repeatedly compared by most Indian writers and also by Deussen and Max Müller. But, as the latter also points out, there is a considerable difference between the ultimate view of Śaṅkara and that of Kant.[2] Śaṅkara does not go so far as Kant in the analysis and detailed subjectification of our mental forms and categories, but his final attitude both to these forms and their products is much more negative. At first sight Kant seems, e.g., to take a more subjective view of space than Śaṅkara. With Kant space is a mental form, although, indeed, by reason of its necessity and universality it may approach objectivity. With Śaṅkara, on the other hand, space is objective in an empirical sense—'the doctrine of its being a nonentity is untenable,' and 'substantiality can be established in the case of space'.[3] But when we consider the matter further, we find that this ascription of objectivity falls wholly within Śaṅkara's provisional refutation of Buddhism, and therefore cannot be taken as his ultimate position. Space turns out to be merely a reality within an unreality. Śaṅkara is

[1] *S. B. E.* XLVIII. 610.
[2] Cf. Müller, *S. S.* 173.
[3] Cf. *Sūtra* II. 2. 24.

more realistic than Kant only provisionally, but much less realistic ultimately. In his attitude to experience taken as a whole Śaṅkara approaches much more nearly to a negative position. Therefore those who adopt the illusory interpretation of Śaṅkara's teaching—whether they are correct or not in this acceptance—cannot defend it by identifying it with the position of Kant. It is a mistake to state the relation between the two orders of knowledge in the Vedānta philosophy, as interpreted by Śaṅkara, as simply equivalent to the Kantian relation between phenomena and noumena. The phenomenal and the illusory have by no means the same philosophical value, and in using the latter term Śaṅkara says much more than is implied in Kant's use of the former. In other words, Śaṅkara is not merely agnostic; he is also condemnatory. As regards the results of our use of the categories it would be just to represent Kant as saying, 'This, though not very much, is the best we can do,' whereas Śaṅkara would seem to prefer to say, 'This is the worst we can do,' or, 'This is what we should not do at all, if we desire the highest wisdom.' According to the latter it is not merely that our knowledge fails but that it does not deserve to succeed, because it is on the wrong lines. Kant again would admit the validity of the intellectual activities which give rise to the categories, and would lament only that they do not succeed in unlocking the door of the mysteries. Śaṅkara, on the other hand, would be inclined to hold that these activities are wrong in principle and that they do not only fail to unlock the door into the real world, but considerably spoil the lock. Further, Kant, however inconsistent this may be with his strict doctrine that causality holds only amongst phenomena, would yet admit that things in themselves are the sources of sense-experience even though not revelatory of themselves in these experiences, whereas Śaṅkara would urge that there is no distributed reality which could possibly be even the remote cause of sensational experience. Identification on this point, therefore, of the Vedantic with the Kantian philosophy would seem to be to a large extent misleading.

It would be interesting to ask whether, if Śaṅkara had written a 'Critique of Pure Reason' from his own point of view, he would have left room, as Kant did, for a 'Critique of Practical Reason'? A consideration of the classical passage in the Commentary on *Sūtra* II. 1. 14 would seem to afford material for an affirmative answer. Here Śaṅkara says, 'The entire complex of phenomenal existence is considered as true as long as the knowledge of Brahman being the Self of all has not arisen. . . . As long as true knowledge does not present itself, there is no reason why the ordinary course of secular and religious activity should not hold on undisturbed.'[1] But while there is a surface similarity here, the fundamental attitudes of the two thinkers are very different from one another. According to Kant, the activities of the practical reason will afford a true access to the deepest reality, whereas, according to Śaṅkara, practical activities in general are purely provisional; they are operations springing from a darkened understanding and should for the most part be disregarded as soon as the light of true knowledge dawns. That this introduces a most important difference in our total attitude to practical activity will be obvious. The distinction is made clear by Solovyof, who points out that, while mere doubt about objective reality would have no effect upon moral activity, dogmatic certainty as to non-existence would certainly have such an effect to a very considerable degree.[2]

Having thus considered a possible affiliation between Śaṅkara's doctrine of *avidyā*, or nescience, and the Kantian philosophy, and having seen that the similarity has been greatly overestimated, we may now return to Śaṅkara's own development of the conception. We have found that ultimately, and perhaps mainly on religious grounds and with a view to the winning of spiritual freedom, he is disposed to assert the unreality of ordinary experience. At the same time in his criticism of Buddhism he has shown his opposition to particularistic subjectivity, or, in other words, his unwillingness to saddle the individual with the whole responsibility for the wrong knowledge in which ignorance consists. An attempt to reconcile the two positions throws considerable light upon the peculiar character of his doctrine of nescience. Although he might not use modern terms, and although our purpose is simply to show the naturalness of the transitions in his thought and we do not attempt to trace in exact details all the windings of his

[1] *S. B. E.* XXXIV. 324.
[2] Cf. Solovyof, *Justification of the Good*, 10.

speculation, yet it may be said that Śaṅkara was very evidently aware of what modern psychologists would describe as the results of intersubjective intercourse. He argues provisionally for empirical realism on the grounds of common perception and the impossibility of providing otherwise, or on the principles of Buddhistic individualism, for the practical concerns of life.[1]

Although a few Vedantists might approach such Buddhistic individualism, yet, as Prof. S. N. Das Gupta points out, 'in the normal Vedantic view the objects of the world are existent as phenomena. . . . The objective phenomena in themselves are of course but modifications of *ajñāna*, but still these phenomena of the *ajñāna* are there as the common ground for the experience of all.'[2] Śaṅkara's reasoning apparently is that, if we make mistakes, other people make the same mistakes. Our ignorance is a common ignorance, and the cause of it, therefore, must lie somewhere beyond ourselves. But in universalizing our ignorance we are at the same time going far in the direction of objectifying it; we are passing from the view of ignorance as an erroneous mental activity to a consideration of the objects presented by that ignorance to us and to others. We thus evade subjective and individual responsibility. We pass from the negation usually implied by the word 'ignorance' to the more positive idea of 'false knowledge', which again, be it carefully noticed, is not a mere private possession. But the two seemingly incompatible ideas of objectivity and unreliability can be held together in the mind only if a principle of falsification can be posited as the explanation of the false knowledge. Why not therefore, the Vedantist philosopher asks, replace our subjective ignorance by a cosmical ignorance and transform a psychological or epistemological principle into a metaphysical one, a disability connected with our human limitations into an ability to create a world? Let us conceive, urged Śaṅkara, of a world-ignorance as well as of an individual ignorance, and let us regard the world-ignorance as so far positive as to be able to produce a phenomenal world. Dr. Barnett traces the transition as evidenced in the individual soul, 'With Śaṅkara and the later Vedānta it is a positive, a false light, a constructive illusion.'[3] Happel puts the matter more

[1] Cf. *S. B. E.* XXXIV. 421 and 428.
[2] Das Gupta, I. 478.
[3] *Brahma-Knowledge*, 39.

objectively and universally. 'The expression *avidyā*, especially if translated as Nescience, conceals the essence of the conception; for the negative expression leads us in a wrong direction, as if the word signified something negative and indicated merely defect. This is an error. *Avidyā* is a mighty power, for through it arise the upâdhis, from which again come the aggregates of names and forms and the instruments of our activity, and hence also suffering, birth, death, age, sickness, and so on.'[1] Thus the same principle which is responsible for our subjective ignorance may also be regarded as the explanation of that objective world which we are supposed to know in the state of ignorance. Here Śaṅkara definitely diverges from Kant. The unreliability of empirical knowledge is found to be due not to the inadequacy of human faculties but to 'the potency of an all-pervading principle of cosmic ignorance'.[2] To suppose a principle of this sort is at once an acknowledgement of inexplicable mystery and a disclaimer of any attempts at explanation. Ignorance is that which because of its very nature *cannot* be understood. He who would understand *avidyā* has been compared to 'a man who should rush to see darkness by means of a far-shining torch'. Moreover the idea of ignorance with its implications of mistake and falsification carries our minds by a natural transition to the idea of an illusory world. If there is a definite suggestion of negation or of the unpermitted in the cause, it is much easier to attach a similar suggestion to the product. Thus *avidyā* and *māyā* have the closest possible affinity with each other.

Śaṅkara indeed ascribes to *avidyā* very much the same functions as he assigns to *māyā*. *Avidyā* is the cause of the *saṁsāra*, or aggregate of world phenomena. In the Commentary on *Sūtra* I. 4. 3 the two ideas are combined. The causal potentiality is of the 'nature of nescience', and also 'of the nature of an illusion'. In connexion with *Sūtra* II. 1. 6 he speaks of the 'fallacious superimpositions of nescience', and in II. 1. 4 he speaks of name and form as 'the presentations of nescience', and in II. 1. 28 of nature as 'a mere figment of nescience'. *Avidyā* is almost personified as a principle of creative error.

In general the connexion between *avidyā* and *māyā* is so close

[1] Happel, *Grundanschauung der Inder*, 89.
[2] Frazer, *Indian Thought*, 88.

that it is difficult to distinguish between them. Thibaut is inclined to identify them, and we have seen that Prof. Das Gupta's opinion is that in Śaṅkara *māyā* means both a principle of creation and the result of this creation.[1] Deussen prefers to regard *avidyā* as the causal principle and *māyā* as the effect. *Avidyā* works by the ascription of *upādhis*, or 'limiting adjuncts', and *māyā* is the resulting totalization of these *upâdhis*, inclusive of the ideas of a personal God, the world, and individual souls. We find also occasionally a disposition to distinguish between *avidyā* and *māyā* on grounds of valuation, the product of the latter being regarded as having a more elevated character than the former. If such views are correct, this just means that *avidyā* has not wholly detached itself from its individual and subjective origin, has not become altogether cosmical. In a later passage Prof. Das Gupta points out that, according to some Vedantists, *māyā* is more distinctively the projective creative force (*vikṣepa*) and thrusts into embodiment the higher attributes, whereas *avidyā* is rather of the nature of a concealing power (*āvaraṇa*), and is responsible for the less worthy attributes. Further, it is sometimes indicated that the pure intelligence of the Absolute in relation with *māyā* produces first of all Īśvara, or the personal God, whilst in relation with *avidyā* it produces the individual soul. Too much stress, however, must not be laid on these minute distinctions, seeing that the Vedantist writers themselves do not always observe them, and for all practical purpose *avidyā* and *māyā* may be taken as simply slightly different ways of describing that mysterious power which produces the more or less unreal world of ordinary experience.

Before going farther it is important that we should notice exactly what degree of commitment to reality is involved in the objectification of *avidyā*. If, from being a merely epistemological concept it is transformed into a metaphysical principle, then its upholders must be ready to accept the consequences of the transformation. They cannot continue to defend the conception against attack as if it were merely negative. Deussen seems not to have observed this caution when he says that the principle needs no explanation just because it is wholly negative, and Prof. P. D. Shastri seems to fall into the same error in his

[1] *Op. cit.*, p. 470.

refutation of the criticisms passed by Rāmānuja upon Śaṅkara. But you must choose between the epistemological and the metaphysical treatment. You cannot treat *avidyā*, or *māyā*, as a principle of metaphysical explanation, and then run away from criticism of it on the ground that it is simply the hypostasis of error and has no true positive existence. It would seem to us that Rāmānuja is wholly justified in claiming that the conception should be treated seriously and that those who use it should not take refuge *merely* in its inexplicability. It may turn out that they are right as regards its inexplicable character, but they should not at one and the same time confess this inexplicability and yet continue to use it as a metaphysical principle which, just because of its inexplicability, is exempt from criticism. They must do one thing or the other. Their principle is either something or nothing. If it is nothing, it cannot be used to explain the world. If it is something, it must be treated as a positive, having sufficient character to stand investigation. Rāmānuja's challenge to the stricter Vedantists seems to be that they cannot be both agnostic and dogmatic. They must choose between the two attitudes, and if they choose the latter they must abide criticism. They must, further, show the relation of *māyā* to Brahman, they must resolve the contradiction between the pure unity of the latter and the admission of a world-principle of differentiation within his being. They must adjust the darkening power of *māyā* to the pure self-luminousness of Brahman. They must show how, if cause and effect are, as they say, identical, Brahman, as reality, can be identical with that which is illusory. If, finally, *māyā* is real—even to the extent of being used as an explanatory principle—it cannot be wholly sublated by the higher knowledge which Śaṅkara aims at, and therefore the way of salvation prescribed by the rigorous monists turns out to be deceptive. You may be wrong in taking nescience as an explanatory principle rather than as an intellectual attitude. But if you choose the former you must consider also the consequences. If *ajñāna* is destroyable, it is not real, and if it is real, it is not destroyable. Rāmānuja points out that if nescience is a part of the Ātman which is Brahman, it cannot be sublated, and adds that 'knowledge cannot destroy a real thing'.[1] In

[1] Cf. *S. B. E.* XLVIII. 116.

short, the sum and substance of Rāmānuja's criticism is, Let *māyā* abide the question, or let it be abandoned as a metaphysical principle.

We seem forced to the conclusion that *māyā* cannot abide the question, if it is taken as a pure principle of illusion, giving rise to an altogether fictitious world. Universal illusionism is impossible. Mr. D. N. Pal in his *Śaṅkara the Sublime* indeed says, 'It is delusion that produces delusion. It is disease that produces disease,'[1] but Śaṅkara himself would, we think, be ready to point out the fallacy underlying this statement, and would allow that in disease there is a positive maleficent agency at work. In general also he would admit that you cannot hang a chain of illusion in the air, that you must get back to reality somewhere, and that only the real can produce anything, even a power of illusion. The logic of the system would seem to demand an ultimate acceptance of reality. As Prof. Das Gupta puts it, 'With Śaṅkara the forms of the external world were no doubt illusory, but they all had a permanent background in the Brahman which was the only reality behind all mental and physical phenomena.'[2] Vedantists are fond of the illustration of the rope and the snake, but after all it is an actual rope which produces the illusion of the snake. Śaṅkara himself says, 'Whenever we deny something unreal, we do so with reference to something real; the unreal snake, e.g., is negatived with reference to the real rope.'[3] It may be said indeed that a rigorous illusionist has no right to the word 'illusion': he ought to confine himself to the word 'hallucination', for all 'illusion' involves an ultimate reference to reality such as we have just indicated, and what is true of a particular illusion is true also of the cosmic illusion. An Indian writer, St. Arulnandi, puts it thus, 'If you say that all knowledge is Illusion, what you call Brahman is Illusion; and, if Brahman is illusion, the assumption of intelligence falls to the ground.'[4] Such reasoning would seem to be incontrovertible: somewhere we must rest in the series of negations. The question comes to be, how far back are we to go in our search for reliable reality? Are we never to call a halt until

[1] *Op. cit.* 198. [2] Das Gupta, I. 168.
[3] Com. on *Sūtra* III. 2. 22, *S. B. E.* XXXVIII. 168.
[4] Quoted in Carpenter, *Theism in Medieval India*, 361.

we have reached a Brahman without qualities and, in our backward look, are we to negate entirely the world from which we have started—sweep it out of existence with the magic word 'illusion'?

Here we come to the centre of our problem. What was it that Śaṅkara did? Was he a thoroughgoing illusionist? Did he escape from every problem through what Carpenter calls 'the backdoor of illusion'? What is the final interpretation of this concept?

> Is all that we see or seem
> But a dream within a dream?[1]

We have seen that some of Śaṅkara's fellow countrymen have taken the conception at its face value, and that he himself frequently uses language which would suggest that he was inclined to flee from the contradictions of the world and take refuge in the conception of universal negation. But such a view would not, we consider, represent the fullness of his thought, and there is much to be said for those who attempt to present the matter in another light, even though at times their conclusions may seem to go beyond the evidence.

The first line of defence is that the whole conception of *māyā* is simply a symbol of humble and reverent agnosticism. As Swami Vivekananda puts it, Śaṅkara was content through this conception to give us 'simply a statement of the fact of this universe, of how it is going on'.[2] It is argued that, like a Scottish philosopher of later days, Śaṅkara felt that 'his line was too short for such vast abysses'. When confronted with the problem of the multiplicity of things, he, like Lotze, could not see 'how a plurality ever arose out of a single principle unless various conditions . . . constrained it to produce here *a* and there *b* or *c*'.[3] The conception of *māyā* was the sign and summary of Śaṅkara's perplexities. The multitudinous things of the world were all a problem and a perplexity. They were and yet they ought not to be; for they were inexplicable. As Prof. Radhakrishnan puts it in attempting to express the attitude of Śaṅkara, 'As for the empirical ramifications which also exist, well, they are there, and there is an end of it. We do not know

[1] E. A. Poe, 'The Sleeper.'
[2] *Jñāna-Yoga*, 10.
[3] *Philosophy of Religion*, 18.

how and cannot know why. It is all a contradiction and yet is actual.'[1]

Māyā was the conception chosen to indicate the inexplicable. But, as we have seen, when that which is inexplicable or indefinable is set over against an abstract unitary being, a depreciatory attitude is apt to emerge in reference to the inexplicable. The indefinable is of lesser worth than the definable; it is something which cannot obviously be connected with the one great Being; which, in other words, ought not to be, and is therefore ultimately dismissible. So *māyā* was made to bear the burden of the mystery, and the conception was itself invested with contradictions, of which perhaps the most important was that it could be said, not at all without meaning, both to be and not to be. And further degradation still was inevitable. From the idea of depreciation to the idea of deception is but a short distance, for when impatience of the inexplicable manifests itself, the inexplicable is soon transformed into the delusive. We cannot hold that whatever is a mystery to us is inexplicable also to God. But for God to cause what is plain to himself to become misleading as far as we are concerned, is to put into operation a principle of concealment and deception. In this way Śaṅkara's perplexity led him to the very edge of the morass of illusionism, although originally and in deepest intention he was a humble agnostic, worthy to have ascribed to him in the words of Prof. Radhakrishnan, 'a touching humility born of intellectual strength,'[2] of which humility and which strength *māyā* is the appropriate expression. This agnostic implication of *māyā* is emphasized by many writers. Dr. Rabindranath Tagore says, 'The word *māyā* is a mere name, it is no explanation,'[3] Prof. Das Gupta describes it as 'a category which baffles the ordinary logical divisions of existence and non-existence and the principle of excluded middle',[4] and Max Müller points out that the 'primeval *Avidyā* is left unexplained, it is not to be accounted for, as little as Brahman can be accounted for'.[5] Further, on the lines of a frequent criticism of the Kantian philosophy, it has been pointed out that we are not justified in raising the question of the cause of Nescience, because causality applies only to that

[1] Radhakrishnan, I. 35. [2] *Op. cit.* 34. [3] *Sādhanā*, 95.
[4] Das Gupta, I. 442. [5] Müller, *S. S.* 171.

empirical world which in its totality is the result of Nescience, and cannot therefore explain the relation between Nescience and the Absolute or between Nescience and the totality of the world produced by it. As Mr. M. L. Bhattacharya puts it, 'We are not justified in raising the question, What is the cause of Nescience? as all our ideas of causality fall within the circle of Nescience, and so to find the cause of it would be like mounting upon one's own shoulders.'[1]

Now it is possible that Śaṅkara was to a large extent the reverent agnostic corresponding to the point of view indicated in these passages. It is possible also that a definite advance from agnosticism to dogmatism was left to later thinkers and that Prof. Das Gupta is right when he says that Śaṅkara only made explicit the doctrine of *māyā* in itself and that it was his followers who were responsible for further metaphysical characterization.[2] But we cannot help feeling that very frequently Śaṅkara himself appears as the negative dogmatist who was not content to say simply that we must leave unsolved the problem of the existence of the many, but went the length of asserting that all plurality *must* be illusory.

The other line of defence is taken by those who adopt the interpretation of the Vedānta philosophy favoured by Rāmānuja, and minimize almost to vanishing point the difference between him and Śaṅkara. Rāmānuja's position is that Scripture does not teach us that Brahman is devoid of qualities, and that when it is said that he is 'without a second', all that is meant is to deny the existence of any other principle separate from Brahman. If, on occasion, it is said that he is without qualities, the intention is only to negate undesirable qualities and nothing more. The plurality which is denied is that which would contradict the conception of the world as being in its entirety an effect of Brahman.[3] Rāmānuja thus sums up his conclusions: 'The authoritative books do *not* teach the doctrine of one undifferenced substance; they do not teach that the universe of things is false; and they do not deny the distinction of intelligent beings, non-intelligent beings and the Lord.'[4]

[1] *Vedānta Philosophy*, 55. [2] Cf. Das Gupta, I. 470.
[3] Cf. Rāmānuja's Commentary on *Sūtra* I. 1. 1, *S. B. E.* XLVIII. 85.
[4] Ib. XLVIII. 102.

Now our differing amount of emphasis upon the particularity of the world may lead us to occupy our minds either with the idea that everything is connected with Brahman, or that there is nothing of value requiring connexion with him. We may mean either that through Brahman all is known, or that there is nothing to be known except Brahman. Those who hold that the positions of Śaṅkara and Rāmānuja are very nearly identical in regard to this matter would choose the first interpretation. If we accept the principle that 'nothing exists unconnected with Brahman', we may of course emphasize the first two words, but if we do so, we, in their opinion, misrepresent Śaṅkara in regarding him as an illusionist who denied the reality of the world. His real intention is to lay stress on the connectedness with Brahman of the things of the world and not to assert their unreality. Śaṅkara's teaching is that we are wrong if we take the plurality in separation from Brahman. The things of the world are indeed unreal in their separate particularity, but in their connectedness with Brahman they partake of his reality. The emphasis which Śaṅkara lays upon the unity and unchangeableness of Brahman is intended to indicate that the world cannot be resolved altogether into particulars but is throughout dominated by the controlling continuity of the Divine Principle. The ultimate Unity is certainly not to be identified with the variety of the world, but on the other hand it is not exclusive of that variety. In order to reach an apprehension of the Divine Unity we may indeed have to negate the diversity, but this negation is only provisional, and the true position is reached, not when we negate all things, but when we view all things in God. This positive movement, it is held, is unmistakably discoverable in the Vedānta. As Kirtikar puts it, 'The finite world is not lost in the Vedantic Brahman, but retains its individuality. Even the individual who has reached perfection is not lost.'[1] From this point of view the Vedānta has been described as a 'philosophy of relative reality'. What is actual has certainly no independent existence, yet it has existence, and is unreal only if we mistakenly ascribe independence to it.

We believe that this may properly describe Śaṅkara's underly-

[1] Kirtikar, 108.

ing thought and that it was the position at which he was ultimately aiming. But he can hardly be said to have reached it. If he had done so, he would not have been satisfied with saying that the 'entire complex of phenomenal existence is to be considered as true' *only* 'as long as the knowledge of Brahman being the Self of all has not arisen'. The truth which he does not seem to have grasped, and which many of his followers also have failed to grasp, was that you cannot teach the essential connectedness of the world with Brahman, and at the same time assert that at some stage or other this whole world must cease to be real. If it is connected with Brahman in its essential character, it must have at least something of the permanence of Brahman. As Thibaut rightly points out, the upholder of the *māyā* doctrine cannot claim that his doctrine means merely that 'we are to look upon the whole world as a true manifestation of Brahman, as springing from it, as animated by it. . . . For him it would be appropriate to say, not that everything we see is in Brahman, but rather that everything we see is out of Brahman, viz. as a false appearance spread over it and hiding it from us.'[1]

Our conclusion then in regard to the realistic aspect of *māyā* which has been emphasized by some defenders of Śaṅkara's position, and which has been outlined in the last two or three paragraphs, is that it represents an ideal at which he was aiming rather than a conclusion which he actually reached. He was prevented from any satisfactory realistic rehabilitation of the world by the mystical trend of his mind, which caused him to be more interested in unity than in diversity. While he did not neglect the latter, and indeed devoted a great part of his teaching to cosmological theory, yet he did not treat the matter seriously enough. Instead of patiently studying the world of ordinary experience and arriving gradually at a unifying interpretation of it, he allowed himself to be too easily disconcerted by its instability and its confusion, and, impelled by religious devotion expressing itself intellectually in intuition, sought for a way of escape from it rather than for a solution of its problems. Thus he was ready to accept the negative and unsatisfactory conception of *māyā*, which, as many even of its defenders allow, is not

[1] *S. B. E.* XXXIV, p. cxx. Cf. also the present writer's *Pantheism and the Value of Life*, 227 ff.

much more than a confession of the insolubility of the problem. He was also hampered by the abstractness of his thought and by his preoccupation with the idea that the Ultimate must be without qualities. This dominating idea not only made his search a hopeless one, but prevented him from finding in the unity for which he was searching any key to the baffling problems of the world. In his conception there stood on the one hand the bare abstract Unity, and on the other the confused world of experience. He could not bridge the gulf—except by the conception of *māyā*, in itself a recognition of the inexplicability of the world and a depreciation of its value.

Still it would be a mistake to regard the conception as wholly a confession of philosophic defeat. It was more than this. It was also a symbolic expression of that mystic consciousness which lies in the depths of religious devotion, and which is content to see the world pass away and the glory thereof, if only it may abide in the Eternal. It is an implicit testimony to the belief that the world is spiritual in its origin and essence.

It shows something of the spirit which, in Merejkowski's novel, *The Death of the Gods*, the philosopher Iamblichus seeks to instil into the youthful Julian, 'Your soul will smile at your body as at a phantasm of the desert. You shall become silence, you shall no more find utterance. And if at that moment the world should crumble away, you would be happy; for what would the world signify to you, since you shall be with him.'[1] The tendency to negation was stronger in Śaṅkara than the tendency to affirmation, and what was wanting in his philosophy was a fuller conception of God which would have led him to see that to overcome the world both theoretically and practically was better than to flee from it. In the words of Happel, 'Not to the destruction of sense or to the loosing of bonds between Spirit and sense is man called, but to the domination and control of the latter. He is called to an ever fuller illumination and understanding of sense through the help of the spirit, so that finally the sensible world may no more detach itself from the Spirit, may no longer show itself as *māyā*, but, itself filled with the spirit, may become an eternal instrument of the spirit.'[2]

[1] *Death of the Gods*, 86. [2] Happel, 225.

The analysis of the implications of *māyā* leads us naturally to a consideration of the distinction which Śaṅkara makes between the Brahman of qualities and the Brahman without qualities. In conjunction with this we must also take account of the opposite view of Rāmānuja, who holds that the distinction is unjustifiable, and a similar view of some of Śaṅkara's own followers who hold that even in their master's teaching the distinction, though it may have been made, was not ultimate.

The depreciation of the world of ordinary experience which we have seen to be implicit in the conception of *māyā* seems certainly to be reproduced in the distinction, emphasized in Śaṅkara, between the higher or attributeless Brahman (*param, nirguṇam*) and the lower or qualitative Brahman (*aparam, saguṇam*). Of the former we can predicate nothing except reality. It is altogether beyond knowledge in the ordinary sense of the term, although it is not unknown to the highest intuition. As the *Taittirīya Upanishad* says, 'The words and thoughts turn back from it and find it not.'[1] In the oscillation of the human mind between the conceptions of *sat* and *asat*, Being and non-Being, it always occupies the side of the relationship farthest away from *māyā*; in other words, when *māyā* is called *sat*, Brahman is *asat*, and when *māyā* is *asat*, Brahman is *sat*. Brahman is, in Deussen's phrase, 'the last unknowable origin of the existent'.[2] It is not a Being which possesses intelligence as an attribute merely, it is itself pure intelligence or self-luminousness. It is thought without any objects, and it can itself never become an object of consciousness. It is essentially independent of all relationships, even though it may enter into them. It is untramelled and infinite, essentially blissful and peaceful in the sense of being free from all influence of variety or change.

On the other hand, the *saguṇam*, or lower Brahman, is the abode of all good qualities, and from these qualities come forth the world and the individual spirits. He is Īśvara, the personal God, and he gives rise to all beings according to the ordinary cosmological processes of immanental theology. Matter and souls are his modes. They exist in God in a subtle state, unevolved so long as the *pralaya* stage persists; but when this comes to an end, God, through an act of will, assumes creational

[1] II. 4.

[2] Deussen, *S. V.* 131.

form and expands himself into all the diversity of the empirical world, which diversity again will be resolved into the original being at the end of every age, or *kalpa*.

The question we have to consider is the relation between these two Brahmans. Śaṅkara insists on a distinction between them, and holds that this distinction is based upon the authority of both the *Sūtras* and the Upanishads. Rāmānuja, on the other hand, pushes the conception of the qualitative Brahman back until it becomes identified with the ultimate Brahman. He has no use for a non-qualitative Brahman such as Śaṅkara posits, and declares that the distinction is not supported either by the *Sūtras* or the Upanishads. In the passage from which we have already quoted[1] he states explicitly that the Scriptures 'do not teach the doctrine of one undifferenced substance'.

Now we have seen that the *Sūtras* seem to support Rāmānuja's position rather than Śaṅkara's, but that there is good reason to think that, though some of Śaṅkara's arguments, as, e.g., those relating to the order of the passages, may be untrustworthy, yet the tendency of the Upanishads is, on the whole, in the direction of an ultimate of abstract or non-qualitative character. At the stage we have reached, however, we are interested not so much in the authority which is behind Śaṅkara, as in the philosophical validity of the distinction itself upon which he lays so much stress. In this connexion it is at least noteworthy that by far the larger portions of Śaṅkara's own treatises are concerned with the relations of the *saguṇam* Brahman to the world and to the individual soul. If his belief in the non-qualitative Brahman had been as whole-hearted as he would have us think, why should he have devoted so much attention to the lower Brahman? Of course, in reply to this it may be said that it is quite appropriate that little space in a philosophical treatise should be devoted to the exposition of a Being who is chiefly revealed in silence, but again the rejoinder is possible that at least the usefulness of what is of the utmost importance should have been adequately set forth, and that, proportionately, what is of lesser importance should not have had so much attention drawn to it.

It is also interesting in this connexion to notice that some of

[1] p. 153.

Śaṅkara's followers have practically adopted the standpoint of Rāmānuja, and have attempted to ascribe it to Śaṅkara himself. They agree that no abrupt contrast should be drawn between the *nirguṇam* and the *saguṇam* Brahman, and they argue that if Śaṅkara himself *seems* to make hard-and-fast distinctions, this was only with a view to refuting those who showed an inclination to lose Brahman in his works, and who failed to appreciate that vast reserve in the nature of Brahman which did not come to expression, and the divine continuity which persisted amidst all the changes of the phenomenal world. If Śaṅkara was apparently depreciatory of the lower Brahman, it was only through fear that, unless emphasis was laid upon the nature of Brahman as he was in himself, the Creator of the world would become merely a diffused divinity, altogether merged in his works. According to Pundit K. Shastri, e.g., it is a mistake to regard Īśvara as distinct from Brahman, and Śaṅkara himself did not make this distinction. What he called illusory was not so much the creative act, but the taking of this act and its products in separation from Brahman. Īśvara is the revelation of Brahman, not complete indeed, because Brahman is inexhaustible, but still a real expression of the ultimate nature of the ultimate God. We should not think first of Brahman and then of a creator, as if they were two separate powers, on differing levels of importance. They are continuous with each other, and we pass from one to the other by an exceedingly natural transition.[1]

It is a little difficult to accept this view of Śaṅkara's teaching. We are afraid that he can hardly be absolved from the charge of attempting, as Lotze would put it, to write a history of the world before creation, and to think of God *apart* from the creation of the world. He is fascinated by the idea of unity and simplicity, and cannot but conceive of any breach in this unity as being to a certain extent a degradation. Because our intellect has not so thoroughly penetrated into the details with which it is dealing as to be able to present them in proper harmony with each other, because, in other words, the diversity is still disconcerting, he prefers to turn his thoughts altogether away from the diversity and fasten them on the unity. The apprehension of

[1] Cf. K. Shastri, 19.

this unity gives him a sense of mystic satisfaction, and when he turns back again to the diversity, it appears as something lower, something almost unworthy. He expresses this feeling in the conception of Īśvara as the first product of Nescience, the primal embodiment of the magic power which is somehow or other attached to the Absolute. In thinking of Īśvara we may but very slightly loosen our grasp upon the Absolute, our conceptions may undergo only the very smallest amount of depreciation, but still there is unmistakably a change. We have taken a step downwards, and we should not attempt to deny it. The idea of the phenomenal, of the unreal, has been introduced into the being of the God of whom we may conceive or whom we may worship. As Prof. Das Gupta puts it, 'In the Vedānta system Īśvara . . . is but a phenomenal being; he may be better, purer, and much more powerful than we are, but still he is as much phenomenal as any of us.'[1]

We may press further the question why, if Pundit K. Shastri is right as regards the valuational equivalence of Brahman and Īśvara, Śaṅkara should so often argue that differences must be negated in order that unity may be preserved. He says, e.g., that 'one and the same thing cannot in itself be affected by differences and not affected', and he considers that the only way out of the difficulty is to say that the differences are illusory. Again he tells us that we may 'now and again for the purposes of worship' treat Brahman as qualified by distinctions, but we must clearly recognize that this is a provisional permission merely and is, strictly speaking, inconsistent with an apprehension of the highest reality.[2] Finally, we may recall the character of the mood which is fundamental in Śaṅkara's thought, and which moves him to declare that he can find satisfaction only in unity and that 'the passages of Scripture about the negation of all differences have a meaning which leaves nothing more to be wished for'.[3] He comes very near indeed on many occasions to the conception attributed by a recent writer to the believers in the old Greek mysteries; 'that the world is not God, or at any rate seems to be not God but a thing apart from God, all shivered by its fall from the Divine into a thousand individual fragments, in fine, that the world

[1] Das Gupta, I. 477. [2] Cf. *S. B. E.* XXXVIII. 402. [3] Ib. 402.

exists at all—that is the primal evil, the original sin, the source of all the sufferings of the world.'[1]

So we come back to the question, whether this conception of the passage from unity to diversity as involving degradation, this determination to place a God of qualities on a lower level than the unqualified Absolute, is a necessary conception. We do not think that it is. We think that Śaṅkara's attempt to press this distinction proceeds from a distrust of human faculties which is indeed reverent, but is not fully justified. It is closely connected with his other distinction between two orders of knowledge which we found had been pressed too far. The human intellect cannot indeed reach the ultimate, but, in so far as it works sincerely and humbly, its procedure is trustworthy. We must not transform the inexhaustible into the inaccessible; and Śaṅkara himself seems to admit that the intellect can in some sense reach the Absolute, seeing that he was able to place the two conceptions side by side and *compare* them. And he should have pointed out more clearly that the intellect is sublimated and not destroyed in intuition. It does not come to a point at which it has to cast away all that it has gained and proceed nakedly on another path. The results of its previous procedure require transformation but do not incur forfeiture in the presence of the Absolute. Śaṅkara's difficulties arise from the assumption that the ultimate must be simple and that our ideal relationship with it is one of unity rather than of communion. He seemed to think that his deep desire for religious satisfaction could be satisfied only by the apprehension of an undifferenced ground of Being into which he could sink utterly. He felt that, wherever qualities remained, these must so affect our attitude that God will become an object and so will remain for ever distinct from the worshipper. He was dominated by the idea that in order to know God we must be God. But surely this is not a necessary consequence. It is indeed true that only God can know himself completely, but this does not mean that God must absorb us into himself. Neither does it imply that, on our part, there is no distinction between us and God, and that only a bare relation of identity can express the highest religious attainment.

[1] Art. on 'Orphic Mysteries', *Hibbert Journal*, Oct. 1922.

We may not have succeeded in bringing all the diversity of our experience as well as ourselves into perfect harmony with God, but it does not follow from this that the harmony can be reached only through a denial of the diversity. The highest unification would surely come through the fullest appreciation of the illimitable qualities of the ultimate Reality, and not from a denial that it has any qualities at all. It would be more satisfactory to regard the quest for identity which Śaṅkara pursued so earnestly and reverently, as a regulative ideal, expressive of the humbling consciousness that our unification with the Divine can never at any stage be regarded as complete. However elaborate our conceptions of the nature of God may be, there is always a 'beyond' to be reached; and however firmly we may establish relations between the Divine Unity and the cosmic multiplicity, there are always further and more fundamental connexions waiting to be discovered and systematized. But we are not therefore called upon to give up the quest and the endeavour. We are not required to say that the highest describable conception of this unity which we may have reached, is merely a fiction of our imagination or the misleading projection of a cosmic magician, separated from Reality by a gulf which is unbridgeable or can be crossed only by means of the cloud-enveloped constructions of *māyā*. There is no necessity fundamentally for this separation between Brahman and Īśvara, or for regarding the latter as simply the first product of deception. Īśvara is surely more than merely 'the presiding spirit of *māyā*, the connecting link between the gross creation and the principle that stands above it'.[1]

It is because we are looking for the wrong kind of ultimate Reality, for some abstraction that would 'maintain its identity unaffected',[2] that we falter in our quest and reach only ultimate fiction instead of ultimate fact. Perhaps we lose our faith in the procedure of the intellect just because, as has been suggested above, we are too purely intellectual. A more active attitude to life would prevent us from being content with abstractions. If we could recover that sense of 'something mysteriously spiritual, not definite, but vaguely *animating the world*',[3] it might be for us 'a presage of what our speculations call the ideal infinite

[1] B. K. Shastri, 81. [2] Ib. 17. [3] Italics mine.

deity.[1] If we could throw ourselves with all the fullness of our being into the life of the world in its onward and upward surging, we might perhaps gain such a sense of the value of its individual constituents that we should not be willing lightly to deny them, but should desire to see them sublimated, restored, redeemed in God, and would find God to be himself the ultimate Reality of the Universe, not requiring to be connected, through the illusiveness of *māyā*, with some further abstract and characterless Being. As Prof. Radhakrishnan puts it, 'The Self in which we are to find ourselves must be shown to be the true life of the whole and not a mere abstraction.'[2] The *Gītā* states for us a more concrete and satisfying conception than is generally to be found in the Vedānta, 'He is knowledge, its object and its end, seated in the hearts of all . . . when he (the worshipper) sees that the separate natures of things are seated in one, and issue from it alone, then he attains to Brahma.'[3] And one of the leaders of modern thought in India definitely departs from an abstract and purely intellectual interpretation of the ancient Indian ideal: 'To attain the world-consciousness we have to unite our feeling with this all pervasive infinite feeling. In fact the only true human progress is coincident with this widening of the range of feeling. All our poetry, philosophy, science, art, and religion are serving to extend the scope of our consciousness towards higher and larger spheres.'[4]

[1] Alexander, *Time, Space, and Deity*, II. 367. Cf. also Pringle-Pattison, *Idea of God*, 113.

[2] Radhakrishnan, I. 157.

[3] *Gītā*, XIII. 17, 30.

[4] Rabindranath Tagore, *Sādhanā*, 18.

VII

THE DESTINY OF THE INDIVIDUAL SOUL. THE PLACE OF ETHICS IN THE VEDĀNTA

FROM the grudging admission of the reality of the world of ordinary experience, which is the utmost that we can extract from Śaṅkara's teaching, we may turn to a consideration of the destiny of the individual souls within that world. In our last chapter we saw that Śaṅkara is dominated by the idea of unity, and that a breach in the unity is almost equivalent to a degradation. In even thinking of a God of qualities—of Īśvara—we have, in Śaṅkara's opinion, taken a step downwards.

Now if this is true in regard to Īśvara, it will be all the more true in regard to the infinite diversity of individual souls. The very recognition of them will be a logical inconsistency, a sacrifice of the esoteric to the exoteric. It is evidently with this thought in his mind that Deussen takes the view that all Śaṅkara's treatment of the individual souls and their relations to God, all his discussions of immortality, all his somewhat hesitating allusions to the doctrine of *karma*, are of the nature of a compromise between his abstract idealism and an uncomfortably insistent realism. From a strictly monistic point of view a consideration of the individual soul and its ethical progress is but a sojourning in a lower and impermanent world, and any attempt at a proof of immortality is superfluous, because we are already immortal—in the only sense of the term which Śaṅkara would approve—in virtue of the essential identity between us and God. Moreover, even from the exoteric point of view, immortality is a vain expectation, because all things that exist in the region of the empirical are subject to the conditions of time. The soul which has its birth must inevitably cease to be, and forms only an unimportant item in the unending process of physical particulars. So neither from the esoteric side nor from the exoteric taken by themselves can we win assurance, and it is only from a somewhat doubtful combination of idealism and realism that we can derive any doctrine of individual existence and development either in this world or that which is to come.

But Deussen's view of the matter does not seem to be altogether satisfactory. In the first place, on general philosophical grounds, there does not seem to be sufficient reason for establishing such an abrupt dualism between idealism and realism as Deussen thinks to be inevitable. Idealism does not necessarily involve an absolute denial of the empirical and actual. Secondly, just as it is impossible for a man to jump off his own shadow, it is equally impossible for him wholly to deny the particularity of the world in which he finds himself, and we have already found reason to think that Śaṅkara, while ostensibly a rigorous monist, is at times vividly aware of the necessity of reaching some accommodation to the world of experience. He builds more wisely than he knows and provides windows through which he may look out upon actuality, even while formally denying their existence or necessity.

About his formal denial of the existence of individual souls there can be no doubt, and we may first set forth his rigidly esoteric position and contrast it with Rāmānuja's. *Vedānta Sūtra* I. 1. 19 speaks of the 'joining of this (i.e. the individual soul) with that (the Self consisting of bliss) on that being fully known (i.e. in the *ānandamaya* state)', and Śaṅkara interprets their 'joining' as meaning identity and nothing else. His comment is as follows: 'If he sees in the Self consisting of bliss even a small difference in the form of non-identification, then he finds no release from the fear of transmigratory existence. But when he by the cognition of absolute identity, finds absolute rest in the Self consisting of bliss, then he is freed from the fear of transmigratory existence.'[1] The doctrine of identity is stated even more explicitly and more emphatically in the Commentary on *Sūtra* I. 4. 22. Śaṅkara selects from the Upanishads that figure which best suits his dominant view and compares the origination of souls from the highest Self to the issuing of sparks from a fire. He declares that the differences between the soul and the highest Self are not real but are due to 'limiting adjuncts' only. We have to do entirely with 'names and forms' and the individual soul, as an embodiment of these, is the product merely of Nescience. In a still more vigorous passage he says, 'As therefore the individual soul and the highest Self differ

[1] *S.B.E.* XXXIV. 71.

in name only, it being a settled matter that perfect knowledge has for its object the absolute oneness of the two; it is senseless to insist (as some do) on a plurality of Selfs and to maintain that the individual soul is different from the highest Self, and the highest Self from the individual soul.'[1] And looking to the future and the question of immortality generally, Śaṅkara takes up the position that the immortality of the individual soul is relative only. It can be expected only by him who is dependent on 'the power of the lower knowledge', and has not 'altogether burned nescience and the other afflictions'.[2]

Rāmānuja, on the other hand, following more or less closely the primary interpretation of the *Sūtras*, but remaining at a greater distance from the general tendency of the Upanishads, holds that the individual soul is real; it enjoys a certain amount of freedom even under the conditions of this life, and passes at death through various stages to the world of Brahman where it will exist, not in a state of indistinguishable identity with the Divine, but in a perfected relation of communion. True knowledge will bring about only the destruction of the separatist spirit in word or in deed. Personality will assuredly continue. The ultimate significance of *Sūtra* I. 1. 19 is that 'the highest Brahman . . . is other than the Being called individual soul', and the contrary opinion is subjected to the vigorous comment, 'To say that any one is identical with that by obtaining which he enjoys bliss, would be madness indeed.'[3] In regard to the future and especially the point raised in *Sūtra* IV. 2. 7, Rāmānuja holds that the immortality there indicated is common both to him who knows and to him who does not know, i.e. the immortality is not merely relative, and perfect knowledge does not destroy individual immortality.

Śaṅkara increases the impression of a depreciation of individuality by certain particular interpretations which he gives of various *Sūtras*. In regard to *Sūtra* II. 3. 50[4] Śaṅkara has no doubt of the applicability of the symbol of the sun and its reflections. The individual soul has no more reality than that of a flickering reflection on a restless piece of water. It may be

[1] *S. B. E.* XXXIV. 282.
[2] Cf. *Sūtra* IV. 2. 7; *S. B. E.* XXXVIII. 370.
[3] *S. B. E.* XLVIII. 237.
[4] 49 in Rāmānuja.

noticed, in passing, that Rāmānuja takes an entirely different view of this *Sūtra*. What Śaṅkara translates as, 'And the individual soul is a reflection only' Rāmānuja translates, 'and it is a mere apparent argument',[1] i.e. the unreality which Śaṅkara ascribes to the individual soul Rāmānuja attaches to the argument by which the unreality of the individual soul is sought to be established. In a slightly earlier *Sūtra* of the same section, we seem to have the unequivocal statement that 'the soul is a part of the Lord on account of the declarations of differences'. Rāmānuja takes this literally, but Śaṅkara, after indicating that the most appropriate symbol is that of the fire and its sparks, says that we must interpret the particular *Sūtra* to mean only 'a part, *as it were*'.[2] The individual soul cannot really be a part of that which has no parts, and to suppose that it has parts and that therefore the individual souls are real, is the result of the universal illusion. Rāmānuja is vigorously of another opinion and brushes aside Śaṅkara's interpretation with the contemptuous remark, 'Truly, if such were the purport of the Veda, what more would the Veda be than the idle talk of a person out of his mind?'[3]

A similar tendency is indicated when Śaṅkara, treating matters from the physical point of view, expresses the doctrine of the identity of the soul and God under the symbol of the all-pervadingness of the former.[4] Rāmānuja, on the other hand, recognizes that the most appropriate symbol for his doctrine is that the soul should be regarded as of atomic size (*aṇu*). This view is supported by the nine *Sūtras* immediately preceding; but Śaṅkara brushes aside the argument of the *Sūtras* by explaining that the atomic view therein indicated refers only to the soul when associated with the organ of intelligence (*buddhi*), and therefore belonging only to a lower state.

From a psychical point of view, Śaṅkara argues, in connexion with *Sūtra* II. 3. 18, that the soul is pure intelligence, i.e. the eternal intelligence of Brahman constitutes the soul's essential nature and leaves no room for difference. On the other hand Rāmānuja translates the same *Sūtra* as 'The Individual

[1] *S. B. E.* XXXVI. 60 and XLVIII. 565.
[2] Cf. *S. B. E.* XXXVIII. 61 and XLVIII. 561.
[3] *S. B. E.* XLVIII. 562.
[4] Cf. Comm. on *Sūtra* II. 3. 39; *S. B. E.* XXXVIII. 42.

soul is a *knower*', i.e. an individual, active, consciously intelligent subject, having distinction from Brahman, and the Sanskrit term used, according to Thibaut, bears out his view.[1]

There seems to be sufficient support, therefore, for the view that on the whole Śaṅkara's admission of the individual soul is of the nature of a concession. From the highest point of view it is, according to him, identical with, or at least not-different from, Brahman himself. It is only from the empirical point of view that we are temporarily justified in speaking of a plurality of souls. But Śaṅkara's own treatment of the matter from the empirical point of view is so voluminous and elaborate (though probably he was constrained to this from the amount of attention devoted to the topic in the *Sūtras* themselves) that we cannot afford to regard it as merely concessional and of secondary importance. And we must also keep in mind in this connexion the contention of many Indian writers that the English words 'identical' and 'non-different' have not the same significance, and that the latter alone is the proper interpretation of '*ananya*', a consideration which may at least incline our minds to a more liberal construction of Śaṅkara's rigorous monism.

The individual soul is constituted—or disguised as Śaṅkara would put it—by the *upādhis*, empirical conditions or limiting adjuncts. Of these the first is the condition of the gross body, which need not detain us, as this is entirely left behind in the migrations of the soul, and all schools of the Vedānta are far removed from materialism. In the conditions which attach to the soul in the existence which persists through innumerable lives, we may distinguish a changing and an unchanging part. The changing part is of vital importance in connexion with the doctrine of *karma*, and includes those moral consequences which have been passed on from one to another in an infinite series of lives and which to a large extent determine the empirical destiny of the soul.

The unchanging part is the nucleus of the soul and consists (1) of that substratum which may be called the 'subtle body' and which is made up of the extremely subtle counterparts of the gross elements. It has a persistence which enables these subtle elements to continue after the death of the gross body. (2) We

[1] Cf. *S. B. E.* XXXIV, p. xcvii.

have the more active aspect of the subtle body, the life-organs or *prāṇas*, the vital breaths of the soul. On the conscious level these include the five organs of sense and the five organs of action, co-ordinated by and under the control of the *Manas*, or central organ of conscious life. But behind these fully conscious aspects of the soul there is posited, with a fine anticipation of more modern doctrines of the unconscious and the sub-conscious, the *Prâṇa* (in a limited sense) or *Mukhya Prâṇa*,[1] the ultimate nucleus of life, both physical and mental in its relationships, subtly supporting the physical processes of respiration and nutrition and rendering intelligible the act of death, but having vague affiliations also with the mental activities of the soul which are below the level of clear consciousness. Indeed one of the most interesting aspects of the Vedānta philosophy is just such an interplay between physical and psychic conceptions. It seems to be left undecided whether the soul is more closely associated with the *Mukhya Prâṇa* or with the *Manas*, and in this hesitation lies much wisdom.

An elaborate account is given of the relations of these various organs of the soul in the three states of waking, dreaming, and dreamless sleep, and also of their fate at death, but into the details we need not enter to any extent. We may note only that at death there takes place a process of involution. The soul gathers the organs of sense and action, or at least the functions of these organs, first of all into the *Manas*.[2] Then the *Manas* is merged in the *Prâṇa*, or breath. The process may be paralleled on the mental side by the retraction from sense-experience which in the lifetime of the individual has taken place during dream sleep and the further concentration which is associated with passing into dreamless sleep. The next stage is more vaguely described. The *Prâṇa* is said to merge in heat (*tejas*) and is also said to merge in the essence of the individual soul.[3] But in both these ways we come near to the idea of the subtle body (indefiniteness here being made to serve the purpose of comprehensiveness). The subtle body is the fine part of the elements, the seed of the body, and constitutes the vehicle by which the continuity of the soul is preserved from one life to

[1] Cf. Deussen, *S. V.* 326.
[2] Cf. *Sūtra* IV. 2. 1.
[3] Cf. *Sūtra* IV. 2. 4.

another, unaffected by death. It is the elementary metaphysical substratum of the departing soul.[1]

With this is closely associated the moral substratum which by reference to past behaviour determines the character of the departing personality and its future destiny. The *karma-âśraya* is the summing up of past experiences, of impressions and the results of actions. When the soul is about to enter on its new life, the past experience is focused as an innate concentrated disposition which gives a starting-point, differentiating the new life from previous lives. As this concentrated effect of the past cannot properly be in actuality until the existence which is passing away has come to a definite end, it may be regarded as something new, something which was not there before. Some writers therefore in this connexion posit an entity called the *apûrva*,[2] half physical and half spiritual, which is described as 'either an imperceptible after-state of the deed, or an imperceptible antecedent state of the result'.[3] From one point of view the doctrine of *apûrva* might be regarded as an attempt to get away from the externality of the notion that judgement is passed upon acts alone, and an anticipation of the more modern view that it is passed rather upon character. Only, in connexion with *apûrva* the character is still left as a somewhat detached entity and is not brought into organic and ethical connexion with the continuing personality of the doer of the action. Śaṅkara himself, however, does not see any necessity for any such mediating conception, and his hesitation is interesting for the light which it throws upon the character of the tradition which he has inherited, as well as upon his view of the doctrine of *karma*.

Before touching upon this latter doctrine we may take into consideration the varying kinds of destiny to which the combination of the elemental and the moral substratum leads the soul. Souls may be divided into three classes: according as they have developed within them knowledge (which, according to

[1] Cf. Deussen, *S.V.* 375.

[2] Cf. *Sūtra* III. 2. 39.

[3] Cf. *S.B.E.* XXXVIII. 182. Cf. also the Vaiśesika doctrine of *adṛishṭa*—the unknown virtue due to *dharma*—described in Das Gupta, I. 283. Cf. also the well-known Vedic idea of *ishṭāpūrta*, a compound word denoting sacrifices and offerings. In the *Ṛigveda* X. 14. 8 it is regarded as something which can be stored up and which will have effect in after-life. Cf. McKenzie, *Hindu Ethics*, 14.

Śaṅkara, is 'lower', but according to Rāmānuja is the highest attainable); according as they have depended only on ritual and moral works; and, finally, according as they have neglected both knowledge and works. The first go by way of the Gods (the *Devayâna*) to eternal and ultimately blissful communion with the qualitative Brahman. The second go by the way of the Fathers (the *Pitṛiyâna*) to the moon, there to receive the reward of their deeds and of all the previous attainments of their souls, the retribution continuing, in varying degrees of felicity or otherwise, until only a residue is left, which residue will determine their future lot upon the earth, and so on and on, until the purification of their souls is so far advanced as to enable them to exchange the path of the Fathers for the path of the Gods.[1] The third class, composed of those who have not sought to acquire merit either by knowledge or by works, go to the 'third place' by 'a path on which they repeatedly return to the existence of small animals'.[2] It must be noticed, however, that the boundaries between the second and the third classes are left comparatively vague, and the idea is frequently brought forward that the evil-doers may also receive their retribution in some kind of intermediate state, their destination being, not the moon, but the abode of Yama, whence, after 'suffering there the torments of Yama corresponding to their evil deeds, they again reascend to this world'.[3]

The important distinction, therefore, is between the first two classes, between those who are worthy to enter the Path of the Gods and those who are not so worthy. In connexion with this distinction the interesting physiological and mythological detail is supplied that of the hundred and one veins of the heart, the one which leads up to the head is the path by which the departing soul of the worthy man goes to the realm of Brahman,

[1] What particular class of works make up this residue is doubtful. It is held by some Vedantists that the stronger works receive their recompense first, i.e. in the intermediate state, whereas the weaker remain with effect sufficient to cause a new birth. Others are satisfied with a purely quantitative idea of the remaining balance, while others again attempt to make the distinction between ritual and moral works, and hold that the former are recompensed in the intermediate state and the latter receive their recompense or retribution in a new birth. Cf. *Sūtra* III. 1. 9; *S.B.E.* XXXVIII. 121.

[2] Cf. *Sūtra* III. 1. 17; *S.B.E.* XXXVIII. 124.

[3] Cf. *Sūtra* III. 1. 13; *S.B.E.* XXXVIII. 122.

whereas the less worthy and the unworthy have to go by any of the other numerous modes of exit.

From these descriptions we may select two topics as demanding further consideration: (1) the doctrine of *karma* as affecting the individual soul, and (2) the ultimate condition of those who reach the realm of Brahman.

We have already referred to the interesting character of *Sūtra* III. 2. 38–41, and the light they throw on the doctrine of *karma*. We discover, on the one hand, a tendency in the direction of regarding the power of the deed in an objective manner, and, on the other hand, towards resolving all power into the hands of God himself. The first tendency implies that those who hold it have, either consciously or unconsciously, served themselves heir to a long tradition in which the conceptions of *ishṭāpūrta*, *ṛita*, *dharma* (all implying continuing effects of deed or conduct, both ritual and moral), as well as the later conception of *apûrva*, have played a conspicuous part, and in the development of which, down to the time of Śaṅkara, Buddhist influence has been strong. For those who think in this way, the fundamental forces of the universe are still animistically or polytheistically conceived, and we are not far from the conception of God as struggling against some power of fate outside of himself. In relation to the *karma* conception, the deeds of men have acquired that independent actuality which invests them with an energy differentiated from that of the central powers of the universe.

On the other hand, Śaṅkara—and Rāmānuja also—wish to centralize all the available power. The actions of human beings do not bring fruit of themselves, either directly or indirectly: it is the Lord who causes this fruit to appear. But if all power is thus vested in God, difficulties immediately arise as to the nature of God and his relations to men. Will he not appear to be oppressively dominating the activity of the individual? The general answer of the Vedānta to difficulties of this nature is to suggest, not that the Divine control should be regarded as diminished, but that its relation to human activity should be conceived of as indirect and not direct. If God can be placed at one or two removes from man, then he may be defended from the charge of oppression and at least a semblance of freedom may be left to human beings. Thus the action of God may be generalized so that its incidence is not immediately upon the individual action but upon the whole karmic process in which the individual and his action is involved; fatalism can be softened by being universalized, the tyranny of a tyrant being replaced by the stern inexorability of a law-giver or judge. Or recourse may be had to metaphors which mitigate the harshness of compulsion and represent God as a cause of a more occasional character. God's control may be likened to the rain in relation to the various shrubs. As the rain provides opportunity for their favourable but diversified growth, so does God arrange 'favourable or unfavourable circumstances for the soul with a view to their former efforts'. We should compare also the commentary on *Sūtra* II. 1. 34, 'For as Parjanya (the giver of rain) is the common cause of the production of rice, barley, and other plants, while the differences between the various species is due to the various potentialities lying hidden in the respective seeds, so the Lord is the common cause of the creation of gods, men, &c., while the differences between these classes of beings are due to different merit belonging to the individual souls.'[1] Still, even metaphors of this kind do not carry conviction, and the almost desperate attempt to remove our difficulties as to the freedom of the individual soul, leads in the same section to what seems to be little more than a bare asseveration of a contradiction. It is conceded that the soul acts by its own activity, and almost in the same breath the concession is withdrawn. 'Although the activity of the soul is not independent, yet the soul does act. The Lord indeed causes it to act, but it acts itself.' Reasoning of this sort is hardly sufficiently cogent to relieve us of the fatalism of a passage like *Kaushītaki Upanishad* III. 8, which Śaṅkara quotes with approval. 'He makes him whom he wishes to lead up from these worlds, do a good deed, and the same makes him whom he wishes to lead down from these worlds, do a bad deed.'

But, putting aside the question of the apportionment of responsibility between Divine and human power, it must be remembered in this connexion that God cannot rightly be charged with pitilessness and arbitrary cruelty. We must

[1] *S. B. E.* XXXIV. 358 and XXXVIII. 60.

remember not only the metaphysical but also the moral aspect of the karmic process. Even though we were to go all the way with the fatalists, even though we were to admit that God provides the all-controlling conditions of each life and acts also in each particular action of the individual soul, yet in the apportionment of happiness or misery he must have regard to the particular place occupied by the individual soul, and will vary the destiny accordingly. Cf. again *Sūtra* II. 1. 34, 'Hence the Lord, being bound by regards, cannot be reproached with inequality of dispensation and cruelty.'[1] He cannot begin *de novo*. He has to observe the existing actualities and the law which emerges in relation to them, even though this law be little better than *lex talionis*, based on a principle of exact retribution. The tyrant gives place to the judge or at least to the administrator of the law. We were perhaps rash in saying above that the judge in this case was also the lawgiver, for at first sight it might seem as if God's righteousness were vindicated by putting him under the constraint of a law external to himself, for which he was not responsible. But there are at least indications of the influence of the idea—afterwards so strongly emphasized by Lotze—that the law is not external to God but is simply an expression of his own nature. He himself, as would appear to be obvious when stress is laid specially upon the all-pervading causality of God, is said to be primarily responsible for the whole course of the *saṁsāra* and the empirical destiny of souls. And although he may also retain the power of graciously granting deliverance from the *saṁsāra* through the saving power of knowledge, yet for the most part his responsibility is discharged in a regular manner. Thus, however we may put the matter, the idea of regularity is conspicuous, and God, being under a law of righteousness, either external or his own, may be defended from any charge of arbitrariness.

But this vindication is immediately countered by another difficulty. Śaṅkara's critics point out that he has simply pushed the problem farther back. God's action, it is said, may be justified by the suggestion that he has to act with reference to the deserts of former lives, but what about these former lives themselves, what about the first in the series? At the beginning

[1] Cf. *S. B. E.* XXXIV. 359.

of the transmigratory process, when there could be no accumulated merit, what justification could there be for unequal creation?[1] Śaṅkara meets this objection with the simple bold statement that the world has no beginning, because, if it had, then God would have to be accused of arbitrariness. Can this carry conviction? It seems to be a barefaced case of circular reasoning. God cannot be accused of arbitrariness because of the existence of the *saṁsāra*, and the *saṁsāra* must exist because God cannot be accused of arbitrariness. But it is not wise to bring a charge of fallacious reasoning against a philosopher of Śaṅkara's quality, and we have the feeling that there is more in his argument than appears on the surface. Is he not struggling with the difficulty of relating the eternal God to the temporal process? May he not be making an attempt to place God above time, or, at least, to get rid of the somewhat crude idea of God as standing at the beginning of creation, looking forward, and apportioning to each soul its destiny through all succeeding aeons of time? Has he not got implicitly in his mind the thought that our temporal categories are inadequate for the representation of God, and that he is to be conceived of rather as an overshadowing and pervasive Presence than as one who stands behind us in time far away at the beginning of human destiny and determining it fatalistically for ever more. And yet Śaṅkara, after looking at the difficulties, seems in the last resort to turn away from them, for his final position is that whatever problems may remain, belong after all to an unreal world, the world of names and forms, and therefore may be disregarded. Why should we worry over apparent injustices in the world or in the Divine control of it when the world itself does not exist?

We come therefore in general to the conclusion that Śaṅkara does not deal adequately with the *karma* doctrine. In so far as he accepts it, he does not relieve it of the charges that it treats each life as subject too much to an individualistic destiny, that it is inclined to hypostatize abstractions under the influence of a persisting animism, that in its more universal aspect its ethical level is legal rather than moral, that it rarely rises above the idea of sheer retribution, and that, despite references to divine grace, it does not escape the danger of impersonal and fatalistic

[1] Cf. *Sūtra* II. 1. 35; *S. B. E.* XXXIV. 359.

domination over the human life. In so far as he rejects it, he leaves his rejection side by side with his acceptance. He leaves unresolved the dualism which the doctrine suggests as to the relation between God and the world. He does not by transforming the doctrine bring the world into organic relation with the eternal nature of God, but turns away from the difficulty as from an unreal problem of an unreal world.

We must now consider the second point that has been reserved, viz. the ultimate condition of those who reach the realm of Brahman. By overcoming the evil *karma* of their past and by scrupulous care that they may not accumulate new *karma*, they may reach this high position. But in doing so, have they reached the ultimate goal, or must they still confess that they have failed to discover the true path of salvation? Which is to be followed—Rāmānuja or Śaṅkara—as regards the doctrine of the ultimate destiny of the soul? In the main they agree as to the preliminary stages. It is in connexion with the final stage of all, and the retrospective valuation of the whole process of the soul's ascent, that the most important differences emerge.

Following their common lead we have found that the souls who proceed upwards on the way of the *Devayāna*, after passing through various stages, at length enter into Brahman's world to abide with him in an eternity of bliss and perfect communion, with participation in all the qualities of Brahman, according to some, or, at least, as Auḍulomi thinks, with participation in the intelligence of Brahman. In this state they enjoy the fulfilment of all purified desires, and their lordship is unlimited, except in so far as it is restricted by the cosmic, creative, and sustaining powers reserved for Īśvara, who, however, also possesses the power to harmonize any incompatible wishes of the pious. There is finality about this state in that it cannot possibly change into anything lower. 'For them verily there is no return to earth life.'[1] But whether it is final in the sense that it cannot change into anything *higher* is just the main question at issue between Śaṅkara and Rāmānuja. We may put the problem in both a narrower and a broader way. We may ask whether the stage which is regarded as highest by Rāmānuja is really final

[1] Cf. *Sūtra* IV. 4. 22.

or not? Or we may raise the question of comprehensive evaluation and ask whether there was really any necessity painfully and gradually to make our way to such a stage at all?

In treating the problem in the simpler way we must bear in mind Śaṅkara's distinction between the lower and higher Brahman, and we may show that his view is that the Brahman with whom the soul enters into perfect communion at Rāmānuja's highest stage, is not the higher but the lower Brahman. This lower Brahman will himself be merged in the higher, and therefore the soul which has entered into communion with the former, will also share in the state of perfect indivisibility with the latter. It will not *reach* unity with God, but will rather discover that unity which has never been lost, that oneness without a second, and, as rivers run into the sea and lose their name and form, so will it merge its identity in the undifferenced Absolute. The character which it has acquired in the painful and gradual stage of its ethical and karmic ascent will be lost in a purely metaphysical absorption.

By treating the question from the broader point of view we may reach much the same conclusion. We must here keep in view primarily Śaṅkara's distinction between the two orders of knowledge, and also his depreciation of the salvational value of works. By those who follow him in this attitude it is urged that there is little to be gained by passing through the various stages of the upward ascent; for, after all, the consummation which is aimed at by this method will turn out to be the reward of the lower knowledge only. Therefore we may shorten the whole process, or, rather, make it superfluous, by reaching the illumination of the *parāvidyā*, the highest knowledge, the immediate consciousness of identity with Brahman, which is possible for us here and now. Such a result is to be obtained by direct meditation, especially concentrated on the formula *tat tvaṁ asi*, which exercise of the soul may have to be repeated again and again if the full significance does not dawn upon the first hearing. Works may be of use as preparatory and purificatory disciplines, but not as a means of securing the illumination. In fact, the man who has won emancipation, and thus possesses the higher knowledge, is independent not only of evil but also of good works. There is 'non-clinging and the destruction of earlier and later sins',[1] and, 'Also of the other (i.e. good works) there is in the same way non-clinging; but at death.'[2] Śaṅkara takes the phrase 'but at death' to be merely emphatic and to signify 'especially at death'. Rāmānuja takes a modified view and explains the phrase as meaning, 'Good works which produce results favourable to knowledge and meditation, perish only on the death of the body (not during the life-time of the Devotee).'[3] The sage, according to Śaṅkara, is thus raised above all conditions of mundane existence. Nothing that is outside of Brahman has any power to disturb him, and he has not to wait for the slow temporal processes of improvement in this life and the next. But why, if Śaṅkara's view is correct, should he have to wait even for the end of this present life? Śaṅkara deals with this difficulty by citing the physical analogy of the potter's wheel, which continues to revolve even after it has completed its work in moulding a particular vessel. But behind this metaphor there is also the theory—not by any means confined to Śaṅkara's teaching—that work effects may be divided into three classes: accumulated (*saṁchita*); current, in the sense that they have begun to affect the soul (*prārabdha*); and finally, those due to the activity of the present life (*kriyamāṇa*). Illumination affects only the first class and the third. Works which belong to the second class, and have already begun to affect the soul, must continue their operation until at death their force is exhausted. Some Vedantists distinguish two stages even within the condition of illumination, the lower being the condition of the enlightened sage even previous to death (*jīvanmukti*), and the higher being the complete stage which is reached in freedom from the body (*videhamukti*).[4]

But in order to accomplish this final merging in Brahman, we do not require, according to Śaṅkara, to imagine at death any semi-angelic flight of the spirit by the Path of the Gods. Time and space no longer exist for the illumined soul when he has reached the point of death. Then,

ends the man
Upwards in that dread point of intercourse,
Nor needs a place, for it returns to Him
What Does, what Knows, what Is; three souls, one man.

[1] Cf. *Sūtra* IV. 1. 13.
[2] *Sūtra* IV. 1. 14.
[3] *S. B. E.* XLVIII. 724.
[4] Cf. Barnett, *Brahma-Knowledge*, 52.

Under such conditions how is it possible to speak of a 'departing' or 'going to Brahman'? 'To what sphere', asks Śaṅkara, 'then belong the scriptural texts about the soul's going? To the sphere of qualified knowledge, we reply. . . . The reaching of another place is out of the question. Statements about the soul's going which apply to the lower Brahman are wrongly put in connexion with the higher Brahman.'[1] Even if we attempt to deal with the matter by means of physical analogies, and speak of omnipresence, there is the same want of suitability, for that which is omnipresent cannot pass from one place to another. And as regards timelessness, the soul need not wait upon the slowness of passing through the various stages. It is *now*, what it eternally has been. So with great earnestness Śaṅkara argues that the proper interpretation of *Sūtra* IV. 2. 13 is that the soul 'does not depart'. This is the plain meaning of Scripture according to him, and those are altogether wrong who try to wrest this meaning and make out that 'do not depart' has reference simply to the relation of the *prāṇas* to the soul and implies that they abide with it in readiness for a conjunct passing out at the moment of death. We are not called upon to decide whether Śaṅkara is right or not in regard to the interpretation of this particular text. There can be no doubt whatever about his own view of the matter, which is, that illumination may confer a non-temporal and non-spatial emancipation, making the sage independent of cosmical processes and ethical endeavour, and raising him above the slow movement of the *kramamukti* (or gradual liberation). Like Iamblichus in Merejkowski's *Death of the Gods*, he would ask, 'Whence comes that beam which falls upon the soul? I do not know. It comes unawares, and when one least expects it. To search for it is useless. God is not remote from us. One must make ready, with a soul becalmed; and simply wait, as the eyes await (according to the saying of the poet) the rush of the sun from the dark ocean. God does not come, God does not go away; He is revealed, He is, what the Universe is not, the negation of everything that exists. He is nothing, and He is All.'[2]

[1] Cf. *Sūtra* IV. 3. 14; *S. B. E.* XXXVIII. 401.
[2] *Op. cit.*, Eng. trans. 81.

The topics which have been treated of in the last few paragraphs throw considerable light upon the Vedantic view of the relation of ethical endeavour to ultimate reality, and to this question we must devote the remainder of this chapter. Does Vedantic doctrine strengthen ethical endeavour, or is it rather indifferent to it? Is the final state which is aimed at by the sage one in which the ethical process is conserved and sublimated? We have already touched upon this topic in connexion with our discussion of the 'place of works' in the Vedantic system, but we must now treat the question from a more general point of view.

If Śaṅkara is taken to be the typical Vedantist, the answer will largely tend to be that the ethical process is cut across and the ethical level is transcended. That which the pious man reaches by his moral striving is not final, and his ethical gains are not carried forward into the ultimate state, but rather put aside as at the most an inadequate approach to what can best be attained by other methods. The Vedantists would for the most part agree with Bosanquet's idea that perfection is a higher concept than the concept of the good, which latter belongs definitely to the stage of finite experience and not to reality as a whole.[1]

With the Vedantist the attitude is closely allied to the implications of a strict interpretation of the doctrine of *māyā*, and to the contention that the Ultimate Reality is without qualities. In closer reference to ethics the essence of the Vedantic doctrine seems to be that, however earnest the ethical aspirant may be, and however widely he may extend his activities so that, in crucifixion of all selfishness, they may be devoted to the interests of others, it is impossible to get rid of egoity in the sphere of ethical endeavour; and yet without deliverance from egoity the final state cannot be attained. Full knowledge does not prevent selfishness and other kinds of evil by directing our desires towards a wider righteousness, but rather by destroying desire altogether. And, in general, ethics deals with 'approach', whereas the enlightened man is concerned with 'recovery'. Ethics belongs essentially to the sphere of duality, and is not in place in any sphere in which activity is denied or transcended.

Śaṅkara, as we have seen, was not so doubtful as St. Paul

[1] Cf. Roger, *Recent American and English Philosophy*, 278.

about the possibility of fulfilling the works of the law, but he held that, even if the law were fulfilled, it was powerless to effect the emancipation of the soul. He thought that ethical endeavour even of the highest kind was impossible except in conjunction with the assertion of individuality and personality; and that, because the ego cannot be got rid of in moral progress, and yet the assertion of the ego renders impossible the attainment of the highest state, the sphere of ethics must be left behind. Morality must be transcended if the end of ethics, viz. perfection, is to be attained. He hardly seems to entertain the idea of a gradual transformation from the incomplete to the complete, from the imperfect to the perfect. As Deussen puts it, 'Moral transformation remained foreign to Indian thought.'[1] A contradiction lies at the very heart of ethics. In order that ethics may reach its goal, the annihilation of the self, ethics itself must disappear.

The argument is that while we remain ourselves, it will be impossible for us to resolve this contradiction. We cannot comprehend how the sphere of the ego may be transcended. But it would almost seem as if the Vedānta, because we cannot understand, gave us permission to be dogmatic about the matter, and to argue that, the transformation of the will being an unintelligible mystery, we are at liberty to pass altogether to another point of view at which the difficulty will disappear, i.e. we may abandon the sphere of ethics. It may be noticed that the attitude to a certain extent implies a confusion between selfishness and 'selfness', and a consequent equal condemnation of them. We have frequently had occasion to consider this view in connexion with the Vedānta philosophy, and it would seem to take for granted that ethical endeavour is and must always be deficient, unless not only selfishness but also selfness can be transcended. The mood is akin to that which Prof. Wenley ascribes to Schopenhauer, 'To gain perfection man must divest himself of his own self-hood, and be received back again into the unconscious reality of will, where nothing is distinguishable.'[2] It is a direct consequence of what we have seen to be the prevailing Vedantic view of the relation of the individual soul to Brahman, and we would thus seem to be justified in linking with this latter

[1] Deussen, 17. [2] Wenley, *Aspects of Pessimism*, 263.

view our treatment of the ethical doctrine of the Vedānta. Depreciation of the individual seems to result inevitably in a depreciation of ethics.

We have already seen[1] that according to Śaṅkara, activity, whether intellectual or practical, does not belong to the essence of the soul, and is alien to the sphere in which the higher knowledge moves. Works can give only transitory felicity and their results are not carried forward into the ultimate condition of the soul. They are ascetic rather than meritorious in that they do not produce the higher emancipating knowledge but simply prepare for it. Good works cannot improve the soul because, being unchangeable, it is incapable of degrees of perfection. Neither can works aiming at the establishment of valuable social conditions be thoroughly efficacious. They may loosen the bonds of selfishness by extending our interests so that they become coincident with those of our fellows and we become more perfect instruments of the common will. But we are instruments still, and therefore not free in our own soul, and we remain in bondage to the temporal, for even the most perfect community is affected by the transitory characteristics of the age to which it belongs.

We must here, of course, repeat our warnings against one-sided judgements, and avoid the conclusion that, because Śaṅkara assigns only subordinate importance to works, this is equivalent to saying that they have no importance at all. We must freely admit, as Prof. K. Shastri so well and so vigorously points out,[2] that there is a close connexion between Vedānta teaching and the practice of the higher virtues, and that, on the other hand, to press a phrase like 'the enlightened man may *live as he pleases*', so as to make it support a charge of antinomianism, is to do a grave injustice to the system as a whole. It may be noticed, however, in passing, that European writers are not the greatest sinners in respect of this charge. We find an Indian judgement of the most severe type, e.g. in R. C. Bose's book on *Hindu Philosophy*. After describing the Pantheism of the Vedānta by the harsh name 'pandiabolism', he goes on to say: 'The system has proved a refuge of lies to many a hardened sinner. The perplexed minds which have found shelter in its solution of the

[1] p. 129.

[2] K. Shastri, Chapter IV, *passim*.

problem of existence are few indeed, but the number of wicked hearts which have been composed to sleep by the opiate of its false hope, is incalculable.' But, surely, in opposition to Mr. Bose, we may be permitted to point out that 'to live as one pleases' may mean, not to neglect morality, but to be independent of rule with the superiority of the artistic to the mechanical spirit and the freedom and joyousness of the former. There is much truth in Prof. Radhakrishnan's saying that 'The pure and perfect are laws unto themselves'.[1]

But at the same time the question remains whether, when all is said and done, the Vedānta can assign that ultimate validity to ethics which would seem to be required if individual and social life is to reach and abide in perfection. Is it indeed necessary to hold that the highest ethical state and the highest condition of the soul must be different from each other? Can we sympathize with Kirtikar when he asks, in reference to the world of ethical action, 'Of what value is a toy elephant to one who understands that it is only a toy?' Or can we agree with the dualism which is implied in his further queries and answers, 'Is philosophical truth to be sacrificed lest its recognition should disturb the ethical ideal?', and again, 'Truth ought not to be sacrificed to practical life'.[2] To many a very different point of view would appeal with greater force; they would hold that if such a contradiction were to arise, we should at least consider the possibility of modifying, not truth itself—which is impossible—but our particular conception of truth. As Rashdall puts it, 'Our conception of the highest good may be inadequate, but we certainly shall not attain to greater adequacy or a nearer approach to ultimate truth by flatly contradicting our moral judgements. It would be just as reasonable to argue that, because the law of gravitation might be proved, from the point of view of the highest knowledge, to be an inadequate statement of truth, . . . therefore we had better assume that, from the point of view of God, there is no difference between attraction and repulsion.'[3]

Our main problem here may be put in the form of an inquiry whether the ethical life can be maintained in its fullness on the

[1] Radhakrishnan, I. 507. [2] Kirtikar, 106.
[3] Rashdall, *Philosophy and Religion*, 68.

basis of that doctrine of abstract and unmodified identity between ourselves and the characterless Absolute which would seem to be the resultant of Śaṅkara's interpretation of the Vedānta? Does not Rāmānuja's guidance seem preferable in this connexion if we are to preserve the health of our ethical life; if, when our precepts are pressed to their logical conclusions, these are not, in the case of the less worthy, to permit of moral deterioration or at least indifference, and, in the case of the more worthy, to bring about the morally reassuring, but theoretically disconcerting result that their practice will turn out to be considerably in advance of their principles. The more worthy seem in the sphere of practical life to live more earnestly than their principles encourage them to do, and as regards them there is much truth in Mr. Archer's saying that 'Hindu philosophy is after all too human to be logical'.[1]

Undoubtedly, the strict Vedantist would show a tendency to answer in the negative this question as to whether ethics is compatible with a doctrine of abstract identity, but, on the ground that ethics does not belong to the highest level, the denial would be made without any serious compunction. On the other hand, this surrender of a valuable constituent of human life seems to us to be without sufficient justification. We are inclined rather to inquire further into the reason for this dualism between the identity conception and the ethical point of view, in the hope that possibly the ideal may be stated in such a way as not to necessitate a depreciation of ethics, which depreciation, we repeat, seems to us to be an implicit criticism of any ideal which involves it.

In citing objections on ethical grounds to this identity ideal we must be careful not to make use of the crude charge of blasphemy, a method of attack which formerly was favoured by critics of the Vedantic position. It used to be argued that to equalize man with God was 'to arrogate divinity for humanity'; and the suggestion was added that such an equation, when applied to the individual, meant that each man could claim that he was already godlike and therefore did not stand in need of ethical improvement. The enthusiastic language of some Vedantists, e.g. that of Swami Vivekananda in portions of his

[1] *India and the Future*, 23.

book on *Jñānayoga*, may have given colour to this criticism. But we think that it is alien to the true meaning of the Vedānta, and that the resulting attitude, though not perhaps the theoretical basis, is more truly given in Prof. Radhakrishnan's language in reference to the Upanishads, 'God is not in man in such obvious fashion that he can possess Him absentmindedly and without a struggle. God is present as a potentia or a possibility. . . . The God in man is a task as well as a fact, a problem as well as a possession.'[1] Moreover, even as regards the theoretical aspect, it is but just to notice that the criticism seems to proceed from a slight misunderstanding of the point of view. The Vedantists were not thinking primarily of ethical completeness but of a fundamental identity above the ethical level. It seems unfair therefore to subject them to charges which can have relevance only on the ethical level. The true point at issue is why they are so unwilling to be judged from the ethical standpoint, and why they are so reluctant to permit our ethical aspirations to find completion in an answering metaphysical reality. We cannot at one and the same time accuse them of transcending the ethical level and condemn them for claiming complete fulfilment of their ethical aspirations. We cannot pass judgement against them in a court whose jurisdiction they deny, though we may quite legitimately ask whether they are justified in denying the jurisdiction, and whether their refusal is not seriously prejudicial to the moral law, which they would desire to have upheld except perhaps when they happen to be in an 'ultra-philosophical mood'. Yet the charge of blasphemy would seem to have at the back of it, not the idea that the Vedantists avoid ethical judgement, but that they claim ethical attainment, and this latter accusation can certainly not be made in general terms. Finally, we must remember that a charge of blasphemy is always apt to provoke a reaction in the form of a counter-charge to the effect that those who argue on the other side wish to minimize the closeness of the connexion between man and God. This would also be unjust, for the objection of the opponents of identity is not to closeness of connexion but to the special interpretation of that connexion as being expressible *only* in terms of bare identity. Emphasis upon the identity conception

[1] Radhakrishnan, I. 209.

is peculiarly disastrous in respect of the claim of ethics to unrestricted jurisdiction and paramount importance in human life. Ethics essentially demands a certain amount of transcendence and objective reference both in the direction of other men and in the direction of God. As regards the first or human reference it is frequently argued that nothing could be more efficacious as a spring of social service than this feeling of identity between ourselves and other men. We can love our neighbour truly, it is said, only if we can realize our oneness with our neighbour, only if we can in thought obliterate all superficial and artificial distinctions. It is possible to obey the injunction to love one's neighbour as oneself only if we can recognize our own self in that of our neighbour. Deussen stresses this argument very markedly, and a recent writer has applied it to modern social conditions: 'It seems at times that we may be approaching a change whereby the universal self-consciousness[1] that inspires life to-day, may be exchanged for a consciousness that sees the whole as one; self-consciousness it is that has built up the form of competitive society which we see everywhere and have seen throughout history. A new reaction to life would produce inevitably a new form of society.'[2] But, in reply to this, it must be noticed that a mere feeling of identity taken by itself may work both ways. It may make us feel—and probably often does so—that we should help our neighbour because he is one with us; but logically it might quite as well enable us to argue that we are justified in promoting our own interests because, our neighbour being one with us, his interests are identical with ours, and therefore in promoting our interests we are *ipso facto* promoting his. It might even, if we were to follow Schopenhauer's application of this thought, be used as a support of injustice. Why should we grieve, he asks, over undeserved suffering falling upon another, for those who suffer on the one hand, and those who, on the other hand, through wrongdoing either escape suffering or cause suffering, are one and the same, and therefore suffering in the last analysis really falls where it is due.

The difficulty would appear to arise from a defect in the concept of identity. It is not differentiating enough to provide a

[1] The word is here used apparently in the narrow and popular sense.
[2] Willcocks, *Between the Old World and the New*, 360.

basis for social ethics. Absorption in another personality is a metaphor derived from physical analogies and is not fully appropriate to the more heterogeneous and more organic relations of human beings. It is to be noticed that Vedantic teaching does not properly detach itself from the original physical significance of the metaphor, and constantly hovers between the idea of absorption on the level of unconsciousness and absorption on the level of consciousness. Social action is dependent indeed on sympathy, but on an intelligent and imaginatively discriminating sympathy which differentiates the object of sympathy from ourselves. Mere identity based on abstraction and negation cannot take the place of sympathy for the different, especially when, over against this comparatively vague and weak bond of association, we have to take account also of the continuing influence of the karmic idea, with its implications of externality and individualism which serve to strengthen the popular assumption of non-transferable destinies. As Solovyof puts it, 'The removal of barriers between the self and the not-self, or immediate identification, is merely a figure of speech and not an expression of real fact. Like the vibration of chords that sound in unison, the bond of compassion between human beings is not simply identity but harmony of the similar.'[1]

Further, an identification with others which is associated with a denial of their reality as individuals is absolutely fatal to ethical endeavour of a social character. If looking at human beings *sub specie aeternitatis* and through the mediation of the concept of strict identity leads us to regard them as small and insignificant, if not almost futile, as individuals, we cannot direct our efforts persistently towards their welfare. We can help men aright only if we can regard them as existences having rights in themselves, 'independent centres of action and sources of feeling', whose interests may not be absorbed in ours but with whom we may enter into the unity of common aims. Social service demands the reality of the social order and its members. As an Indian writer puts it, 'To live and work for the essentially untrue is hardly an inspiring and convincing creed, and to think of others when there is none else to be thought of, is almost to make a mockery of intelligence.'[2]

[1] Solovyof, *Justification of the Good*, 68.

[2] B. K. Shastri, 229.

In reference to God also, ethics, if it is to be properly established, demands transcendence and objectivity. The essence of the ethical spirit is aspiration, and aspiration is possible only in connexion with the 'other'—the 'other' which is also the higher. The conception of identity is useful in giving us confidence that we have within us the potentiality of the divine, and that therefore ethical endeavour is not meaningless. But if this conception is pressed too far or too exclusively, it is apt to result in a view which might render the ethical life superfluous. Prof. Radhakrishnan has foreseen this danger and has done his best to guard against it in the passage which we have quoted above.[1] But the danger is apt to recur with disconcerting frequency in connexion with the Vedānta. If we are already one with God, there is little point in striving ethically to become Godlike. When there is identity, sufficient room is not left for the stages of approach. When we have already arrived at a destination we do not concern ourselves very much with the toilsome and dusty road. It is an outgoing of desire and love which alone can inspire ethical action in times of crisis, and indeed on ordinary occasions also; and if the love is simply another form of the love wherewith a man loves himself, its uplifting force is diminished. An Indian writer protests in another connexion against the charge that the Vedānta rouses no enthusiasm for God, by pointing out that 'it is obviously wrong to suppose that (the devotee) has no love for Brahma, unless one is prepared to say of him that he does not love himself'.[2] Now at first sight such a statement has a superficial resemblance to Spinoza's doctrine that our highest love to God is the love wherewith God loves himself. But the emphasis is different, and this difference of emphasis is all-important from the point of view of ethics. Our starting-point makes all the difference. If, when we are thinking of the identity of human and divine love, we think first of the love wherewith God loves himself, we may lose little in respect of inspiration as we carry the thought downwards to human life. But if, on the other hand, we begin by saying that our highest spring of action is a love similar to that wherewith we love ourselves, then our ethical endeavour would seem to be weakened at its very source; for to love oneself—in the case of

[1] p. 185. [2] Kirtikar, 121.

the weak man at least—may demand very little effort. Ethics cannot exist except in association with a feeling of uplift, and it would seem to demand such an interpretation of aspiration towards God as is given by Solovyof: 'However complete', he says, 'the feeling of our inner unity with God may be, it never becomes a consciousness of mere identity, of simple merging into one. The feeling of unity is inseparably connected with the consciousness that the Deity with which we are united, and which acts and reveals itself in us, is something distinct and independent of us, that it is prior to us, higher and greater than we.'[1] And in ethics there is further involved, as the essence of the process, the establishment of harmony between the imperfect in us and the objective perfection in God.

This leads to another thought. It may be argued that identity, even though it leaves no room for 'approach', yet does not rule out progress, inasmuch as it provides for recovery and return, for 'a becoming of the soul what it has always been, a revival of its true nature'.[2] This would certainly relieve us greatly of our difficulty, were the recovery based upon identification with a God possessed of all perfect qualities. But when we have to do with a characterless Brahman, recovery of identity with Him means nothing that has importance for ethics. It implies a relapse upon quietism, a virtual abandonment once more of the ethical point of view. Now we are quite willing to admit that this abandonment of the ethical struggle may frequently arise from a vivid apprehension of the grace of God, and from a profound and praiseworthy feeling of dissatisfaction with our own attainments, from the consciousness that what we actualize in our character can never be adequate to the ideal. But is abandonment the only possible outcome of this feeling? Because we are dissatisfied, need we cease to struggle for satisfaction along the lines which our duty has hitherto prescribed for us? Because moral aspiration is insatiable, must the moral level be altogether transcended? Must we sink our ideal in the characterless unknown depths of our own being, vaguely recognized as identical with the Being of God? Should we not rather project our ideal on to the heights of the Divine Reality, justified thereto by what would seem to be the direct and obvious answer to the simple

[1] Solovyof, *op. cit.*, 164. [2] Müller, *S. S.* 168.

question as to whence came our ideal? Surely our sense of the inadequacy of our objective moral achievement does not demand that we should become merely subjective and negative. Rather does it send our thoughts onward to the thought of a fuller objective realization, not in us but in God.

But if this is so, then ethics refuses to be satisfied with a characterless Absolute. It demands a Reality having a character which may constitute our goal, however distant it may be from our present attainment. And so we are led to ask whether the difficulties in the way of finding a moral ideal in God are so insuperable as many Vedantists would make out. Such objections may be first of all connected with the depreciation of activity in general. Action, according to the Vedantists, is irrelevant in connexion with the highest knowledge, because action has to do with what has not yet come into existence, whereas knowledge has to do with that which eternally is, that which is not susceptible of increase or decrease, or of any kind of alteration. From this it follows, according to the argument we are considering, that the Eternal self cannot be improved by the addition of good qualities or the removal of defects. Therefore moral predicates are out of place in connexion with any ultimate and unchangeably real existence; for the conception of goodness is unmeaning except in connexion with activity, and unless a distinction of good from evil is allowed. The idea underlying the reluctance to make use of moral characterization would thus seem to be that goodness emerges from a sense of incompleteness and consequently from desire, and that when incompleteness and the longing to be rid of it are ruled out, then goodness has no place.

But over and above our reluctance to accept the view that desire is inherently evil, and the suspicion, which we share with Mr. Archer, that the demand for the annihilation of desire is a kind of 'hedging' against destiny,[1] we cannot agree with the further assumption that the goodness of a thing depends on our desiring it. It is not good because we desire it; it is rather desired because it is good, because it has inherent value, objectively and not merely subjectively, because it seems to have an inalienable right to a significant place in a scheme of reality

[1] Cf. *India and the Future*, 73.

having a definite character. Our sense of value is an appreciation of objective conditions; and desire implies a recognition of a standard of values not dependent on the desire itself. Thus, even if we were to grant the contention that desire ought to disappear, the value would remain as a recognition of the ultimate meaning of the world. If, on the other hand, we are indisposed to go the length of allowing that all desire is evil, our demand that there should be objective justification for our highest desires is correspondingly strengthened. Further, although we may be in the habit of applying the word 'good' to what shows signs of a satisfactory measure of approach towards an ideal, yet the word may also be applied simply as a description of the highest we know; and the inapplicability to the Absolute of the first sense need not preclude the application of the second.

Not only may we apply ethical predicates to the ultimate, but it seems to us that we *must* do so, if our ethical struggle is not to be meaningless and futile. Ethics, as we have contended, demands a sphere of reality in which it may work, and a reasonable faith that the basis of this reality may be characterized in such a way as to give strength and encouragement for the struggle with certain disconcerting aspects of experience. Prof. Radhakrishnan illustrates the need in his criticism of Buddhism when he says that 'Buddhism establishes the enormous difficulty of having a pure morality independent of spiritual values'.[1] The problem of ethics is to deal with the evil and sorrow of the world, and these cannot be dealt with adequately simply by relegating them to a sphere of unreality. As Principal Galloway puts it, 'Spiritual selves claim to be real, and our consciousness of freedom and our sense of moral evil decline to be relegated to the category of illusion.'[2] Evil cannot be overcome by denying its reality, especially when this is accompanied by a denial of the reality of the good as well. Evil cannot be overcome by negation, but only by a positive reality. We cannot agree with Prof. Shastri that an unreal life can be worthy in the highest sense.[3] Selfishness, e.g., can be overcome not by merely thinking about its disappearance but by an assertion or at least a consciousness of objective unselfishness. All great virtues are the

[1] Radhakrishnan, I. 608. [2] *Religion and Modern Thought*, 216.
[3] Cf. B. K. Shastri, p. xxi.

results of faith in a positive impact of goodness; and, ultimately, we arrive at the necessity of a belief that the quality of goodness can be used to describe the deepest reality of the universe, and that we are not without justification for the assurance that help for the combating of evil may come to us from the innermost shrine of the Being of God.

To be told that, on the emergence of true knowledge, evil will necessarily be *thought* out of existence is hardly sufficient to comfort us whilst we are still struggling under untoward conditions of everyday life; and in the face of actual sorrow, especially that which comes to us from the suffering of others, whom we love, to tell us that this suffering is an illusion is not far removed from pitilessness. We cannot, e.g., place ourselves very readily at the point of view of Prof. Das Gupta, when he says, 'The sorrow around us has no fear for us, if we remember that we are naturally sorrowless and blessed in ourselves. The pessimistic mood loses all terrors, as it closes in absolute optimistic confidence in one's own self and the ultimate destiny and goal of emancipation.'[1]

The emphasis here is still laid upon deliverance and negative freedom, upon the cultivation of a mood of philosophical detachment. And when, in the inevitable clash between such a mood and the ordinary experience of life, our thought swings over to the opposite extreme, we are not much helped, as regards ethical support, by the doctrine of *karma* in the form in which it appears in the Vedānta. This doctrine was intended by Śaṅkara to save us from uncomfortable questioning about the justice of God. But we establish our theodicy—if, indeed, we do establish it—at a very great price. Even if we slur over our difficulties about the beginning of things, and accept the explanation that there is no beginning, we find that we are the resultants of previous conditions which have been unfolding themselves for untold ages. We are bereft of the privilege of responsibility even for the evil that we do. We find that all causality, after all, really belongs to God; or that we are in the grasp of an inexorable destiny within whose processes there is only cyclic change, and with regard to which there is no hope of progress except in the negative sense that we may attain ever

[1] Das Gupta, I. 77.

more completely to the true knowledge which will give us, not victory, but escape. Nothing seems to be provided between the extremes we have indicated. It is a case of either bondage or abstract freedom. We can escape only by thinking of our imprisonment as a dream, and not by breaking down the walls of the prison-house. We do not sublimate or consecrate the conditions of the actual, but stand apart from the perplexing problems of ordinary life, apart in theory at least, if—fortunately—not always in practice. And does the freedom which we are promised satisfy the aspiring soul? Is it the freedom that we desire, or—to go one step farther back—can we rest in this theoretical knowledge that there is a freedom without our prison-house? Rather is it the freedom of the desert, of the wide empty spaces or the boundless sea:

> So lonely 'twas that God himself
> Seemed scarcely there to be.[1]

And it is just possible that by its very vacuity such freedom may become a new kind of bondage. Activity which can find no outlet produces subjectively the same kind of feeling as restraint. A character in a recent novel seems to express such a mood, '"Ah", she mocked, "wait till you're so free that you just daren't do what you like. Wait till you're so free that you can be here one minute and there another. Wait till you are so free that you can see the four walls of your freedom and the iron-bound door that will let you out into the open air of slavery, if only there were some one to open it."'[2] A similar mood is set forth by another writer who speaks of the great hours of experience when 'the soul of man has . . . suddenly hated its so-called freedom and returned to some bondage dearer than freedom', and of the transition 'from a condition of "liberty" to some blessed state of bondage'; adding the reflection, 'perhaps the truth is that we are made for bondage, but it must be bondage to something which moves or to someone who loves'.[3] These quotations suggest that there is a higher freedom than merely abstract and negative freedom—a freedom which is hinted at in the well-known words, 'whose service is perfect freedom', a freedom

[1] *Ancient Mariner*. [2] Michael Arlen, *The Green Hat*, 131.
[3] Dr. J. A. Hutton, *Guidance from Francis Thompson in Matters of Faith*, 49.

which is allied with interest in the actual, with a discernment of the problems of the actual, and an attempt to solve these through the inspiration of a faith that the ultimate purpose of the actual and its essential meaning is the establishment of the good. In other words we desire a freedom which will not merely tell us that there is liberty outside the prison-house of our lower desires and mundane existence, but which will enable us to break down its walls and pass out, having victorious strength of character in ourselves, and so desirous of the salvation of our fellows that the prison walls may not so easily close again either upon them or upon us.

Asceticism and negation generally are meaningless, except as they are steps on the way to moral affirmation. We must pass from negative to positive freedom. The former, when reinforced by indifference, may give way before the downward persistence of our lower desires; the latter lays hold on the principle of life, and cherishes the faith that all moral endeavour will be taken up into and transformed by the deepest Power and Order of the world—there shall not be one lost good. We must not, of course, lose sight of the value that underlies the negative attitude to morality. It is right that we should not, through over-scrupulous attention to the means, lose sight of the end of our moral endeavour; and negation may simply be an exaggeration of the warning against legalism. But it is equally necessary that we should not transform a subject attitude of caution into a metaphysical conclusion, and deny to morality any place in the ultimate end; we should not so conceive the end as to deprive the means of all importance. It is for us rather to

> Learn, by a mortal yearning, to ascend—
> Seeking a higher object.[1]

If our aim is simply to get out of the *saṁsāra*, then we shall not be encouraged to faithful observance of the stages of the process. A doctrine of metaphysical emptiness may not be very far removed from moral indifference, unless we are willing to look upon morality not merely as a disciplinary struggle, but as a positive achievement. After all, *end* and *means* are correlative conceptions, and the end can have significance only if the means

[1] Wordsworth, *Laodamia*.

also are taken as real. As has been said, 'It is the peril of the Mystic that he is inclined to forget the Way in the end. The peril of the man of Reason is that he cannot see the end for the dust he raises by the way.'[1] We may add that it is the duty of the moral philosopher to avoid the extremes of both the Mystic and the man of Reason.

We have been urging that, if morality is to have a proper basis, it requires objectification or a reaching outwards to a Divine Reality of positive moral character; but we must emphasize also the necessity of a feeling of reality in regard to our subjective point of initiation. Ethics cannot be secure if associated with a depreciation of personality. And we demand not only a feeling of reality but a feeling of value. It should be impossible to describe the individual soul in the words even of Rāmānuja—usually inclined towards a more positive attitude—as 'a mere wretched glow-worm'.[2] In drawing attention to the need of personal persistence we must not be thought to be laying ourselves open to the charge of selfishness or concern with material reward either in this world or the next. Despite any possible misunderstandings, we cannot relinquish the idea that the completion of personal efficiency is an essential element in the moral ideal, or the demand that we shall be allowed to find ourselves again in an eternal Reality receptive of the good. Personality must be regarded, not as an accident or anomaly, but as normal to the universe. In fact we may relate the argument to the present tense rather than to the future, and we may point out that our present appreciation of reality is essentially bound up with the exercise of our personality, and that we cannot sacrifice this without reducing our life, as well as our hopes, to the vagueness and instability of a dream. So from the present we may pass to the future as to an extension of the same consciousness, and, considering both present and future together, may quite naturally point out that if the life of the individual is not to be continued in the future, a feeling of *impuissance de vivre* will descend upon him, and he will be inclined to take up an attitude of indifference even in regard to the present. We are not urging that, with the loss of the hope of personal im-

[1] Joergens, art. in *Time and Tide*, Sept. 1924.
[2] *S. B. E.* XLVIII. 469.

mortality, the fear of hell will be lessened and the expectation of reward will disappear. Our argument has a deeper basis; we are thinking rather of contribution than of claim, and all that we ask is the continuance of the opportunity to make that contribution. If, as we think is the case, our contribution cannot be separated from ourselves and consists rather in what we *are* than in what we *give*, all that we ask is that this gift of our personality itself may be assigned a place of permanent value in the ultimate constitution of things. We believe that the perfection of the whole cannot be secured without the perfection, permanence, and utmost expansion of the parts—which parts we are. And if the high philosopher still shakes his head in unbelief, and speaks, wistfully, if not contemptuously, of pious wishes divorced from facts, we may quote in support of our contention for the reality of the individual the common-sense appeal of Sir Oliver Lodge: 'If any philosopher tells you that you do not exist, . . . that you are an automaton without free-will, that all your actions are determined by outside causes—then appeal must be made to twelve average men, unsophisticated by special studies. This is not an appeal to the mob as against the philosopher, but an appeal to the experience of untold ages against the studies of a generation.'[1]

In our discussion of the place of works in the Vedantic system we have already spoken of the difficulty, within that system, of arriving at any practical conception of the Kingdom of God. Works of social service are regarded certainly as one of the best means of purifying the soul, but as little more. In fact the further idea is hinted at that, if the permanence of the results of unselfish labours is dwelt upon, the individual will become the prisoner of the good he has wrought and thus fail to win deliverance. It were better therefore, it is urged, that this world should be regarded simply as a place of sanctification and atonement, and that no thought of the establishment of a kingdom of righteousness should obsess the soul. It were better that the enlightened man should remember that 'all relations lose their significance in the one eternal life'.[2]

In such a position once more the foundations of ethics would seem to be weakened. At our highest, we strive for the estab-

[1] Quoted in the *Hibbert Journal*, July 1926.

[2] Kirtikar, 122.

lishment not only of personal but of social values, and, unless we can feel that there is a promise of the permanence of the results of such efforts, in the upbuilding of a community of free and noble spirits, the efforts themselves are apt to slacken. We desire that from our ultimate ideal we may derive an incentive for the service of the community; and we feel that, if the way is blocked in this direction, our moral life in its highest exercise will become futile, and bereft also of the inspirational value of association with the good in other lives. From the conception of the true Self which is so strongly emphasized in the Vedānta, such a way of expansion ought to open out. As Happel puts it, 'The true Ego is present only in elementary form in separate human individuals. It is only in organic communion with others that it wins its higher potentiality, and it attains its complete fullness only in the personality of God, in communion with whom separate personalities can reach their truest development and independence, so that God then truly is all in all.'[1]

But our final question is whether in the Vedānta such a way of emergence and expansion has been left open? We are doubtful if this question can be answered in the affirmative. In application to the Vedānta there is much truth in the words of Caird, 'To remain at the negative point of view is as disastrous as never to have reached it. For to deny the place of passion and desire is to cut oneself off from all concrete human interests; to shut the spirit up in the cell of its own self-contained independence instead of finding a home for it in the wide world of human good.'[2] Eucken also complains in special reference to the Vedānta of the cleavage which it introduces between 'the height of the inner life and the rest of existence', and complains that by its method 'man attains a purely inward life and that there is no path leading from this inwardness to the wide field of life'.[3] For a judgement of much the same character as Eucken's, but in our opinion excessively severe, we may compare Archer's *India and the Future*, 73.

'There is something no doubt in the rule of practical philosophy which bids us not found the livability of life upon external satisfac-

[1] Happel, 175.
[2] *Life of Caird*, 314.
[3] Cf. also the present writer's *Pantheism and the Value of Life*, 331 ff.

tions but rather upon internal resources of which nothing can deprive us. Up to a certain point this is true wisdom; carried beyond that point it lands us in sheer inanities of egoism which strike at the root of all human association. This is so evident that Indian thinkers have expended a great deal of ingenuity in the attempt to reconcile a philosophy which denies all value to life with an ethical system based, as all ethical systems must be, on the assumption that life is supremely valuable and the test of all other values. . . . The doctrine of detachment, passionlessness, indifference, as a cure for the inherent evil of existence, is not a profound one at all, but is merely the exaggeration of a common and somewhat pusillanimous mode of procedure. In its exaggerated form it is violently anti-social and consequently incompatible with any rational system of ethics.

The demand for modification and reconstruction which we have made from the point of view of ethics really leads us on to the religious demand that God should be brought, not into negative, but into positive organic relation with the world; that He should enter into contact with history and the present endeavours of men, that He should take into and upon Himself the burden of the suffering and evil of the world and of our misuse of human freedom, that He should redeem us from our unfitness and our evil, and welcome us to fullness of communion and service and to a permanent place of value in His kingdom. A love of the world and of the human beings in it, a trust in it and in them planted at the very heart of God, and a readiness to give His very self for the redemption of the world, or in the language of the New Testament 'to give His only begotten Son', can alone satisfy the hearts of men.

We shall consider the religious value of the Vedānta in our concluding chapter, but before we go on to this most important topic of all, we may set our whole discussion in clearer light by devoting a chapter to a comparison of Vedantic teaching with certain conceptions of modern philosophy.

VIII

SOME COMPARISONS BETWEEN THE VEDĀNTA AND MODERN PHILOSOPHICAL THOUGHT

EVEN the briefest study of speculation in other parts of the world will have the result of deepening the impression of the unity of human thought. It is possible to find parallels to Vedantic teaching in many Western systems, and illustrations of cases in which like elements in fundamental assumptions are followed by conclusions also similar serve to make more obvious the essential and wholly natural implications of such elements. In this section we shall take 'modern' in the wide sense usually accepted in histories of philosophy, and for the most part, though not entirely, we shall confine our attention to those philosophies which present broad similarities to the Vedānta, especially in respect of intellectualistic tendency.

A study of the Vedānta inevitably invites comparison first of all with Spinoza amongst 'modern' philosophers. Even in the diverse judgements which have been passed upon him there are suggestive parallels, for, just as in the Vedānta, it seems difficult to assess the comparative importance of the mystical and intellectual elements. On the one hand he has been called 'a God-intoxicated man'. When Renan unveiled the Spinoza monument in The Hague, he pointed reverently to the windows of the house where Spinoza died, and said, 'Maybe it was from there that God was seen nearest,' and a recent critic, who was, in general, not given to emotion, had to confess that 'one cannot read Spinoza in cold blood'.[1] On the other hand he has been described as an atheist and as 'caring little for the world provided it were only one'. In 1678, one year after his death, his *Opera Posthuma* was anathematized as 'a godless book the like of which did not exist from the beginning of the world till now' and there have been echoes of this judgement ever since. The starting-point of Spinoza's philosophy is to be found in that aversion from the ordinary point of view, that discontent with the merely given, which we have found to be characteristic of the Vedānta, and his goal also reveals that close unity between

[1] Iverach, *Descartes and Spinoza*, 132.

philosophical and religious interest which we have found to be characteristic of the earlier school of thought.

It might be said with some amount of truth that Spinoza combines in himself the tendencies manifested both in Śaṅkara and Rāmānuja. He shows affinity with the former, in that he also regards God as the characterless infinite, in relation to which all determination is negation; and he connects himself with the latter in conceiving of God as the abode of all auspicious qualities, as that which 'has absolutely infinite attributes of which each expresses infinite essence in its own kind'.[1] Spinoza wavers between a negation of the world which is reminiscent for us of Śaṅkara's strict monism, and an accommodation to ordinary experience which recalls Rāmānuja's rehabilitation of the actual world. The relation between the individual and God is stated by him at times in terms of the identity relation of Śaṅkara, and at other times he attributes to the individual an internal self-activity which is compatible only with Rāmānuja's ideal of communion as the final phase of religious attainment. It must be confessed, however, that the self-activity has no real place in his system, and his want of adequate provision for this reminds us of Rāmānuja's difficulties in adjusting divine and human causality, and in connexion with Spinoza himself it provoked the reaction towards individualism which followed immediately in the philosophy of Leibniz. But on the whole the closer affinity is with Śaṅkara rather than with Rāmānuja, at least if we confine ourselves to the logically consistent parts of Spinoza's system. Although there is not in Spinoza the same abrupt separation between the higher and the lower orders of knowledge as in the Indian thinker, yet the higher, for the most part, turns out to be the negation of the lower rather than a development out of it. In both philosophers there is a strict adherence to the intellectual point of view and an almost exclusive reliance upon the activity of the mind as a means of obtaining deliverance. The means of escape for Spinoza are 'adequate ideas', and, when in the individual life disturbance and misery are caused by our passions, it is by the power of the understanding that we may escape from their sway. 'There is no modification of the body whereof we cannot form some clear and distinct

[1] *Ethics*, I. 16.

conception,' and, 'An emotion, which is a passion, ceases to be a passion, as soon as we form a clear and distinct idea thereof.'[1] Here we have a close parallel to Śaṅkara's principle that 'the feeling of pain is due merely to the error of false imagination'.[2] At the same time we may notice in passing a slight difference in the operation of the enlightened understanding in the two philosophers. Spinoza is more inclined to dwell upon the application of knowledge to particular cases of the incidence of passion, and would attribute efficacy to the systematizing of the causes of passion according to ordinary scientific procedure; whereas Śaṅkara is much more uncompromisingly negative, and is occupied with the general or total effect of emancipating knowledge in delivering us from the sum of conditions under which passions can be detrimentally operative.

But although there may be a difference in degree of intensity of application, the acosmistic tendency is strong in both philosophers. By obedience to the higher knowledge we are to turn away our attention from the things of the world and withdraw into the depths of the soul. And just as in the Vedānta the root idea is the identification of Ātman and Brahman, so with Spinoza also it is by the deeper knowledge of the self within that we reach unity with the universal Self or God. This intense aspiration after unity leads Spinoza to a negative attitude towards the world and to a more or less abstract conception of God. Spinoza certainly bids farewell to the world with greater reluctance than Śaṅkara, and his unity is always more open in the direction of diversity. His highest knowledge has been described as 'thoughtfulness matured to inspiration', and the idea of maturity very properly suggests the idea of gradual growth. But still, though the departure may be lingering and ultimately so formal as to permit of surreptitious return, the farewell is an important gesture. We are made to feel that extension as admitting of divisibility is a defective category, and that duration as permitting degrees is inapplicable to God. Our ordinary conceptions and classifications which aid us in our apprehension of the particular modes of being belong after all to the realm of illusion; it is in unity alone that we can find satisfaction. On the intellectual side there is perhaps a parallel

[1] *Ethics*, V. 3 and 4.

[2] *S. B. E.* XXXVIII. 64.

between Śaṅkara's conception of Ultimate Being as self-luminous, and Spinoza's idea that Substance cannot be knowable except as self-luminous, because, if it were otherwise luminous, it would have qualities implying its dependence on other things.

So negative and abstract is Spinoza's thought that he really provides no proper passage from the undifferenced unity of Substance to the variety of the attributes. In striving to effect such a transition Spinoza finds himself in difficulties which have, in turn, involved his interpreters in seemingly interminable controversies as to the relation of attributes to substance within his system, exactly the difficulties over again of the Vedantic transition from the non-qualitative to the qualitative Brahman. Do the attributes constitute the essence of Spinoza's substance or are they only fictions of the human intellect? If the former, what becomes of the doctrine of the undifferenced unity of Brahman; if the latter, whence came the minds capable of constructing the fictions? If all ordinary experience belongs to the region of names and forms—to borrow a Vedantic phrase—will not the imaging intellect also be a mere reflection, and partake of the general illusoriness, and whence can come the energy necessary for framing the illusion and becoming dissatisfied with it, as well as that general capacity for persistence which is so fundamental an element in Spinoza's philosophy? If it is suggested in reply that these difficulties are themselves illusory, and will disappear with the disappearance of the illusion, we are simply compelled to press the question farther back and ask whence came the illusory point of view at all, for even an illusion must have a cause.

In attempting to deal with this latter question—implicitly or explicitly put—Spinoza finds himself in much the same difficulty as Śaṅkara in relation to the doctrine of *māyā*. If the Absolute has first of all been defined as undifferentiated and changeless, it is impossible to get any creative energy out of it. And yet our ordinary experience—just because it is *our* experience—demands some explanation—demands the establishment of some relation between that experience and the ultimate reality. This demand can be speciously satisfied only by a conception which, like the Vedantic *māyā*, hovers between being and non-being; or, like the infinite modes of Spinoza, bridges only very ineffectively the gulf between static unity and dynamic multiplicity. Both are illogical attempts to prevent the finite world becoming, as Prof. Rogers puts it, 'a mere impertinence in the system',[1] but into the further details of this parallel, theoretically illegitimate but practically most useful, it is not necessary to enter.

We are more concerned with the effect of Spinoza's views upon the importance of the individual both now and in any life —or lives—to come, and here we get another illustration of the fundamental deficiency of any purely intellectual system. Spinoza leaves no true place for the individual. As Caird says, 'The idea of God on which Spinoza's whole system is ostensibly based, is one which involves the denial of any reality or independence to the finite.'[2] And Spinoza obtains deliverance from the distressing aspects of the world—from its pain and its sorrow and its evil—partly by indifference and partly by acquiescence. In actual life he was detached from ordinary human concerns; he lived through one of the most exciting periods of European history, and yet practically no reference to public affairs is to be found in his works. As Prof. Santayana puts it: 'Lodged in his corner of the great house of nature he felt himself humble, pensioned and at peace. He was proud of that great house and its glories; he venerated its economy, and never dreamt of reforming it.'[3] This outward indifference was but the reflection of the internal attitude which seeks the solution of problems in thought alone and ends in escape rather than victory. For him distinction between good and evil was but a conditional and purely human contrivance, and was transcended in the Absolute. But although Spinoza had a stronger sense of the importance of society and a more modern and more sublime conception of the significance of natural law as revealed by science and interpreted by art, and, in consequence, never surrendered himself to the Vedantic extreme of indifference, yet when the pendulum of his thought swings over to an acknowledgement of the reality of the cosmos, he was apt, in his reaction from indifference, to fall a victim to a conception of inexorable necessity and a denial of any true freedom to man. There is a parallel here to Śaṅkara's transition from negation to a

1 *History of Philosophy*, 305. 2 Caird, *Spinoza*, 298.
3 Introduction to Spinoza's *Ethics*, p. ix.

modified acknowledgement of the law of *karma*. But neither in the negation of evil nor in the admission of its necessity, nor in freedom so restricted as almost to pass over into its opposite, can there be any abiding satisfaction for the soul of man.

The freedom which he allows is that of complete identification with the Divine thought, and he expresses the unity through the help of the conception of the 'intellectual love of God'. The choice of the term might seem to arise from a sense of human worth and an inescapable consciousness of the reality of human endeavour, and it suggests the possibility of establishing a real and enduring relation between the individual and God. But Spinoza does not bring out the full significance of the term. Our love to God turns out to be the love wherewith God loves himself. In a very real sense Spinoza believes that a man becomes that of which he thinks. To think high thoughts is indeed the important influence in moral elevation. But when the process reaches the highest level, we find that (according to him) to think high thoughts is to become identified with our thought. The relation of identity is predominant and all differentiation disappears. In this way we get, no doubt, assurance of immortality, for 'the spirit shares the fate of the object with which it identified itself, . . . and in caring for the eternal, it has ceased to care for that part of itself which can die'.[1] But our permanence is simply the permanence in God of our true thought, and does not carry with it the permanence of the thinker who formed the thought. Prof. Pringle-Pattison speaks truly of Spinoza's 'substitution of the eternal life of thought . . . for immortality in the usual sense of a continued personal existence',[2] and it is this depreciation of continued personal existence which seems to be significant of the total effect of Spinoza's system.

It might be interesting by way of contrast to follow out some of the consequences in the immediately succeeding Leibnizian philosophy of a revolt against this depreciation of the individual, and to find in the transition from Spinoza to Leibniz a parallel to some of the more striking differences between Śaṅkara and Rāmānuja. Leibniz, like Rāmānuja, was disturbed by the fact that in the philosophy which preceded him the whole had seemed

[1] Santayana, *op. cit.* xviii.

[2] *Idea of Immortality*, 150.

to swallow up the parts. Leibniz wished to hold fast to the principle of continuity, which might be said to be the result on the scientific level of a monism showing signs of a modification of its strictness. He also allowed, with Spinoza, the inadequacy of many of our ordinary categories, holding, e.g., that the form of space, because of the infinite divisibility of any extended substance, would not enable us to reach any distinct reality of the individual. But at the same time, he was unwilling to abandon the reality of the individual, and conserved it in his doctrine of monads, which emphasized the idea that the reality of substance was intensive rather than extensive. He thus showed a tendency *in the same direction* as Rāmānuja, although he went very much farther than the latter in his search for a satisfactory basis of individuality.

It is curious also to notice that the difficulties which we have found to emerge in the Vedānta regarding the proper distribution of responsibility for the suffering and evil of the world between God and man reappear in Leibniz. We found that Śaṅkara in treating this problem had to take refuge in what was little more than a bare contradiction—'The Lord indeed causes it (the individual soul) to act, but it acts itself.'[1] Similarly, Leibniz, while showing that the soul is not determined to act from outside, yet, inasmuch as he holds that the individual is determined by the law of its own nature and that for that nature it is entirely dependent on God, escapes no more than Śaṅkara from the necessity of refunding all causality ultimately into God.

Before leaving Leibniz we may call attention to an interesting contrast between him and the Vedānta in respect of the former's law of the three stages of development. In the Vedānta we found that there were three stages of the soul's progress—from ordinary waking consciousness, through dreaming sleep, to dreamless sleep. In Leibniz there are also three stages through which the monads may ascend from the lowest to the highest kind of perception. But the order is exactly reversed. The lowest are those which exist in a state of slumber or swoon, the middle class have attained to the phase of confused dreaming, whereas the highest of all have arrived at clear waking consciousness. The point is of small importance in itself, but it may

[1] *S. B. E.* XXXVIII. 60.

illustrate the great difference in total mental attitude between the Leibnizian philosophy and the Vedānta.

From this digression we may turn back to systems presenting more of similarity with than of contrast to the Vedānta. We have in the course of our discussion already touched at considerable length on possible comparisons between the Vedānta and Kant, and we may devote a few paragraphs to the consideration of the philosophy of Fichte, which will, we think, afford further illustrations of the diminishing importance of the individual in any system of mystical or intellectualistic speculation, having identity as a fundamental concept.

Prof. Rudolf Otto, in one of his recent addresses, speaks of the likeness between Śaṅkara and Fichte as being so striking that one might almost speak of the rebirth of Indian philosophical speculation in a German personality.[1] There is of course no direct relationship, but the gaze of both thinkers is turned in the same direction. With both, the pure Being, which is pure thought, is an absolute unity without variety, and relationship with it is attained by a higher kind of knowledge or intuition which is to be very carefully distinguished from the ordinary operations of the understanding. The ultimate Being is unchangeable and without creative energy, and in order to pass from it to the ordinary world we must posit a power which Fichte describes in terms almost identical with those which Śaṅkara applies to *māyā*. This appears to Prof. Otto to be the most surprising parallel of all, and it is indeed so striking that Fichte's actual words may be quoted: 'There is only the One, unchangeable and eternal, and there is nothing beyond Him. All changeable and alterable is therefore most certainly nothing. And its appearance is most certainly empty illusion. That I know.'

On the other hand, Fichte is less inclined than Śaṅkara to favour the idea of a world-illusion, and emphasizes rather the idea that the responsibility for the illusion rests upon the conceptual and discursive understanding of the individual thinker. Also, Fichte, notwithstanding his acceptance of the principle of unchangeableness, does not keep so consistently to this as does Śaṅkara. He is inclined to modify it to a far greater extent and

[1] Cf. *Mitteilungen der Deutschen Akademie*, Dec. 1925.

opposes resolutely the idea of a God who is lifeless and static. Although our salvation is still according to Fichte based upon the relationship of identity between us and the divine, this relationship will express itself in a life of action, even under the conditions of our present existence. The door of admission to the active service of humanity is opened wider with Fichte than with Śaṅkara, because he conceives of God as active. But on the other hand, because the ideal relationship is for him still one of identity, the door is not opened quite far enough, and, because of ultimate metaphysical negation leading to a depreciation of the individual, the desire for entrance is greatly weakened. As Schelling puts it in his interpretation of Fichte: 'The goal of the finite Ego is enlargement of its sphere till the attainment of identity with the infinite Ego. But the infinite Ego knows no object, and possesses, therefore, no consciousness or unity of consciousness, such as we mean by personality. Consequently, the ultimate goal of all endeavour may also be represented as enlargement of the personality to infinity—that is to say, as its annihilation. The ultimate goal of the finite Ego—and not only of it but also of the Non-Ego,—the final goal, therefore, of the world—is its annihilation as a world.'[1] This quotation brings together in significant conjunction abstraction as regards the ultimate principle and negation as regards the world and the individual.

Before turning to the broader and more intellectual development associated with Hegel and his followers, we may, in slight alteration of chronological order, make a passing reference to Schopenhauer. He is specially interesting for our purposes because of the vehemence with which he avows his indebtedness to Indian philosophy, not so much for explicit statements of detailed conclusions as for the expression of a general spirit and of fundamental principles. He considers that his own principles are almost exactly similar to those of the earlier thinkers, and would independently lead to the same results. We find both in him and in them the same detachment from the ordinary interests of life, the same yearning after deliverance,

[1] Schelling, *Vom Ich als Princip der Philosophie*, quoted in Seth's *Hegelianism and Personality*, 59.

the same abstractness of procedure, the same inclination towards an annihilating identification with a characterless infinite Reality. It is interesting also to notice the close connexion which Schopenhauer suggests between himself and Spinoza. He prides himself on having been born exactly one hundred and eleven years and one day after Spinoza, and evidently considers that the mantle of the earlier philosopher had fallen upon his shoulders.

Schopenhauer finds it easy to reach the point of view at which the world appears to be an unreality. He tells us that 'he to whom man and all things have not appeared as phantoms, has no capacity for philosophy'.[1] Consequently, he disregards altogether the temporal developments of history, crushing the centuries together as he would the sections of a telescope, on the principle that we can learn nothing from the things of time except the necessity of going beyond them; and no doubt remembering also his conviction or experience that the transition from common knowledge to enlightenment cannot be a gradual attainment but takes place suddenly. The ultimate reality is will; not consciousness, as in the Vedānta, but this will, equally with the Vedantic ultimate, is characterless, and the ideal relationship with it is absorption. In regard to this absorption there may indeed be several degrees of completeness, but the goal is that we should sink into a sheer sense of identity with the Ultimate. Even in stages before the final 'the true world in idea arises only when subject and object reciprocally fill and penetrate each other completely'.[2] Further, 'whoever becomes so absorbed and lost in the perception of nature that he only continues to exist as the pure knowing subject, becomes in this way directly conscious that, as such, he is the condition, that is, the support of the world and all objective existence, for this now shows itself as dependent on his existence'.[3]

This identification (set forth almost in Fichtean language) with the underlying restless striving will can provide no support for a sense of the value of the individual. His consciousness of individuality is a mere illusion, and immortality can consist only in the destruction of this illusion. Meanwhile an anticipation of essential identity may, as we have seen, make one patient in

[1] Schopenhauer, 497. [2] Ib. 235. [3] Ib. 234.

suffering injustice and unperturbed in inflicting it, just in so far as the doer or the sufferer is influenced by the consideration that those who inflict injury and those who suffer it are one and the same.

Yet identity with this cosmic will cannot give final peace and rest according to Schopenhauer, for even the cosmic will is not absolute. Beyond the striving of the will he seems to descry a state of being in which it returns upon itself and ceases to be. Nothingness, at the dark impression of which he tells us we must not be alarmed, seeing that it is that 'which we discern behind all virtue and holiness as their final goal', would seem to be the consummation of our striving and our final verdict upon the world.

In approaching the Hegelian philosophy it is tempting to rush at once to comparisons and allow the Hegelian opposition between Being and non-Being to remind us of the Vedantic *Sat* and *Asat*. But the parallel would hardly be exact, seeing that the Being of the Vedānta (whether unqualified or qualified) is the ultimate reality, whereas with Hegel Being is merely the simplest and least adequate interpretation of reality. Further, the relation between the two terms is on the whole more exclusive and finally oppositional in the Vedānta than in Hegel. We might be on surer ground, indeed, if we were to compare *māyā* with the Hegelian principle of negation from which Hegel shows a tendency to derive a principle of actualization. Kirtikar, e.g., describes *māyā* and *avidyā* as 'neither more nor less than this negative aspect of Being explaining the Becoming'.[1]

It will perhaps be most useful to place Hegel in relation to the Vedānta through the mediation of a consideration of Schelling's position. The latter, after the manner of the stricter Vedānta, practically sacrifices difference to unity. He is inclined towards an Absolute which is like 'the night in which all cows are black' —to use Hegel's phrase. It is the vigour of the human imagination which is responsible for the differences which emerge in our construction of experience, and these differences must, if regarded from the proper point of view, be taken as unreal in comparison with the one pure identity. Hegel is altogether

[1] Kirtikar, 10.

opposed to the abstraction which results in this annihilation of difference. The ultimate identity must be one which goes out into, and realizes itself through difference. As he puts it, 'the Absolute is to be apprehended not as Substance but as Subject', and he interprets this to mean that, as in the unity of our self-consciousness we can hold together a diversity of presentations, so in the Absolute the particularity of the world may persist without the suppression of difference, so long, at least, as we consider the relationship between unity and diversity in its static and not in its developmental aspect.

But, on the other hand, in this statement Hegel puts himself alongside the Vedantist in respect of the centrality of thought in the universe. A Subject is essentially a thinking being, and it is therefore through thought alone that we reach penetration into real being and arrive at an identity comparable to that of the Vedantic formula, 'That art Thou'. Indeed, so centrally important is thought in Hegel's system that he has been accused, as is well known, of turning a Logic—or at least an Epistemology—into a Metaphysic, and reducing reality to a 'bloodless ballet of categories'. Prof. Pringle-Pattison definitely accuses Hegelianism of 'converting an identity of type into a numerical unity of existence',[1] i.e. of passing from the consideration that all men think uniformly in their unifying processes of thought, to the idea that a unitary thinker thinks in all of them and that they and all their experiences are nothing but thoughts of this Universal Mind. He holds that the Hegelian position is 'reached by hypostatizing the notion of self-consciousness and not by any progress from reality. There is, in fact, no bridge between this hypostatized conception and the world of real things and real men.'[2] To a very considerable extent we may agree with this criticism, but, in passing, it may be noted that it rather leaves out of account the consideration that, after all, identity of type means something. Men do not think alike unless there is something in their nature which constrains them to do so, and therefore the uniformity of their thought is significant of their place in the universe, and may be a fact of such importance as to be worthy of metaphysical status.

[1] *Hegelianism and Personality*, 69. Ib. 171.

But be this as it may, the parallel between Hegel's conception of thought as fundamental and certain Vedantic ideas is sufficiently striking. As the Vedānta speaks of the creative forth-bursting force of the Word (and of the underlying thought) so Hegel speaks of the idea 'freely letting itself go' into the externality of space and time, and of the idea as 'resolving to determine itself as an external Idea'. 'The absolute freedom', he says, 'of the Idea consists in this, that it resolves to let the element of its particularity go forth freely from itself as Nature.'[1] Kirtikar compares this, as was indicated above, to the 'Vedantic conception of Being projecting itself through its power called *Māyā*'.[2] It resembles also the Upanishad passage, 'Let me be many, let me go forth.' It is doubtful, however, whether Hegel, in emphasizing the centrality of thought, would have reached the same abstractness in regard to thought as Śaṅkara did. He would not, e.g., have abolished the distinction between thought and a thinker, but would rather have taken up the position of Rāmānuja, and associated the universal thought with a universal thinker. In this he would have agreed with Prof. Pringle-Pattison when the latter says, 'Thought *exists* only as the thought of a thinker; it must be centred somewhere. To thought *per se* we can attribute neither existence nor causal activity; and, this being so, it can have no place in existence as a theory of Being.'[3]

Neither would Hegel—ostensibly at least—have assigned to this pure identity of thought in which all things originate that position of aloofness and almost of superciliousness which we find in the rigorous monism of the Vedānta. There is with him at least no explicitly expressed idea that, when we turn to the particularity of the world, we are launching ourselves on a process of degradation. In fact, he says in his *Philosophy of Religion* that 'spirit which does not appear, *is* not'.[4] He seeks to preserve the unity of significance and value even amidst the differences. Even though he desires to begin with the purely philosophical point of view and would almost say, as Caird points out, that we can only reach the infinite if we deny or cast loose from the

[1] *Werke*, 414. Cf. Pringle-Pattison, *Hegelianism and Personality*, 112.
[2] Kirtikar, 66. [3] *Hegelianism and Personality*, 78.
[4] Vol. I. 26 (Speirs and Sanderson's Trans.).

finite,[1] yet he does not separate so abruptly as Śaṅkara between lower and higher orders of knowledge. He recognizes the unbroken continuity between the scientific and the philosophical procedure, and holds, as Caird again points out in another connexion, that, 'if philosophy requires of the individual that he should lift himself into the pure ether of thought, on the other hand the individual has a right to demand of philosophy that it should let down a ladder on which he may ascend to this point of view; nay that it should show him that he already has this ladder in his own possession.'[2] Hegel's aim is to show the reality as well as the rationality of the whole, and not merely the exclusive reality of pure undifferenced Being and the corresponding inferiority and illusoriness of particularity. Pure Being, with Hegel, instead of being the highest, is the lowest of the categories, and his polemic is continually directed against the folly of attempting to interpret the universe simply by such an inadequate category. He urges that we must interpret reality as an articulated system in which every part shall have its own proper and persistent place. Being must open out into Becoming, and the processes of nature must be given their place in the whole and regarded as calling for ever more and more adequate interpretations, until all the particulars are found to be unified under a supreme principle to which we find ourselves most akin in the highest development of human personality, and so break down the differences between the knower and the known and attain the completed ideal of knowledge.

Yet though the Vedānta exhibits a much greater bias in favour of unity as opposed to difference, and Hegel arrives at a much fuller reconciliation of unity and difference than does Śaṅkara, yet Hegel is not altogether free from bias in the same direction. Although he formally repudiates the idea of degradation, yet we cannot help feeling that his almost purely intellectualistic attitude leads him into positions not far removed from those of the Vedantists, and that he is apt by logical exclusions to reach conclusions of an abstract character almost irreconcilable with actual experience and destructive of a serviceable attitude to the world in which we live.

One of Hegel's fundamental ideas is that of development;

[1] Cf. Caird's *Hegel*, 56. [2] Caird, *Spinoza*, 58.

and, in considering this, the difficulty at once arises as to whether all stages of the process are equally real. Hegel was confronted with an awkward alternative, and whichever alternative he chose, he, with his intellectualistic presupposition, was in danger of depreciating the value of the individual. He found himself compelled to regard the individual either as an insignificant part of a naturalistic cosmic process, or as losing reality altogether over against the sole reality of the Absolute in its final expression.

On the one hand, in his reliance upon the centrality of thought alone, he found that this thought was apt to dissolve into negligible thinness in face of the developing actual, and leave us with nothing above the process itself. As Prof. Pringle-Pattison puts it: 'The metaphysical priority assigned to the logical system pales before the imperious reality of the senses.'[1] The Absolute is being developed in the process, and therefore there is at any moment nothing higher than the stage already reached. To quote again from Prof. Pringle-Pattison: 'The circle is closed, finality is attained; the ideal is real and we see that it is so.'[2] We seem committed almost to a deification of the actual, and to the acceptance of a system of naturalism and determinism. From this point of view a recent writer is not far wrong in describing Hegel's ethics as 'a remorseless naturalism'.[3]

As is the case in connexion with the doctrine of *karma*, to which the Vedānta in its less strictly philosophical moods gives its assent, we human beings are in the grasp of a pitiless process, and no freedom is left for us. Hegel may view the developing process more scientifically, but with him also the exclusion of freedom seems to be equally rigorous. Moreover, it is impossible to designate evil as evil, if every part of the developing process is equally real, and there are no marks of progress in the world. In such circumstances reforming zeal is out of place, and our only truly sensible procedure is to legalize custom and justify all existing institutions as well as the actual achievements of individual men. But surely for ethical health it is necessary, as one writer puts it, to 'abstract from the concrete and actual humanity of our experience, from the real men and women

[1] *Hegelianism and Personality*, 201.
[2] *Op. cit.* 208.
[3] Macintosh, *Hegel*, 211.

whom we know, and know to be imperfect, to have failings as well as virtues and excellences of character, whom we love even in their weakness and perhaps even because of it, but whom we cannot worship or regard as the complete embodiment of the moral ideal'.[1] We cannot allow the ideal to lose itself in becoming identified with the actual, instead of being regarded as identifiable with the real, i.e. as the further truth of the actual which has not yet been attained.

The other alternative with which Hegel is faced almost compels him to deny the reality of all stages in the process of development except the last. Here we find a close parallel between Hegel and the Vedānta, and an approach on the part of the former towards a doctrine of illusionism. Of course, there is a difference between the Vedantic view of the illusoriness of all the variety of the world, and the particular form which this attitude assumes in connexion with the Hegelian doctrine of development. But some kind of depreciation of detailed experience seems inseparable from the intellectual point of view, even when applied definitely and seriously to cosmic process; and the reason of this probably is that, when dominated by intellectualism, we are inclined to identify the motive of practical progress with the ideal of the attainment of truth. When, however, we are concerned mainly with the movement onwards from error to truth, we are apt to regard the stages of error as *ipso facto* swept out of existence as soon as truth has been attained.[2] We are compelled to regard every stage except the last as an inadequate and therefore unreal thought-construction. From a purely logical point of view, an unsatisfactory hypothesis fades away into unreality as soon as truth has been discovered; and when the logical conception controls us, we are apt to take up the same attitude towards the practical activities of our lives. We come, e.g., to regard inventions which have been improved upon and institutions of which the limitations have become obvious, as unreal in the same sense as a discarded hypothesis. But surely an engine which has been found to be out of date does not cease to be real in the same sense as an erroneous hypothesis; and, in general, the practical determina-

[1] Seth, *Ethical Principles*, 409.
[2] Cf. the present writer's *Pantheism and the Value of Life*, 562 ff.

tions of our life-activity have a more abiding reality than the errors through which we pass on the way to the attainment of truth. In other words, it is not possible to apply a non-temporal and merely logical judgement to the contents of the temporal process without depriving these of reality and significance to an altogether illegitimate extent. It is not permissible to occupy in thought the highest point of view and then sweep back from that to the temporal with a depreciatory condemnation of the reality of our ordinary experience.

And yet this is what Hegel often seems to do. He too frequently regards the various phases of the finite world and of human activity therein as merely a series of illusions. He is dominated by 'the fearful power of the negative', which always seems to treat reality as a negation of that which is actual at any stage in the process. Even the motive of our most serious struggles and highest aspirations is at times represented by him as a kind of illusion. 'The consummation of the infinite End,' he says, 'therefore, consists merely in removing the illusion which makes it seem yet unaccomplished. The Good, the absolutely good, is eternally accomplishing itself in the world, and the result is that it needs not wait upon us, but is already by implication, as well as in full actuality, accomplished. *This is the illusion under which we live.*[1] It alone supplies at the same time the actualizing force on which the interest of the world depends. In the course of its process, the Idea creates that illusion by setting an antithesis to confront itself, and its action consists in getting rid of the illusion which it has created.'[2]

The effect of such an attitude upon ethical and social endeavour can hardly be doubtful. It may indeed create in us a superficial optimism in that it enables us to be secure in the confidence that all is already accomplished and persuades us that we need not worry overmuch about the defects of temporal existence. We may be permitted by it to take up an attitude of practical indifference towards external happenings however disconcerting these may be. We may deal with evil in a quick and superficially satisfactory manner by denying the total sphere in which it appears. We may get rid of uncomfortable details by bringing them under the category of the contingent, and thus

[1] Italics mine. [2] *Encyclopaedia*, Section 212.

virtually refusing to recognize their reality. In fact all the difficulties of the actual may be got rid of by classifying them as untrue existences which, therefore, do not merit serious attention.

Now this may be satisfactory so long as the philosophic mood persists, but when it weakens and the claims of the actual become insistent again, our placidity is apt to be disturbed, and we find ourselves without a refuge from the sorrow and sin of the world. And, when we are confronted with actual emergencies, our indifference will not longer be taken as a sign of philosophical elevation, but rather as a proof of ethical deficiency—an evidence of pitilessness in regard to the urgent needs of humanity. Once more, as we have had occasion to notice in connexion with the Vedānta, intellectualism is found to be insufficient for individual ethics or for the uplift of society; and we are inclined to agree to a certain extent with the verdict of the writer who exclaims with reference to Hegel somewhat bitterly, 'To the strength of his logic—his mere logic—tears and blood and sins are negligible quantities.'[1]

But the point of comparison between Hegel and the Vedānta which is most important as regards ethics, and as we shall see also as regards religion, is the identity relation between man and God which is established in both systems. Śaṅkara reaches identity with God by the way of abstraction, and Hegel by emphasis on a self-consciousness which turns out to be more divine than human, but in either case it is an identity which practically destroys the reality and freedom of the individual. Hegel, as we have seen, assigns much more importance to the diversity of the world than does Śaṅkara, but it is not sufficient for true individualizing significance. For Hegel, individuality is after all of little value. The importance of the thinker is apt to be swallowed up in that of the thought, and 'our minds are no better than shifting heaps of percepts, principles and syllogisms'.[2] Therefore it matters little what becomes of us so long as our thought persists; and the suggestion is not far away that even the desire to continue otherwise than in the immortality of our thought is a sign that we have reached only a comparatively low philosophical level. To such an attitude Hegel was led by the course which his reasoning has taken. As has been so clearly pointed out by Prof. Pringle-Pattison, the system

[1] Macintosh, *op. cit.* 14. [2] Ib. 180.

starts with the Kantian synthetic unity of apperception, with the idea of consciousness as such, set over against the manifold of perception. The next step is to turn this unity into a metaphysical principle by universalizing it and identifying it with the divine self-consciousness. As Prof. Haldane puts it, there is in Hegel's system 'potential identity of man and God in a single subject of knowledge'.[1] This means that all that is left on the human side is the manifold and shifting content of perception; and from such a position the transition is easy to regarding the human consciousness with all its variety of experience as a mere thought of the divine thinker. Or we may put it more generally and say that the universe tends, in Prof. Pringle-Pattison's phrase, 'to shrink together into a logical process of which individuals are merely the foci'.[2] The individual is sacrificed to the universal, and, instead of hoping for personal immortality, has to be content with his persistence as a thought in the mind of God: he becomes, according to Lotze, a mere 'selfless state of the creator'. And as on this line of thought coalescence with the object known is regarded as the ideal of knowledge, so this idea of coalescence is applied to existences also. Identity expressed in association with the thought of absorption, however unsatisfying religiously this may be, comes to be conceived as the highest relationship between the soul and God; and the conclusions of Hegel in this respect may very well be placed alongside those of the Vedānta. In both systems it has been shown that, so long as we occupy a purely intellectual point of view, so long is it impossible to provide adequately for human personality or to find a fully satisfactory basis for the religious relationship. All that Hegel can say in reference to this is that 'religion is the Divine Spirit's knowledge of itself through the mediation of finite spirit. . . . Religion is not a transaction of man, but is essentially the highest determination of the absolute idea itself.'[3]

We may trace the same tendency to sacrifice the individual in much of the later thought which is based upon Hegel—the thought which according to Mr. Bertrand Russell follows the

[1] *Pathway to Reality*, II. 169. [2] *Hegelianism and Personality*, 118.
[3] *Philosophy of Religion*, I. 206.

'classical tradition' and shows an inclination to make thought constitutive of reality instead of limiting it to the function of deciding between alternative possible interpretations of reality.[1] The result of the intellectualistic procedure in more recent philosophy also is that the thinker is of less importance than his thought, and the thought of the individual becomes a thought of the Absolute and the Universal. For Bosanquet the Absolute is the only true individual, and all so-called finite individuals are merely incomplete phases of the whole. He indeed indicates his approval of the idea that the main purpose of the universe is the 'making of souls', and he quite fully appreciates the doctrine that souls differ, not merely as separate numerical entities, but because of their diversity of content. In this he seems to take a step towards a recognition of the concrete individual, but on the other hand he neutralizes any tendency in this direction by the emphasis which he lays upon the *contents* of the individual consciousness. He regards the contents as of far more importance than the container, and he draws unwarrantable conclusions from the consideration that in all the great experiences of life, in all our sharing of institutional and custom-born social organization, in all our aspirations after a more ideal state of our own selves or of society, we inevitably transcend the individual. With the purest and most elevated souls, this constantly happens, and according to him it is what ought to happen in all cases. As if any assertion of finite individuality necessarily implied a selfish spirit, he speaks rather contemptuously of those who 'try to divide up the unity and tell how much comes from "you" and how much from "God"'.[2] The contents of our personality *ought* to merge in the universal; our progress consists in an ever-nearer approach to this goal, and it should be a matter of regret and of conscious failure if we do not merge altogether.

> Our destiny, our being's heart and home
> Is with infinitude, and only there.

Our aim is to be an 'element' in the Absolute; we should not claim even to be a 'member', lest the latter term should suggest too definitely a continuing individuality.

[1] Cf. Preface to Bertrand Russell's *Our Knowledge of the External World*.
[2] Cf. *What Religion Is*, 20.

Bradley also, while occasionally accommodating himself to the demands of ordinary experience, and admitting the criterion that 'a result, if it fails to satisfy our whole nature, comes short of perfection', and that 'if metaphysics is to stand, it must take account of all sides of our being',[1] yet shows, on the whole, a definite inclination to sacrifice the individual. 'Incompleteness, unrest and unsatisfied reality, are the lot of the finite. There is nothing which, to speak properly, is individual or perfect, except only the Absolute.'[2] 'The plurality of souls in the Absolute is, therefore, appearance and their existence is not genuine.'[3] And again, the same attitude is taken up as regards the goal of endeavour, 'The finite disappears in being accomplished.'[4]

He makes great use of the idea that the attainments of the individual are merely adjectival in relation to the Absolute, and thus seems almost content with the implication that the individual is nothing but a bundle of qualities. These are temporarily conjoined in him, but do not belong to him, as it were, in his own right. They are merely held in trust for the Absolute, and, when the trust is fulfilled, the individual will surrender the qualities altogether for attachment to the Absolute. This will be his contribution, and in making this contribution the individual will fulfil his destiny. In such a position, however, there seems to lurk a contradiction. If the contribution is merely of qualities, these qualities, merely as such, might be supposed to be already possessed by the Absolute and therefore cannot be contributed. The idea of contribution has meaning, only if the individual can give also himself, in whom the qualities can have that independence which alone can constitute them a gift in any proper sense of the term; for one cannot give as a gift that which is already possessed by him to whom it is given. This difficulty, however, does not deter Bradley from reaching the conclusion that the true destiny of souls is absorption or transmutation into the Absolute.

It is easy to see how such an attitude will empty the region of moral endeavour of much of its meaning. If there is no distinction between us and the Absolute, and if, in respect of the Absolute, Bradley can say, 'Nothing perfect, nothing genuinely real, can move; the Absolute has no seasons, but all at once

[1] *Appearance and Reality*, 148. [2] Ib. 246. [3] Ib. 305. [4] Ib. 419.

bears its leaves, fruits and blossoms',[1] then the heart is taken out of the ethical struggle. In an earlier passage Bradley animadverts upon the divorce between religion and morality with a view to showing that neither morality nor religion can be ultimate. He tells us that 'if, flying from the discord, religion keeps its thoughts fixed upon harmony it tends to suffer once more. . . . The truth that devotion even to a finite object may lift us above moral laws, seduces religion into false and immoral perversions. Because for it all reality is, in one sense, good alike, every action may become completely indifferent. It idly dreams its life away in the quiet world of divine inanity, or, forced into action by chance desire, it may hallow every practice, however corrupt, by its empty spirit of devotion.'[2] The curious thing is that Bradley does not seem to see that the same consequences as are indicated in the last sentence may follow from his own position. If we are at best engrossing ourselves with a play of appearances, our final view of consummation will leave us without energy for the arduous stages of the process towards that consummation. As in the Vedānta, so with Bradley, the ethical level is found to be transcended, and goodness must be regarded as 'a subordinate, and, therefore, a self-contradictory aspect of the universe'.[3] If everything is already accomplished, or if nothing that is accomplished has any prospect of continuance, the life of the individual and of humanity is emptied of meaning, and, as we shall see, little place is left for any truly religious relationship. Very naturally did the almost pitiless intellectualism of Bosanquet and Bradley lead to a reaction in the direction of pluralism. But it does not seem necessary to pass in such extreme fashion from absorbing unity to inorganic particularity, and our concluding chapter will be occupied with an attempt to show that, while there are dangers associated with the ideal offered to us by the Vedānta system and philosophies broadly similar to it, it is possible also to conserve the religious value enshrined in the ideal and, perhaps, by certain modifications to enhance it.

Hitherto we have been trying to trace the main tendencies of the Vedānta as these are reflected in its attitude to authority and within the scope of the doctrines of the two orders of

[1] *Appearance and Reality*, 500. [2] *Op. cit.* 444. [3] Ib. 420.

knowledge, the notion of God both unqualified and qualified, the validity of external experience, and the place of the individual both in this life and that which is to come. We have found that the inclination of speculation has been strongly in a monistic direction and that it has been associated with a predominantly intellectualistic point of view. We have seen that the same tendency is strongly marked in the philosophies of Spinoza, Hegel, Bradley, and Bosanquet, &c., and that the most striking resultant might be described as, in general, a merging of the part in the whole, a sacrifice of the Many to the One, and of the individual to the Universal. Our study of parallels between the Vedānta and other allied modes of thought has compelled us to recognize the principle of identity as their fundamental conception. We are thus brought round once more to the point at which we left our main argument at the close of last chapter. There we found that the Vedantic basis for ethics which this principle affords, was decidedly insecure, and we have reached practically the same conclusion as regards the Hegelian school of thought.

The underlying idea that the relationship between us and God is one of identity may indeed diminish the distance which seems to separate us from God and may deliver us from that coldness in our subjective attitude which a more external relationship might induce. Yet we have also become aware of undesirable consequence of various sorts. The finite has been absorbed in the Infinite, and a sufficient basis has not been left on which our individual personality may become effective. Intellectualism may save us from the bondage of the sense world and ordinary desires, but it also presents a strong similarity to naturalism, in that, equally with the latter, it leaves us under the sway of determinism. It provides no sphere for the free creative activity of the spirit, and, if our experience is one with the experience of God, we come under the control of laws of thought which are not so much principles of our own action as superior determinations of that action, inasmuch as they are laws of the universal. The importance of the generalized point of view turns our attention away from the particular and thus tends to rob us of the vitalizing effect of action in reference to the particular. The result is a dream-like attitude to life, along with that sense of futility which attaches to dreams and the consequent evaporation of ideals. The ethical life is thus robbed of the necessary energy for dealing with it, and because this life belongs essentially to the sphere of duality, we are required altogether to pass beyond it in reaching the goal of identity. The distinction between good and evil ceases to be the most urgent of contrasts, and presents itself not so much as a stimulus to effort as an opportunity for acquiescence. For, if we are one with God, and if in our search for universal concepts we have risen above the movement of time and yet in our practical life have still got to live under the conditions of time, we are apt to satisfy our desire for eternity or timelessness by arresting definitively the movement of time and crystallizing the momentary into the permanent. But when experience is thus theoretically conceptualized and practically made static, the ideas of further possibilities and progress are apt to disappear from it. We find ourselves confined to the charmed circle of the actual, occupied with perpetual analysis and re-analysis of given conditions and relations, and powerless to move forward to projects of reformation. And from out the far distance there comes to us a vision which further robs our ideals of their effectiveness, for if we are one with God we are also complete in Him. Despite the warnings against ethical sluggishness which the moral intensity of certain writers on Vedantism compels them to emphasize, we yet cannot altogether escape from the conception that perfection on such presuppositions is not something to be attained in the long run, but something which we already possess. Almost inevitably the question arises in our minds as to why, if we have annihilated the temporal distance between ourselves and the goal, we should any longer submit to the exhausting conditions of the race.

But enough was said in our last chapter in reference to this point, and we are now left with the final question whether the same insecurity which we have discovered in respect of ethics will attach also to the only religious relationship for which the identity conception seems to leave room. We may focus our thoughts on the value of the identity principle by asking whether the relationship which emerges from it is sufficient for the purposes of religion, for, after all, the degree of religious satisfactoriness ought to furnish a supreme criterion of any system. This problem will occupy us in our concluding chapter.

IX

THE RELIGIOUS VALUE OF THE VEDĀNTA, AND SOME CONCLUSIONS

IT is probable that the applicability of such a criterion as we have just proposed, viz. the test of religious satisfactoriness, will be at once disputed, either on the ground that any test at all is superfluous or that this particular test is illegitimate and misleading. Those who assign the first reason for objection argue that the identity relationship is inevitable, and that therefore it is useless to discuss whether it is adequate or not. Such a relation is said to be the ultimate position to which we must come when we fully analyse the conditions of knowledge, and is a necessary deduction from the fundamental assumption of idealism. If an object is known only through thought, then the object itself is thought, and, when we are constrained to deal with thought alone, the identification of subject and object, and on broader lines, of the finite and the infinite, is the only form which our ideal of completed knowledge can take. The relation of subject and object, it is said, is that with which we start, and development will consist in overcoming the 'otherness', by means of the expansion or deeper knowledge of the subject. The western mind, which is inclined to idealism, will probably think more of expansion and the eastern of deepening, but the result in both cases is the same, and the ideal ought to be the same, viz. the identification of the subject and the object, and the entire removal of duality. As an Indian writer says: 'One of the universally admitted maxims of Hindu philosophy is that the mind assumes the form of what it perceives, and, therefore, necessarily becomes what it perceives.'[1] To know a thing is to become that thing, and, universally, to think properly of, or to know, the Infinite is to become the Infinite. Our aspiration in knowledge and in every spiritual activity is to

Close with all we loved
And all we flow from, soul in soul.

True knowledge places us on a level with God, or, rather, makes us one with God. It is an ideal of knowledge which in western

[1] R. C. Bose, *Hindu Philosophy*, 169.

philosophy has come down from Aristotle, who holds that the only activity which can appropriately be ascribed to the Divine Being is the activity of the thinking mind, and that the characteristic of such thought is that 'it becomes its object in the act of comprehending it'. For Spinoza the knowledge wherewith we know God is also the knowledge wherewith God knows himself, and the fundamental principle of Hegel is that in the highest thought we reach potential identity with God. We come across the same principle in the *Muṇḍaka Upanishad* III. 2. 9, 'He who knows Brahman, becomes Brahman', and that such an ideal underlies the Vedantic conception of *tat tvam asi* is so obvious as to need no further comment.

It is therefore asked why, in view of all this, we should take the trouble to apply the criterion of religious satisfaction which we have suggested. If we are faithfully to analyse the conditions of knowledge in their highest exercise, it is urged that no other relationship is possible except the relationship of identity, and that if this is not religiously satisfying, so much the worse for us. We have got to accept the inevitability of the facts of the case.

In answer to this contention we may say simply that the epistemological assumption does not seem to us to be valid. We shall return to this point a few pages later, but in the meantime we may consider the position of those who object to the test of religious sufficiency on the ground that such a test is illegitimate and misleading. The reason which they give is that, even if we admit that a test may be applied, it is philosophy which must supply the test and not religion. Religion is definitely on a lower level than philosophy; it is a stage through which the philosopher must pass, and failure to satisfy the needs of the lower is to be welcomed rather than deplored, inasmuch as unsatisfied need is a spur to the requisite progress from the lower to the higher.

There are many instances in Vedantic teaching, and in Indian thought generally, of this depreciation of religion in favour of philosophy. Prof. Radhakrishnan thinks that if we try to remain at the religious level we shall be involved in an inextricable dilemma. Personality is essential to the religious relationship of worship, but yet personality is a limitation of the perfection of the Absolute. Thus we are compelled to say that 'if God is perfect, religion is impossible. If God is imperfect, religion is ineffective', the reason of the ineffectiveness being that 'we cannot have with a finite limited God the joy and peace, the assurance of victory and the confidence in the ultimate destiny of the universe'.[1] Prof. Radhakrishnan's regret is noteworthy, as it implies an ideal of an effective religion which would seem to be indispensable for a completed attitude to the universe, but yet on the whole he extricates himself from the dilemma by holding that religion must be transcended. 'The end of religion', he says, 'is the transcendence of religion,' and again, 'Religious worship has to be accepted *until* the perfect condition is reached.'[2] The main theme of an earlier work of his is to show that philosophical 'deviations from the "high road" of absolutism are all due to the "reign of religion in philosophy" '.[3] It is true that later in the same book he says that 'true religion and true philosophy will agree',[4] but his vote would be in favour of a religion turned philosophy rather than in favour of a philosophy turned religion, and the reason of this would seem to be that a proper regard for the identity relation and for the consideration that, in order to know God, we must be God, does not admit of what is usually regarded as the religious attitude. Kirtikar is still more uncompromising as to the desirability of the dominance of philosophy over religion. Although he also leaves room for the ultimate identification of religion and philosophy, he is emphatic in his disregard of the ordinary religious consciousness. 'Ethics, morality and religious life', he says, 'admittedly belong to the sphere of relativity—to the world of the One and the Many,' though they may be 'as much necessary to the development and spiritual progress of man as the initial stages in the development of a child are to his attaining manhood'. And he asks rather indignantly, 'Is philosophic truth to be sacrificed lest its recognition might . . . shake the very foundations of religion?'[5]

[1] Radhakrishnan, I. 97.

[2] Ib. 235; italics mine. There seems to be a modification of this view in his book on *The Hindu View of Life*, which has just appeared, and in which he apparently suggests that religion has to do with a reality beyond all differences and is therefore ultimate.

[3] Cf. *The Reign of Religion in Contemporary Philosophy*, Chapter VII.

[4] Ib. 22.

[5] Kirtikar, 106 and 107.

It is obvious that, according to views of this kind, religion is given a place at all only on condition that it should be philosophically transformed, and should thus cease to be what we ordinarily regard as religious. The result will be of an exceedingly refined character, and of such a religion only a few chosen souls of a philosophical cast of mind will be capable, whilst the bulk of humanity by the very nature of the case will be excluded. Now it is noteworthy that this depreciation of the demands of religion takes place in connexion with adherence to the monistic Vedantic ideal of identity. We thus have an implicit admission that the conception does not satisfy ordinary religious requirements; and, even though the additional suggestion be made that it does not matter very much whether the test succeeds or not, the admission of failure remains significant.

But we may ask, Is it so immaterial that religious demands should remain unsatisfied by a conception taken to be metaphysically fundamental? Despite the slightness of emphasis on this consideration which would seem to be indicated by the quotations just made, it would be a mistake to suppose that the Vedantists themselves are, in general, regardless of what they consider to be religious needs. We have seen how it was possible to say that no people on earth took religion so seriously as did the people of India.[1] The whole attitude of the Vedānta might be described as an attempt to do the work of religion, even though it be by means of a philosophy. Śaṅkara has been described as 'a great philosopher who fully grasped the necessity of religion to the world',[2] and this by a writer who contends that the Vedānta was intended to be only a philosophy and not a religion. We have noticed both in Prof. Radhakrishnan and in Kirtikar a strong desire to identify religion and philosophy, which shows that, provided religion is kept in a proper relation to philosophy, they by no means wish that the religious test should be altogether abandoned. The former encourages himself with the consideration that 'the monistic conception is

[1] Cf. Deussen, *S. V.* 49; cf. also Heiler, *Sunder Singh*, p. 211: 'India has been for centuries the land of religion. As hardly amongst any other people of the earth there is amongst the people of India a wonderfully strong sense of the transcendental world and an earnest desire to sacrifice everything to this supersensible world.'

[2] Worsley, *Concepts of Monism*, 90.

also capable of developing the highest religious spirit';[1] and the latter admits the principle that 'the richness of an abstract conception depends upon its efficacy in awakening the religious consciousness in man'.[2] They would seem to be in almost complete agreement with the dictum of Hegel that 'philosophy only unfolds itself when it unfolds religion and in unfolding itself, it unfolds religion'.

Why then are they in such difficulties? Why have they either to depreciate religion as a test, or, if they admit it, why have they to distinguish so carefully between religion in general and philosophical religion, even while it has to be admitted almost despairingly that such a philosophical religion cannot be 'for the bulk of humanity but only for the chosen few'?[3] Is it not because there is something essentially antagonistic between the identity principle which they cherish and the religious consciousness in general? They seem to be faced with the alternative either of giving up the religious attitude, except in a very attenuated and almost purely philosophical form, or of giving up the principle. The reluctance of these very philosophers themselves to accept the first alternative encourages us to refuse the admission that the religious test is either illegitimate or misleading. We do not consider that the objections to the test are sufficiently convincing to lead to its abandonment. Religious value must be considered and not merely philosophical or religio-philosophical value. We are therefore back again at our central problem, as to whether the principle of identity offers such satisfaction to the human spirit in its highest development as to make it worthy of retention.

Now it would be unfair to deny in any uncompromising way the religious value of the identity concept. It is indeed, as we have seen, reached through negation, both theoretical and practical, and through abstraction. But negation is, after all, the expression of a consciousness which is at the bottom of all religion, a refusal to indulge in a superficial optimism, and a recognition of the truth that 'strait is the gate, and narrow is the way, which leadeth unto life'. And, on the other hand and more positively, identity is often regarded as the speculative basis of

[1] Radhakrishnan, I. 98. [2] Kirtikar, 24.
[3] Worsley, *op. cit.* 168.

that mystical consciousness which must be an element in every true form of religion.

It is undoubtedly true that religion emerges from a mood of 'divine discontent' and is the indication of an insatiable quest. Whenever the religious consciousness becomes vividly and intensely awake, the soul is always inclined to say, 'It is not here, it is not here—that which I seek'; and, in contrast to the urgency of the aspiration and the importance of its objective, the world of the actual is apt to assume a dream-like and illusive character. The Vedānta in its negations expresses very nearly the mood described by Wordsworth, when

> The gross and visible frame of things
> Relinquishes its hold upon the sense,
> Yea almost on the mind itself, and seems
> All unsubstantialized.

The intensity of religious devotion expresses itself in a singleness of aim which is intolerant of the variety of ordinary experience, and conscious only of the inadequacy of that experience to reveal the ultimate Unity towards which the quest is so earnestly directed. If in such a mood the multiplicity of ordinary experience engenders a sense of confusion, perplexity, and mystery, it is perhaps natural that a solution of the problems should be sought, not in further examination of the ordinary, but in turning away from it, and assigning the mystery—now become a source of attraction—to a detached Ultimate Being, in contact with whom, and in intuitive apprehension of whose nature, we may find that peace which the world cannot give—as we reach

> that blessed mood,
> In which the burthen of the mystery,
> In which the heavy and the weary weight
> Of all this unintelligible world,
> Is lightened.[1]

Perhaps occasionally it is true that the mood we have sought to suggest indicates that less worthy mental condition of lassitude or weariness of spirit which has moved a writer in *Das Licht vom Osten* to exclaim, 'How tired must the Indian spirit have been of all Being, that no other deliverance was discovered by

[1] Wordsworth, *Tintern Abbey*.

him.'[1] It is necessary, as we shall see, that we should obtain some means of distinguishing between lower and higher mystical moods, but on the whole we should prefer to derive the prevailing mood not from lassitude but from a sense of the unreality of time, from a consciousness that we are passing beyond both spatial and temporal limitations, and that the permanence or eternity which we long for in religion is not some abode of bliss which we reach after the struggle of untold years, but something in which we may participate even here and now, just in so far as we realize the insignificance of the spatial and the temporal, and

feed this mind of ours
In a wise passiveness.[2]

That it is not *mere* lassitude is shown by its association with the more volitional idea of self-denial. The Upanishads describe him who knows as him 'who has no desires', and it is felt intensely that the way to religious attainment lies through sacrifice and the emptying of self. We must 'noughten all else' that would keep us from God, in the spirit which T. E. Brown suggests in the following lines.

But thou art all replete with very 'thou'
And hast such shrewd activity
That when He comes, He says, 'This is enow
Unto itself, 'tis better let it be:
It is so small and full,
There is no room for Me.'

But the identity concept has value, not only in respect of the negations through which it is reached, but in regard also to the consummation which it indicates. It expresses undoubtedly an abhorrence of externality in religion. In these days we are somewhat weary of the idea of a God set at a distance from the world and from ourselves. A deistic God is alien to our thoughts, and we demand that God should be conceived as in the world and especially as in us. It is felt that religion must be subjective or it is nothing at all. It must be *ours*, our own attitude. If God is to mean anything for us, He must be brought from outside of us to the very inside, as it were, of our heart. And here the Vedantic formula, *tat tvam asi*, with its emphasis upon community of nature between the human and the divine, would

[1] *Op. cit.* 92. [2] Wordsworth, *Expostulation and Reply.*

seem to promise satisfaction for our aspirations. It strengthens both our refusal to allow any longer that we are separate, self-centred, independent beings, and our claim that divinity is within us or that we are within the divine. God is all in all, and we are absorbed in the All—there is no longer any difference to disturb our religious contentment. 'From death to death goes he who sees plurality anywhere,' and we are encouraged to add that from life to life goes he who has abolished plurality and overthrown this mosaic wall of separation. It has been said that 'in middle life God becomes far less an object than an atmosphere'; but such an experience surely may belong to all stages in the development of the soul.

Thus we may freely admit the beauty and attractiveness of this religious conception of identity. It seems to represent the consummation of our religious yearning; and, even though we may be constrained to point out that it tends to embody the emotional resultant of normal religious relationship rather than to describe the religious relation itself, and that it throws into permanent metaphysical form what is a momentary, though oft-repeated, subjective and emotional experience, yet it cannot be denied that, for some minds, the identity relation with its mystical possibilities supports the intensest form of religion. And it may be said again that it is not by any means only the result of spiritual lassitude or even of exhaustion, but represents rather a positive and active spiritual awareness, 'the rest of infinite unrest', as it has been called, an experience which is real, however wrongly conceived it may be through the influence of the particular thought-form under which it is subsumed. Even if it were on the whole more passive than we are willing to admit, it still, as Prof. Paterson says, 'remains a possibility that the God who giveth his beloved in sleep, could make some gifts in the Yoga-trance to those who sought Him therein with a pure and sincere heart'.[1] Perhaps also as Max Müller puts it, 'if it is true that "those also serve who only stand and wait", then we may hope that even the quiet in the land are not so entirely useless as they appear to be'.[2] And surely even the most actively inclined religionist would hardly venture to evacuate of all meaning the classic description, so Vedantic in spirit, which

[1] *The Nature of Religion*, 187.

[2] Müller, *S. S.* 193.

Plotinus gives of mystical attainment: 'It is a state in which you are your finite self no longer—in which the Divine essence is communicated to you. It is the liberation of your mind from its finite anxieties. Like only can comprehend like. When you cease to be finite, you become one with the Infinite. In the reduction of your soul to its simplest self, its Divine essence, you realize this Union, nay, this Identity.'[1]

Yet we still wonder whether this identity relation, despite all its beauty and spiritual satisfyingness, adequately represents the true conditions of spiritual communion and attainment. Something fuller seems to be demanded. We cannot be altogether content, e.g., with such a phrase as 'the reduction of your soul to its simplest self'. In such a phrase—which is typical—there seems to lurk a certain suggestion of abnormality, of negation beyond what is essentially necessary, and of too purely intellectual abstraction. We may ask whether in realizing and taking precautions against these dangers we may not reach a more adequate and more religiously valuable statement of the relation between ourselves and God.

We have seen that the negation through which the identity is reached is to a certain extent commendable and necessary; but, if it is pressed too far, the accompanying advantages seem to be lost. Often it appears as if so much stress were laid upon the negation and abstractness of the means that they have infected with their emptiness the end which it is sought to attain. We have already referred frequently to this negative process as applied to the external world, and we are now more immediately concerned with it as it affects the relation between the self and God. We discover a tendency to reduce both sides of the relationship to their lowest terms, and thus to reach an identity of zeros so far as determinate qualities go. As regards anything more, we are left only with the affirmation of an indescribable experience, the product of an intuition alleged to be above the level of the intellect. It is by no means impossible to believe in the truth of such an experience, but we fail to see the necessity for such profound silence regarding its character, and it would be more satisfactory if it could be established, not in separation

[1] Quoted in Kirtikar, 170.

from or in opposition to ordinary experience, but in organic connexion with it. Unless such an organic connexion can be shown, we cannot conceive of the identity relation being able to afford such a permanent basis as is necessary for religion.

Denial must never be merely for the sake of denial; it must always have reference to a positive. It has its proper place only when something supremely valuable is apprehended in comparison with which everything else is of lesser value or negligible, when there is discovered, as it has been put, 'a reality so intense, so encompassing, so absorbing that beside it all other existences grow dim and at length fade into nothingness and illusion'.[1] But when the mind, as in excessive mysticism or asceticism, falls in love with denial for its own sake, and, faced with the difficulties of the actual, attempts to meet these only by way of negation; and, moreover, continues the same procedure with regard to the soul itself, the result cannot be satisfactory. When thought, devoted to abstract procedure, sets out upon its search for the 'mythical Absolute', for some unknowable substance hidden behind the qualities of the world, or some mysterious soul lurking beneath all the processes of the mind, and when, failing in the quest, it is disposed to deny the reality of all the products of its exploring experiences, it may reach the conception of identity between that *which has not been found* in either direction of the search. But a result which is so closely and consciously associated with scepticism is hardly likely to perform adequately the function of removing scepticism, and yet this is surely one of the functions we naturally assign to religion—we expect it to give us at least some rock to which we may cling in the midst of our sea of doubt. It is significant in connexion with this line of thought that Sriharsa, a commentator of the Vedantic school who flourished about the end of the twelfth century, after dwelling constantly upon the contradictory character of appearances and the untrustworthiness of our faculties, reached a doctrine of Real Being which could be distinguished only with difficulty from a doctrine of the void.

Now all healthy philosophy must begin with a certain amount of scepticism, and we must not try to minimize the difficulties of gaining a knowledge of the soul. As Oscar Wilde says: 'To

[1] *Hibbert Journal*, art. 'Centripetal Realism', Oct. 1926.

recognize that the soul of a man is unknowable, is the ultimate achievement of wisdom. The final mystery is oneself. When one has weighed the sun in the balance and mapped out the seven heavens, star by star, there still remains oneself.'[1] And Bradley teaches over and over again that the 'subject in the end must be felt and it can never be perceived'.[2] The self is so deeply ourselves that one can hardly sound its depths. All this is true; but we exaggerate the difficulties if we persistently distrust our faculties, if we make, as it were, a cult of scepticism and by way of it hope to reach unity with real Being. Such procedure savours of abnormality and will be followed by some kind of retributory reaction. If we have found only vanity and illusion in the world, we have accustomed ourselves to the darkness, and one may come to expect that the self will be enveloped in the same darkness, in which we shall have to be content with blurred outlines and vague indeterminate forms of being. Or, to change the metaphor, we may make 'a desert of the soul and call it peace'.[3]

In this darkness or desert, this vagueness and indeterminateness, there lie great dangers for the soul filled with a haunting sense of emptiness. It may be tempted to the repose of death rather than of life. If such a result seems to follow from the depreciation of our faculties, which again is the consequence of disillusionment, then, as hinted above, the result may be desired, not out of a grim determination to reach truth, but simply from lassitude of spirit. As Prof. Paterson again says: 'Repose may be the index of very different types of character, and the by-product of very different activities. It may be akin either to the peace of the saint or the sage, or to the placidity of the cow or the slumber of the tired horse. The pursuit of rest may be every whit as selfish as, and may entail even more injury to others than, the pursuit of wealth, and may have its roots in sheer indolence and cowardice.'[4]

Now in commenting upon the attractiveness of the identity ideal we have already indicated, as emphatically as possible, that it may correspond to the subjective 'peace of the saint', but the danger is that the abstractness of the result will not rule out

[1] *De Profundis*. [2] *Appearance and Reality*, 108.
[3] Cf. Prof. Paterson, *The Nature of Religion*, 205. [4] Ib. 205.

lower motives with sufficient strictness. If the result of the operation of both higher and lower motives is a featureless identity, we cannot from the result derive a criterion which will enable us to decide which type of motive has been operative. But this is unfortunate, and surely it is legitimate to demand that the result should have such positive character as will show it to be the outcome only of pure and elevated religious concentration. We must be able to distinguish between the destinies of the saint and the sluggard, and yet, in reference to an ideal which is largely described by negations, it is difficult to secure such differentiation. Thought that is abstract is always poor, and the poverty of our thought about the Absolute may make it impossible for us to refute the cynical reflection that unity with such an Absolute means that one lot happens to saint and slothful sinner alike.

The course of our whole discussion has revealed a closely allied danger, also showing the religious inadequacy of the identity ideal. It encourages, not explicitly but implicitly, the use of lower categories. As Jeroboam, king of Israel, 'made of the lowest of the people priests of the *high* places', so do we make use of the lowest of our thoughts when we enter the shrine of the mysterious indescribable Reality of all things. The identity conception may seem to express the highest spiritual attainment of the soul, but the terms which it uses for expression are often based merely on physical analogies. A similar defect of course attaches to all use of language to express spiritual experiences, but the influence of the physical analogy seems to cling to the key-words of identity religion with more than average closeness. 'Absorption', e.g., retains more of physical than of psychical association, and suggests something like the 'plop' of a raindrop in a pool of water. Bergson has drawn attention to this tendency of the intellect in abstract procedure, and has argued that the inadequacy of abstraction can be shown by the fact that the results of abstraction can be expressed only through spatial metaphors. What is psychical and vital cannot be reached by abstraction; but yet, as we make the attempt and think away one concrete determination after another, we come inevitably to the idea of illimitable spaces, filled only with emptiness, and are left with the feeling of our own loneliness and helplessness and insignificance—we count for as little as a wave of the vast ocean or a speck of sand in the far-stretching desert. Even as we struggle upwards in our thought, we find it difficult to get away from the dominance of the physical. We may think of filled space rather than empty space, but the result is only the unsatisfactory conception of God and ourselves as forming 'one block' so to speak. Even biological categories yield only the idea of God as a vital principle, and ourselves as physically participating in his life. The point is that, if we insist on negation and depreciation of personality, we become prisoners of the lower categories of our thought, and these react so as to increase the depreciation and prevent fullness of relationship between us and God. We come to think ultimately in terms of material atoms and physical forces. Our relation to the universe is interpreted almost entirely in a quantitative manner. Not in our higher endowments of human character and personality do we realize our closeness to the divine, but rather in those of our faculties which are nearest to unconsciousness and our physical nature. No room is left for the uniqueness or the freedom of personality. We are swallowed up in God, and when we inquire who *we* are, no answer comes from out the silences of the boundless spaces.

We are thus left without guidance, and into the emptiness, into the house of the intellect thus swept and garnished, undesirable guests may enter. If our fundamental belief presents us with no deterring positive characters, we are at the mercy of arbitrary authority, superstition, and even of our own capricious invention. We have no criterion by which we may try the spirits and see whether they be of God. From our distrust of our faculties we draw also the conclusion that if *nothing* matters in the sense that nothing is reliable, *anything* may matter and be allowed to become dominant. Distrust of our faculties may produce a permanent and disconcerting mood of scepticism in which we despair of arriving at any universal standard. If a man is told that the deepest reality is without character and reached only through cohesion between the human and the divine in a featureless blank, or if he is told that in any case a satisfactory apprehension of it is impossible, then, seeing that he cannot exist in a mental and spiritual vacuum, he is apt to embrace any theory or any object of devotion which lies to hand without scrutinizing it too closely. When the intellectual activity abandons its task through lack of content with which it may deal, or for sceptical reasons, it is apt to give way before an anti-intellectualistic reaction, and the house of the soul may be filled with phantoms and extravagant products of unrestrained construction.[1]

The further steps may be left to the influence of custom. The mere habit of keeping a theory loosely in the mind tends to engender a certain liking for it. He who entertains it becomes loath to part with it, and the bigotry of superstition finds its opportunity. The pendulum swings over very easily, if not always in the same individual, at least in the same society, from agnosticism to credulity; and the transit has frequently been observed in the land where the philosophy of abstract identity is most naturalized. Bradley speaks of finding vanity and illusion in a world which is self-less and of then returning 'to one's self into congenial darkness and the equivocal consolation of some psychological monster'.[2] Sometimes, however, the consoling—and also terrifying—monsters may not be merely psychological hypostases, but exceedingly realistic projections of the imagination which acquire a fictitious objectivity through the association of communal and traditional beliefs. Yet they do not satisfy with any permanent satisfaction even those who cherish them, for as has been said: 'No religion can permanently take refuge in the glamour of vagueness and fluidity of conception and uncorrelated elements.'[3]

Further, as we have had occasion to point out in connexion with our discussion of the ethical effects of the Vedānta, the identity conception may occasionally produce a mood approaching to subjective complacency or even conceit. Emphasis may be laid upon ourselves rather than upon God; we may take upon ourselves the burden of the universal consciousness, and seeing that this latter has been left destitute of content, it affords no defence against individual caprice. The individual may invest himself with the authority of the universal, and, intellectually

[1] Cf. the present writer's *Pantheism and the Value of Life*, 299 ff.
[2] *Appearance and Reality*, 120.
[3] Angus, *The Mystery Religions and Christianity*, 263.

and religiously, may do that which is right in his own eyes. An opportunity is thus afforded for that arbitrary perversion of the prophetic consciousness whereby a man claims specific illumination and absolute authority for his own views and practices, and, in short, becomes a law unto himself in the realm of metaphysics and religion, like the 'stateless man' of Aristotle's political conception. What Clutton Brock says of the ascetic is also true in a measure of such men. They 'are the worst egoists of all, thinking about nothing but their own souls, which means their own selves, living a life of inner conquest and adventure, which is all *artificial*.[1] Their interest, because they refuse it to external reality, is the more intensely concentrated on themselves; their very God to whom they incessantly pray, is but an idol made and set up within the temple of the self, and has no likeness to the real God, if there be one.'[2] But surely, as another writer says: 'The great individual is not the man who grows up in nearest approach to isolation; whoever does this will remain the nearest approach to a perfect idiot. The great individual is the man who is reacting to the greatest number of elements in Reality, the greatest variety of its aspects.'[3]

This brings us to the further consideration that identity which relies mainly upon negation is open to the charge of abnormality. We must apply this criticism with the greatest care. We must not take ourselves too seriously and regard ourselves as the type of the normal. But by normal we may be allowed to mean that which takes account of all aspects of experience, allows the fact of existence at least to create a presumption in favour of the continuance of that existence, and regards it as a justifiable assumption that the faculties we possess are meant to be used in an harmonious and systematic way, demanding that no one of them should be elevated at the expense of the rest. Normally we aim at the widest possible grasp of experience, and, if a negative movement in our thought seems necessary, we ask that it should be supplemented by a positive. As Prof. B. K. Shastri says, the truly religious man 'pleads for a simple natural course of religion in every department of life, action, thought and emotion. . . . The ideal, the rational ideal, will first

[1] Italics mine. [2] *Essay on Religion*, 86.

[3] Bishop Temple, *Christus Veritas*, 55.

spiritualize, will first rationalize, the whole scheme of life, the so-called material and the non-material, and will, as a corollary to the truth thus established, vitalize and vivify the whole. . . . To work for human life, is to work for the whole world of life.'[1]

Now we do not think that the religious relationship we have been considering is able to satisfy this test. The element of agnosticism which is associated with it seems to be in conflict with the normal demands of the religious nature. It puts a man out of touch with the universe in which he lives, and denies him an object whom he may invest with beauty and goodness, and thus worship and serve. And denial of the world leads to a denial of God or at least to the assertion of a merely characterless God, altogether unsatisfying. One abnormality leads to another. As Dr. Tagore suggests: 'Flight from the world is flight from God. Flight from the world means an abrupt separation of the creature from the Creator.'[2] The abnormality shows itself also in detachment of the individual from his society. It encourages him in the thought that the main object of his endeavour should be the salvation of his lonely soul. Within the soul, also, there is an abnormal elevation of the intellect over the other faculties, and this results in an abstract view of the self which empties it of all reality. In practice it leads to a non-evangelical indifference to the religious needs of the common people. When for religious purposes we rely entirely, or chiefly, upon the intellect, it must necessarily follow that the majority of men are excluded. A mediating view may of course be adopted, viz. that what does not satisfy the intellectual man may yet be good enough for the masses. But such a view cannot be permanently held without weakening the religion of the multitude, or, for the sake of its preservation, inducing hypocritical observance on the part of the intellectuals. It is curious how frequently a predominantly intellectual attitude has had associated with it a claim to a monopoly of divine truth and a jealous guarding of it from the intrusions of the vulgar. But such religious dualism is unfortunate whatever form it takes. Religious indifference which is born of intellectual superiority,

[1] B. K. Shastri, 214, 225, 248.
[2] Quoted in Heiler, *Christ and Indian Thought*, 29.

or an assumption of this, does violence to our deepest desires both for ourselves and others. Those who are outside of the privileged class must of necessity feel that they are for ever excluded from the highest state of religious blessedness, whereas the noblest of those who are inside the favoured group will be depressed at the thought that others cannot share the privileges which they themselves enjoy.[1]

But can we accept this abnormality of over-emphasis upon the intellect, with its indifference to evangelism, and the wider abnormality of which it forms a part, according to which it is assumed that ordinary experience is something to be got away from and that if we are to reach identity with God it will be by denial of the concrete wealth of our personality, by distrust or depression of the faculties which we possess, by deadening down or destruction of our desires, instead of by their sublimation? It seems impossible thus to reject the religious validity of our ordinary activities in their fullness. Religious salvation means essentially the attainment of the health of the soul, the expansion of the normal powers of the whole man. 'A free life', as Prof. B. K. Shastri puts it, 'ever seeks to be full in its freedom; free life and full life are indeed interchangeable terms.'[2] It is life and more life that we want, and not death, and our hearts will turn instinctively to such a Revealer as can proclaim that He came to give life and to give it more abundantly.

Thus we come by many ways to the conclusion that the identity relationship between man and God, while it contains within itself much attractiveness and beauty and power, and while it describes significantly and valuably the emotional resultant of the true religious attitude, yet, because it has to lay aside so much, cannot adequately embody the fundamental

[1] Prof. Wright has expressed himself vigorously on the relation between this attitude and religious adequacy. 'If a religion', he says, 'becomes the private possession of a highly cultivated class, and is inaccessible in its higher insights to the masses of men, it will be bound ultimately to fail. The masses are in the majority, and the purer faith of the esoteric few will in turn become corrupted by the baser notions of the many. Only through active service of the needs of all can a religion permanently be successful in maintaining itself. And a religion cannot endure in its higher forms if it idly regards the lower form of religion in the nation with complacent toleration and makes no honest missionary effort to enlighten all and bring them up to higher levels.' (*Philosophy of Religion*, 84.)

[2] B. K. Shastri, 226.

conditions of religious experience. It may turn out to be true that 'the soul of man has not one centre but two; his own eternal entity—and God'.[1]

Let us try to reduce the relationship to its simplest terms, and by analysis to discover its real nature. We prefer to proceed along the lines of the knowledge relationship, and also practical relationship, of subject and object. This seems to us indefeasible; we cannot get beyond it, and do not require to get beyond it, even for the sake of the fullest religious attainment. Just as in the simplest act of knowledge a subject implies an object and an object a subject, so must it be in religion. God is our religious Object, and will for ever remain such; and we hold that this relationship can satisfy our most intense religious aspirations, not by way of identity, indeed, but by way of communion.

Of course there are difficulties in the way of thinking of God as Object. We must beware of likening Him to the ordinary objects of sense, or of claiming that we can take up towards Him the same attitude of predominance or even of equality that we take up towards ordinary objects. But, on the other hand, a completed form of religion certainly does not demand either that the Subject should be fused with the Object or the Object with the Subject. However much *more* than a mere object God may be, and to whatever extent His reality may penetrate us or stretch beyond our comprehension, yet these considerations cannot destroy the distinction and yet connexion between us and Him which is involved in the subject-object relation. We must use our knowledge-giving faculties in a normal way; and in religion this means that we must regard God as an Object distinct from ourselves, however similar He may be to us in nature, and however many bonds of connexion, closer than any we have yet comprehended, remain to be discovered and appropriated by us.

Thus in laying emphasis upon the subject-object relation we do not at all contradict our admission, made a few pages back, that in true religion God cannot remain a mere external object. Further—and this is much more important—we are quite

[1] Cf. Hutton, *Francis Thompson*, 50.

aware that we shall be immediately confronted with the negative principle of Śaṅkara, that we cannot ascribe subjective qualities to the object or objective qualities to the subject; and also with the positive central principle of the identity between the self within and the self without. It will set our position therefore in clearer light if we try to discover the real truth which underlies these principles. Surely they need not carry with them the denial of the relationship of subject and object. Rather are they intended to negate any abruptness of contrast, any utterly disconcerting dualism. They emphasize rightly and impressively the spiritual kinship between us and God, and also between us and the world which God has made. The first principle has an effect dissolvent of differences, preventing us from setting the world over against us in permanent rigid outlines, from accepting it in its particular actuality, and so failing to reach its inner spiritual and friendly meaning, that meaning which proves its kinship with ourselves. In the same way it also prevents us from 'concretizing' and characterizing our own self with such definiteness as to encourage a distancing distinction between it and the universal Self. Thus the negative principle in its twofold application prepares the way for the identification which take place according to the positive central principle, *tat tvam asi*. Now, though the explicit aim of this cautioning and recommendation may be the assertion of identity between ourselves and the world-principle, all that is effectively done, and all that ought to be done, is the breaking down of barriers and the removal of the feeling of alienation. 'The saint's rest', as it has been said, 'comes not from the discovery of anything hitherto unsuspected in himself, but rather because he has found that his spiritual nature is not wandering in an inhospitable universe, but has a home, and that in God. The *rest* lay not in what he would be, but in what One already was—an actual present fact.'[1]

But this does not mean that we are called upon to deny the subject-object relation; it only means that we are encouraged to discover and realize that there is a unity between ourselves and the whole which is as overwhelmingly certain as the reality of our individual self, and that no strangeness, no foreignness, can

[1] Dunning, *God and The Absolute*.

continue to exist within that unity. We are asked to share with intensity in that sympathy which binds together the things of earth and the things of heaven, and also unites us with the rest of the universe which we inhabit. Religiously it ought to mean that the whole world is sacred for us, because it is the home of God, and it should suggest that we also are the temple of his spirit. But we do violence to the character of this intense consciousness of religious consummation when we compel it to constitute also the conditions under which it may arise, when we transform a feeling of closeness with the divine into an intellectual assertion of identity and thus press it into the service of a particular epistemological or metaphysical theory.

It is surely, e.g., an extreme to say that, because our knowledge cannot be complete until we reach the point of view of God, therefore complete knowledge involves the conclusion that God and we are one. God's perfect knowledge—which may be taken as our regulative, but infinitely transcendent ideal in the realm of knowledge—does not mean that God takes us up into identity with Himself, but only that the relations between Him and us are perfectly understood. Even when perfectly understood, they do not cease to be real relations involving distinguishable terms, and it does not follow that the two sides of the relation should fuse into one. Because God knows us perfectly, it does not follow that we are God. Moreover, we should be careful not to interpret our regulative ideal wrongly. Because the divine knowledge may be our ideal, this does not necessarily imply that perfect human knowledge must be exactly the same as perfect divine knowledge. Our knowledge may not be the knowledge wherewith God knows himself, but for all that it may be none the less valid. Even at its highest our completed knowledge is our own, not God's. Thus the presupposition from which we try to reach an assertion of identity along this line of thought is not particularly satisfactory even as a starting-point, and does not legitimately reach the conclusion intended. It is not possible to establish the position, as a deduction from the ideal requirements of knowledge, that, in order to know a thing, we must become that thing, or, in order to know God, we must become God. That 'dread point of Intercourse', however mysterious and unfathomable, in which the soul, tending upwards, 'holds, is upheld by God', is still intercourse, and not fusion.

When we are faithful to the subject-object relationship, we find, on a direct analysis of experience, that it is quite unnecessary and, indeed, impossible, to deny the reality of the subject or to merge that reality, irrecoverably, into a larger Reality. In fact it is just by descending into and affirming our own selves that we get our fundamental sense of reality. The Vedānta teaches this emphatically, but then goes on to assert that we know our own reality only as merging, or as merged, in the Universal Reality. It is this further step that we are unable to take; the self which gives us our hold upon reality is an indefeasible self. It is through the consciousness of our individual self that we are able to extricate ourselves from that dreamlike mood which is apt to creep over us when we first become aware of the puzzling and often disconcerting character of our experience. It is in the earnest quest of life which emerges in connexion with our self-activity that we establish a sense of true life, that we refuse to 'take a dream for a truth' and find that 'The world and life's too big to pass for a dream'.[1] Within our active experience we reach definiteness and concreteness which we cannot afterwards let go from us. As has been said, 'Only when we lose sight of this connexion of thought with action, can we suppose ourselves able to rest content with appearances as a substitute for what really is.'[2] And, invertedly, Kirtikar admits the truth of this principle when he says that 'until the sense of "I" has completely disappeared, man has no right to deny the reality of the universe',[3] which is equivalent to saying that, so long as the sense of 'I' remains, man cannot deny the reality of the universe. We can prove illusion only theoretically or on paper. In our activity we are brought into contact with a real world and become growingly conscious of its reality as we deal with its problems.

But this consciousness of the self, though indefeasible, is not isolating in its effects. As has been said: 'There is something within us . . . which may be said to come into being only at the approach of God. . . . The deep and solving idea is that the final

[1] Cf. Browning, *Statue and the Bust* and *Fra Lippo Lippi*.
[2] Rogers, *European and American Philosophy*, 255. [3] Kirtikar, 4.

thing in the human soul is not that it is alone, but that it is in eternal fellowship; that we have each one of us one final companion, and that final companion is God. That man is a duality. That man is not a "thing in himself". That he is a relationship. That his soul is, you might say, a state of tension between his conscious being and another. In short, that he lives and moves and has his being in God. The unit of the human race is not a person, it is that person's communion with another.'[1] In the real essence of ourselves, especially in the real activity of ourselves, we reach beyond ourselves, and we do not do this in any spirit of annexation. Because we have found so much of importance in the depths of ourselves, and because we have recognized our essential kinship with the universal, we do not claim to *be* the universal. The fundamental significance of the self within us does not warrant us in dragging all reality within our subjectivity. Rather in our activity, especially in its noblest aspirations, do we become conscious of outlets to a wider reality. 'Having renounced the unworthy reality, I ought to replace it by what is worthy of existence.'[2] In our moral striving we are conscious of setting up an ideal, but at the same time we know that this is not our own construction, but that we have drawn it from a reality beyond ourselves. As Suso says, 'He who finds the inward in the outward is a more spiritual man than he who can only find the inward in the inward.'[3] What we supremely value is not merely ourselves; the good for which we strive is part of the good of the universe. We are humbly and reverently conscious of the great Other from whom our inspiration is derived. 'Self-realization', as one writer has it, 'must be balanced, not with a pantheistic, but with a transcendent conception of God, for only thus can a man be saved from the worship of self to the worship of God.'[4]

And as our intensest subjective activity is sublimated into worship, we are conscious of the Object of our worship, not as ourselves, nor as the projected image of ourselves, but as something beyond ourselves, immensely attractive and immensely elevating. The essence of worship is the love of God, and love

[1] Dr. Hutton, *Francis Thompson*, 108.
[2] Solovyof, *The Justification of the Good*, 245.
[3] Quoted in *Hibbert Journal*, Jan. 1925.
[4] G. Gardiner, *Vision and Vesture*, 127.

is not merely a subjective feeling. It is not directed towards our own selves. It is directed outwards far more than inwards, towards that which is supremely valuable in the universe and in ourselves, but is never *merely* ourselves, seen through the haze of self-esteem rising from the mists of complacency.

And so in worship we pass, naturally and inevitably, from the reality of the self to the reality of the Divine Object, recognizing once again, and now especially in the sphere of religion, the fundamental character of the subject-object relation. The love that is worship and the worship that is love are alike impossible except as a relation between two terms, and the relation cannot be maintained if these are fused together into an identity. In whatever way the inclination to this fusion manifests itself, it renders true worship impossible. If the stress falls upon ourselves, it is obvious that we cannot make ourselves into an object of worship. If we allow the stress to fall upon the object almost exclusively, and permit ourselves to be merged in the object of our adoration, it is equally obvious that *we* cannot offer the worship, for we have left no foundation in ourselves upon which we may set up our altars. Worship essentially implies a going beyond ourselves in devotion towards and adoration of a Divine Being from whom we all the while distinguish ourselves. The adequate relationship can be established only if we approach it with a vivid consciousness of the reality both of ourselves and God. Subject and Object must both be given their rights in religion as elsewhere.

But in speaking of the rights of the individual in this connexion we must beware of the danger of irreverence, of which danger the Vedānta has done so much to warn us. As already hinted, we cannot claim for ourselves greater importance than, or even equal importance with, the religious Object. While our relation to God must be one of co-operation and confident response, it must also be one of humility. The greater importance must be attached to the Object. Prof. Paterson tells us that it must be 'taken for granted by all who believe religion to be a reality that God is the all-important member of the sacred association, and that there has been a contribution from the divine side which makes the religious relationship immeasurably to surpass, both in content and in promise, the most intimate and enriching form of human union'.[1] God is above us and beyond us, and in our approach to Him we must lay our hands upon our mouths and keep silence. It is here that we reach the truth of the Vedantic emphasis upon the uselessness of our ordinary categories of thought and understand the inner meaning of negation, asceticism, and mystical self-forgetfulness and abandonment. We approach God by the way of a sense of the insufficiency of the finite self, as well as by way of a confidence in our limited self-sufficiency. We are dependent as well as independent, and our dependence is greater than our independence.

It is here also that we reach the truth of the Vedantic reliance upon authority which has seemed to some to be pressed to extreme lengths. For if we believe in the greater and the absolute Value of God, and yet believe also in his kinship to us, we are bound to take up the position of learners by slow degrees of the mysteries of his divine nature and purposes. We come also to the further confidence that in the course of the world's history God has not left himself without a witness, and that his revelations may be made through others as well as through ourselves, a collective authority thus being constituted which we neglect only at our great loss and peril. In learning this lesson of humility we may begin to understand the truth of that saying of Jesus Christ that those who would enter the Kingdom of Heaven must become as little children. And as we realize that we are not sufficient unto ourselves, we shall be the more ready to place our confidence in those whom He has sent to be the prophets and teachers of the world, and pre-eminently, it may be, to believe in Him who came forth from God, and in whom are 'hid all the treasures of wisdom and knowledge'. There is much truth in the lines of T. E. Brown:

> If thou wouldst empty all thyself of self
> Like to a shell dishabited,
> Then might he find thee on the ocean shelf
> And say, 'This is not dead',
> And fill thee with himself instead.

And we must not forget the complementary aspect of the truth. Again the negative must always be in relation to a positive. It is not because of the emptiness of God, or even because of his

[1] Paterson, *Nature of Religion*, 448.

indescribableness, but because of his fullness of qualities and the richness of his glory that we bow ourselves in adoration.

But while we are on our guard against irreverence and self-assertion, we must also beware of another danger in this connexion, if we place excessive emphasis on the transcendence of God. We must not carry humility and reverence to such an extreme as spiritually to grovel in the dust before the majesty of God. The faculties which we possess have after all been given us by God. Some one has said that 'genius in man is the Godhead in distribution'; and 'what is true of genius is also true of more ordinary qualifications'.[1] The Holy Spirit may mean the collective and Godward aspect of the human soul as God made it, and before man marred it, and the continuing help of the Holy Spirit may symbolize the idea that the channel of communication between God and man has never all down through the ages been altogether closed, although man may often have behaved and acted as if he were alone in a lonely universe. Man has in his nature and set right within his heart an indefeasible power to attain to God, and this power should be his glory and his confidence. The summons to the old Hebrew prophet was, 'Son of man, stand upon thy feet'; and the voice may be listened to as a challenge to all humanity.

Although their idea was not so much to cultivate humility as to prepare the way for absorption, the danger is linked with that depreciation of human personality which has so often suggested itself in connexion with Vedantic teachers. They have increased the danger by their over-emphasis upon negation, but perhaps they have also suggested a way of guarding against it. We may develop further their teaching as to the community of nature between us and God, and in such a way as to provide the warning rather than increase the danger. Through this community of nature we possess interpretative rights in the universe; we are organic to the universe, as Prof. Pringle-Pattison has so often and impressively told us. We can claim to understand something of the nature of the Divine Object just because He is not alien to us. Our typical actions, both intellectual and practical, are significant of the nature of the Absolute. Our thought-procedure, e.g., is one of the

[1] W. Robertson Nicoll, *People and Books*, 210.

constituent elements in reality—an aspect of the truth which we do not think has been sufficiently recognized in Prof. Pringle-Pattison's otherwise extremely valuable criticism of the Hegelian transformation of a logic into a metaphysic. Principal Oman puts the matter thus: 'The more we have stood upon our own feet, and thought and felt and acted for ourselves, the more the whole universe has responded to us.'[1]

Our interpretations must be based both on our humility and our confidence. Because of our humility we shall think of God as infinitely transcending us in resources, as corresponding *only* to our best and not to our worst, and as ready to supply the deficiencies indicated in our intellectual and practical limitations. But, because of our confidence, we feel that we may regard the elements of our personality as revealing the nature of God, that we may proceed from the best within to the best without.

And so, discriminatingly and humbly, we make use of our own nature in order that through it we may know God. We demand liberty for comprehensive interpretation, encouraged thereto even by an intellectualist like Bradley, who admits that 'if the main tendencies of our nature do not reach consummation in the Absolute, we cannot believe that we have attained to perfection and truth'.[2] We cannot be content with thinking of God, after the manner of the Vedantists of Śaṅkara's school, as merely intelligence or self-luminousness. Rather do we, following Rāmānuja, tend to think of him as the abode of all auspicious qualities, or—in more modern and more comprehensive phrase—as the home of all values. Especially do we think it natural and necessary to carry with us into the region of the Absolute, our good—our actually accomplished good, and our most unfettered anticipations of it. We claim interpretative rights for our ideals as well as for our attainments. The exceeding naturalness of this procedure of our thought is illustrated strikingly by Clutton Brock when he says, 'The word provoked by evil is "why?", but that word is never provoked by good.'[3]

[1] *Science, Religion, and Reality*, art. by Oman.

[2] *Appearance and Reality*, 148. Cf. also Solovyof, *The Justification of the Good*, 245: 'Truth which is thinkable only and not realizable—truth which does not represent the whole of life—is not what is demanded, is not absolute perfection.'

[3] *Essays on Religion*, 71.

This illuminating good we seek to comprehend in all its variety, and, combining it with other qualities both intellectual and aesthetic, we present it before our worshipping spirits in the unity of a Personality whom we reverence as Divine. One of the most impressive philosophies of the nineteenth century has taught us that perfect personality is in God only,[1] and this apprehension of the essential character of cosmic reality corresponds to the felt need of humanity all down through the ages; for, as Renan puts it, 'Humanity seeks the idea, but it seeks it in a person and not in an abstraction.'[2] And the thought of the French writer is an echo of the cry heard in an eastern land from the lips of Tuḷsidas, 'The worship of the impersonal laid no hold upon my heart.' We refuse to be content with an absolute blank, and we fill up the emptiness with qualities drawn from our own personality, having a not unwarrantable confidence that these qualities are divine; for personality is our most valuable possession, and we hold fast to a belief in the ultimate identity of value and existence.

And in taking up this attitude to God, we think of Him above all as active and of 'the whole course of things as the expression of his unceasing will'.[3] Prof. K. Shastri argues that even Śaṅkara would attribute activity to God, to the underlying real Self, and that it is only *change* which he wishes to deny. Prof. Shastri says: 'Whenever Śaṅkara denies agency to the self, it is always the *passive* agency (if such a term can be used) of the empirical self. Śaṅkara never denies anywhere the free active agency of the real Self.'[4] But apart from the difficulty of reconciling the conceptions of activity and changelessness, we have already seen reason to think that it would be difficult for Prof. Shastri to establish such a position and that the prevailing tendency of the Vedānta is almost to overlook this active aspect. In any case it is pure or theoretical activity which Prof. Shastri has in view in his particular argument rather than concretizing activity having purposeful results. But, notwithstanding this, we think that Prof. Shastri is not wholly wrong if we take into account the spirit and implications of the terms used rather than the explicit utterances in which these terms are embodied. For

[1] Cf. Lotze, *Philosophy of Religion.*
[2] *Marcus Aurelius*, 582.
[3] Cf. Wright, *Philosophy of Religion*, 432.
[4] K. Shastri, 60.

the unfolding of our conception of the divine activity it is certainly possible to borrow terms from the Vedānta as well as from the Gospel of St. John. We may, e.g., consider the divine energy as bursting out of the charmed circle of mere thought—through the Word, the Logos, the *śabda*, uttered eternally as well as in time. Through the Word of his Power, God makes the primary transition from His thought to actuality. It reaches embodiment first of all in sound—a mere vagueness, but, inasmuch as it is the vehicle of possible 'commands', containing within it the germs of the idea of purposiveness. It passes to greater definiteness in the concrete existences of nature and of history, revealing moral characteristics, and indicating progress, in the greatness of promise for humanity when the 'Word became flesh', and in potentiality for all men in the power given to them 'to become Sons of God'.

As we think of God along the lines of what is best within us and in the light of historic revelations of his nature, we regard the divine activity as dominated by love. This is in accordance with our principle; for it is the love of God which expresses most fully the truth of the subject-object relation in religion, as well as the superior importance of the Object, and at the same time the Vedantic truth of the nearness of God to men in the affinity of nature and the incidence of grace. It is love which saves us from the dangers of the identity conception, and by establishing both terms of the relation, gives substance to the idea of communion between God and man and prevents it from being a mere sentimental human yearning.

And as applied to God, love means the outflowing activity of God, in trustfulness, towards a world which He has made, and expresses our belief that He gives to the world such reality that He would not be God without it and without satisfying its needs. He looks upon the particular as a trustee for the whole, and Himself makes possible the fulfilment of the trust. The conception seems to emerge from a metaphysical necessity; and even Bradley, with all his intellectualistic tendency, admits its validity as a deduction from an adequate conception of the universe. 'If other things remain equal,' he says, 'a definite place in, and connexion with, the temporal system gives increase of reality. Not to appear at all in the series of time, not to exhibit one's nature in the field of existence, is to be false and unreal. And to be more true, and to be more real, is, in some way or other, to be more manifest outwardly. For the truer is always the wider. There is a fair presumption that any truth which cannot be exhibited at work, is for the most part untrue.'[1] The same idea is expressed by a recent writer in words which provide an association with, and a contrast to, the Vedantic conception, 'All may be *māyā* until one has found the Central Reality; after that, reality, meaning, value, radiate to the last electron and the remotest star, but above all and in a far higher degree, to "the least of these my brethren".'[2]

Now this expansion of reality, this concern of the centre for the circumference, with an almost humanistic interest in the individuals between the centre and the circumference, seems to be best expressed through the conception of Divine Love. We should stress the connexion between the divine love and activity. We should not think of God as simply the attractive object or magnet for human love, but as Himself descending in the service and expression of His own personality, streaming outwards in His loving-kindness, annihilating the separating distance between the throne of His infinity and the turmoil of existence. Under such a conception it is impossible for us to entertain the idea of God as depreciating the world or treating it as a mere dream or system of appearances. Philosophy (as represented in a Bradley) and religious needs unite in helping us to regard the world as the real condition of the existence of real spirits and the possible environment of an Incarnation of the Divine, both in humanity and in a very special sense. Here, it seems to us, we approach the metaphysical idea which may be taken to underly that central text of Christianity, 'God so loved the world that He gave His only begotten Son'—implying an utter trust of the Divine in the world-conditions of humanity and in humanity itself.

For religious purposes this metaphysically justified trust in humanity is of the utmost importance. It arises from a full acceptance of the principle—enunciated by Lotze and accepted by Ward—that creation has little meaning unless it means the

[1] *Appearance and Reality*, 381.
[2] *Hibbert Journal*, art. 'Centripetal Realism', Oct. 1926.

creation of creators; and implies a full appreciation of the significance of the individual both for time and for eternity, as well as a refusal to merge him, undistinguished, in the divine existence or to treat him as a mere phase of the divine consciousness. We feel, with Bishop Temple, that 'it is impossible that things or persons should wholly constitute one another'.[1] This principle also involves a recognition of the importance of history, or, in other words, a realization that the activities of individuals in relation to one another have had value in the past, and have had consequences continuing their effectiveness to the present and into the future, which will be accepted by God as contributing to the unfolding of His purposes.

Nor do we think it illegitimate to pass from the idea of general benevolent activity of God to special expression of His mercy. This is simply to unfold the implication of the idea of communion between God and man and to press further the Vedantic idea of divine grace and pity, taking these ideas out of the region of mere contemplation of the miseries of man, out of the region of sentimental compassion, and placing them as active forces in the region of the actual. As Bradley says, 'We must not admit the possibility of an Absolute, perfect in apprehension, yet resting tranquilly in pain.'[2] The Divine Love aims at communion, but, seeing that men are not perfect, and that, misusing their freedom, they have gone far astray in the paths of error and of sin, the love of God has to deal with the consequent suffering and evil; and communion can come only as a result of restoration. In its idea of the unity of the human and the divine the Vedānta suggests conditions for redemption; why should not these conditions be constrained by concrete Divine activity to yield up the possibilities that are in them? In the *Gita* we find the idea that God incarnates Himself again and again for the benefit of suffering and sinning humanity; why should not this idea of redemption be dissociated from somewhat meaningless repetition and unreality, and dignified by connexion with a continuous, unitary, and actualized divine purposefulness? An Indian writer says, 'Krishna's incarnation is a camouflage, but it is for the well-being of the world.'[3]

[1] *Christus Veritas*, 57.
[2] *Appearance and Reality*, 158.
[3] B. K. Shastri, 393.

Courtesy to the adherents of another faith would not permit us deliberately to select such a term, but the important point is the connexion in the mind of this writer between camouflage and the well-being of the world. Such a connexion hardly seems to provide a solid basis for religious faith, especially if it is possible, as we have tried to show, that the camouflage may be transformed into an actuality. We would press the idea of redemption back into the very heart of reality, and would take the fullest meaning out of an earlier statement of the same writer that 'every item of creation is really an item in a great scheme of God's self-sacrifice for me and for the world'.[1] The highest soul of the universe can be, nay, has been, proved to be not indifferent to men, but takes their weakness up into his strength, and sends downwards his strength and his purity to redeem them from their sinfulness. Those who enter most fully into the spirit of the Divine sacrifice are so inspired by it that they desire to reproduce it in that evangelism which by word and deed will proclaim the good news of salvation to others—even to the most unlikely, the degraded, and the outcast, 'the least of these my brethren', and will accompany their words by service which will bring nearer the redemption of mankind. As Prof. Radhakrishnan says, 'The great souls of the world address themselves to the task of rousing the divine possibilities in the publicans and the sinners',[2] and his thought corresponds to that of the writer we have just been quoting from: 'Individual life engaged in sacrifice helps in the fulfilment of self and the world.'[3] This represents a great advance on the earlier attitude of the commentator Madhusūdan, who in speaking of 'the vice which enters so largely into the composition of human society', says, 'the least that one can do is entire indifference. If he can help to cure . . . it is sacrifice of a superior kind, but generally indifference is the best attitude to maintain.'[4]

Vedantism in relation to those aspects we have just been considering does not seem to satisfy those of its adherents who are most affected by modern influences. In general there seems to be a striking parallel between the attitude of St. Augustine to the philosophical teaching of his day and the possible attitude

[1] Ib. 195.
[2] *The Hindu View of Life*, 71.
[3] B. K. Shastri, 197.
[4] Quoted in K. Shastri, 168.

of many modern thinkers in India and elsewhere to the Vedantic view of life. Speaking of the Platonic books in Book VII, Chapter 9, of his *Confessions*, St. Augustine says:

'Therein I found that "in the beginning was the Word, and the Word was with God, and the Word was God", and that God, the Word of God, is the "true light that lighteth every man that cometh into the world". But that "He came unto his own",—this I found not there. Also I found that God the Word "was born, not of flesh, nor of blood, nor of the will of man, but of God". But that "the Word was made flesh and dwelt among us", this I found not there. I could discover in these books, though it was expressed in other and in varying phrases, that "the Son was in the form of the Father and thought it not robbery to be equal with God", because by nature He was that same substance. But that "He emptied Himself, taking upon Him the form of a servant, and became obedient unto death, even the death of the Cross"—this those books do not contain. . . . For thou hast hidden these things from the wise, and revealed them unto babes, that they that labour and are heavy laden might come unto Him, and He might refresh them, because He is meek and lowly in heart, and the meek He guideth in judgement, and the gentle He teacheth His ways, looking upon our lowliness and troubles, and forgiving all our sins.'

The Vedānta will afford such satisfaction to the human spirit as it can give, mainly in the intellectual and practical sphere, but concretely and practically, in the realm of history and ethics, it seems to be too detached from the need of men. It moves in worlds of its own not realized by ordinary humanity; it does not base itself on reality and from its comprehension of reality derive strength for the deliverance of men, nor does it view the problems of humanity with that steady gaze which is necessary if a solution is to be discovered. It is so completely baffled by speculative hindrances that it is unready for the practical crises; a denial of reality does not predispose our minds to reform. Just because it takes the way of action as well as the way of thought, Christianity is not in like measure prevented from getting into touch with actuality. Ideally—though those who name the name of Christ have so frequently failed to express His spirit—Christianity comes nearer to the concrete problems of life and provides more fully for relief from the sins and sufferings of men. But while it is in touch with the actual, it is not forgetful of the possible, it is not content with a finished and limited vision, but one of its central beliefs is that 'eye hath not seen nor ear heard, neither hath entered into the heart of man what God hath prepared for them which love Him'. It doth not yet appear what we shall be, but certainly our vision of the future under the guidance of Christianity does not include the gradual fading away of the outlines of our personality into the being of God. The nearer we approach to God, the steadier will be the concentration of our gaze and the more rapt will be our communion, but we neither hope nor desire that we shall become God.

Yet in this connecting of the possible and the actual, in this linking of human potentiality with divine purposefulness, in the proclamation of the possibility, and the hastening through service of its realization, Christianity seems to continue and make available and valid for all men the central teaching of the Vedānta. The great and fundamental truth of the latter—the *tat tvam asi*—'That art Thou'—finds its counterpart and its completion in the message of the New Testament, symbolized in the name given to Him whom we believe to be at once Son of God and Son of Man. The *tat tvam asi* seems like a question sent out by abstract thought into vague immensity, and in the name *Immanuel*, God with us, there comes back an answer which satisfies also the longing of our hearts. Is it too much to believe that in Christ India may find the goal of her searching, the satisfaction of her desire to realize the nearness of God, a consciousness of which is fundamental in the teaching of the Vedānta?

Thus there would seem to be a remarkable affinity between the Vedānta and much Christian thought and life, and a not irrational basis for the idea that the Vedānta naturally reaches forwards towards, and welcomes, the transformation which may be wrought by the presentation of essential, and not merely conventional, Christianity. But in this close relating of Christianity and Vedantism there is need of great care. Premature synthesis and sentimental breaking down of distinctions do more harm than good. The Vedānta is not Christianity, and never will be—simply as the Vedānta; but it is a very definite preparation for it; not a preparation for the acceptance of the particular dogmatic and institutional forms in which Christianity has often been presented, but for the Christ Himself. For we who belong to nominally Christian communities cannot pretend that Christ has not frequently been despised and rejected by us; neither can we claim that we have allowed Him to appeal in all His essential attractiveness to the Indian mind and heart. But we believe—and we are strengthened in our belief by a study of the Vedānta—that when he does so appeal in simplicity and directness, He will in India draw the hearts of all men unto Him, and reveal Himself as the Desire of the nation.

We ought to recognize more fully than we have as yet done the service which Indian thought may render in the interpretation of Christianity. As Max Müller said long ago, 'Vedantic teachings may bring us very near to the earliest Christian philosophy, and help us to understand it, as it was understood by the great thinkers of Alexandria'.[1] And what is true in reference to the earliest Christian thought ought to be still more true of the latest. The thought of India is influencing more and more pervasively the thought of those who are occupied with the unfolding of the truth that is enshrined in Christianity, and we should not be unready or unwilling to acknowledge the debt. We have a Saviour whom we believe to be the Saviour of the world; and all men must help forward, in unity of aim and accomplishment, the understanding of Him.

Further, we need to appreciate more fully than we have yet done the general religious aptitude of India. In the very denials of her thought, in the very intensity of her ascetic abnegation, she has expressed something of the deepest need of the human soul, that sense of loneliness and of mystery and of helplessness over against the immensity of the universe, which are a preparation for the overwhelming Presence of God. And as regards developments of the religious consciousness which we may look for in the future there is a good deal of truth in the words of Prof. Vasvani of Bombay: 'The West will come to the East to learn its age-long wisdom, in order to develop its own mystical sense, to look upon Nature no longer merely as a field of scientific experiment, but as the sanctuary of the Spirit, to exercise itself in meditation so as to grasp the spirit of idealism and realize the presence of God in social life.'[2]

[1] Müller, *S. S.* 124. [2] Speech at the Berlin Religious Congress.

There is need also of more serious and systematic attempts to relate the thought of Christianity to the thought of India. Prof. J. S. Mackenzie says, in the pages of a Western journal, 'For us here at the present time there is probably nothing more important than the attempt to bring together the light that has been gathered by Western science and that which has been set forth by the saints and sages of the East', and he adds pointedly, 'perhaps it is chiefly in our religious and moral outlook that mutual understanding and toleration is important'.[1] Christian theologians have spent much labour in relating their doctrines to the thought of Greece, but they have hardly made as yet sufficient efforts to systematize their teaching or think out its principles in relation to the philosophy of India. Perhaps Prof. Heiler of Marburg lays too much stress on systematic elaboration, but nevertheless many will agree with him in his appeal for sustained intellectual effort: 'For the lasting conquest of the spiritual world of India,' he says, 'the simple evangelical proclamation of the Word and life is not sufficient. For this there is need also of a theological labour on a gigantic scale, which shall link the fullness of the Christian revelation with the religious and philosophical possessions of India. . . . There is need of a new *Summa Theologica*. . . . And this theological synthesis is in relation to India more difficult and more important than it was in the West (in the days of Aquinas) just for the reason that the religious and philosophical treasures of India are far older and richer than those of Greece. Without a theological work of this kind Christianity will never succeed in becoming to the Indian world what once it was to the Greek and Roman world.'[2] And in similar fashion, but naturally with more intensity of emphasis, an Indian theologian writes: 'Jesus Christ came not to destroy but to fulfil, and God who at sundry times and in divers places spake to His children in India, does not desire that His word to our fathers should be made of none effect. In the same manner as the ancient philosophy of the Greeks was consecrated to Christ, will the Indian Church make an effort to present her thought to the world, sanctified and made complete by the power of the living Christ.'[3]

[1] *Hibbert Journal*, art. 'International Unity', Oct. 1926.
[2] Heiler, *Sadhu Sunder Singh*, 228.
[3] Coomaraswamy, *International Review of Missions*, art. 'The Indian Church'.

It is our belief that the living Christ will sanctify and make complete the religious thought of India. For centuries—more centuries of civilization and culture than have been granted, perhaps, to any other nation—her saints have been longing for Him, and her thinkers, and not least the thinkers of the Vedānta, have been thinking His thoughts. Often they have not known His name, but they have been deeply conscious of His spirit, and their age-long thirst for communion with the living God and for realization of the nearness of His Presence will one day be satisfied. Then will the words of Jesus Christ become true also of India and her people: 'Whosoever drinketh of the water that I shall give him shall never thirst; but the water that I shall give him shall be in him a well of water springing up unto everlasting life.'[1]

[1] John iv. 14.

INDEX

Abnormality, 225, 229 f.
Absolute, 34, 45, 59, 62, 113, 128, 145, 153, 176, 182, 194, 201, 202, 205, 210, 211, 217, 224, 239, 240, 244.
Absorption, 120, 179, 213, 226, 239.
Abstraction, 116, 200, 202, 223, 226.
Academic aloofness, 402.
Āchārya, 60, 61.
Acosmism, 193, 213.
Activity, Depreciation of, 182.
Activity of God, 216.
Activity of Knowledge, 122, 174.
Activity of Self, 109, 110, 122, 241.
'Adequate Ideas', 192.
Advaita, 55, 58, 63, 98.
Agni, 12, 14.
Agnosticism, 135, 143, 230.
aham Brahma asmi, 31.
Aitareya U., 23.
Aiyar, Mr. C. N. Krishnaswami, 52, 64.
ajñāna, 138, 141.
ākāśa, 48.
alātaśānti, 48.
Alavandar, 61.
alayavijñāna, 96.
Alexander, Prof., 110, 155.
All-gods, 14.
Alloy, 34.
Ālvārs, 61.
Ānānda, 112, 157.
Angus, Prof., 228.
annamaya, 33.
Anti-intellectualism, 228.
Antinomianism, 125, 174.
aparā vidyā, 30, 113.
Apostolical succession, 37.
apûrva, 162, 164.
Araṇyakas, 5, 8, 11.
Archer, 176, 182, 189.
Aristotle, 78, 216, 229.
Arlen, Michael, 185.
Arulnandi, St., 100, 142.
Arundhatī, 100.
asat, 57, 131, 149, 201.
Asceticism, 23, 125, 174, 186.
Āśmarathya, 43.
Aśvaghoṣa, 94.
Atharvaveda, 6, 19, 20, 131.
Ātman, 17–27, 31, 132, 141, 193.
Atonement, 188.
Attributes, 194.
Auḍulomi, 43, 168.
Augustine, 11, 246.
Authority, 27, 37, 50, 66, 75 f., 227, 238.
āvaraṇa, 129, 140.
avidyā, 30, 36, 128 f., 201.
avidyā, as cosmical principle, 30, 48, 57, 138 f., 198.

Bādarāyaṇa, 42, 71, 72.
Barnett, 36, 131, 138, 170.
Being, 1, 17, 34, 57, 111, 131, 184, 198, 201, 204, 224.
Being and non-Being, 1, 18.
Benares, 54, 55.
Bergson, 226.
bhakti, 61, 62.
Bhāgavatas, 44.
Bhāgavata Purāṇa, 62.
Bhandarkar, Sir R. G., 72, 132.
Bhāshya, 51.
Bhattacharya, M. L., 145.
Blasphemy, 177.
Bliss, 33–4, 157.
Bloomfield, 20.
Boehmen, Jacob, 106.
Bosanquet, 172, 210 f.
Bose, R. C., 174, 215.
Bradley, 108, 210 f., 225, 228, 240, 242.
Brahmacārin, 20.
Brahman, 16, 27, 31, 33, 34, 57, 63, 68, 111, 120, 129, 142, 147, 155, 193.
Brahman, higher and lower, 67, 69 f., 86, 129, 149 f., 169, 196, 212.
Brahman, with qualities, 43, 58, 62, 145, 163.
Brahman, without qualities, 43, 45, 57, 113, 134, 143, 172, 192.
Brāhmaṇas, 5, 6, 11, 21.
Brāhmans, 37, 216.
Brahma-sūtras, 39 f.
Breath, 16.
Brevity, 39.
Bṛihadāraṇyaka U., 23, 27, 34, 36, 38, 69, 86, 115, 125.
Brock, Clutton, 229, 240.
Brown, T. E., 221, 238.
Browning, 235.
Buddhism, 5–46, 53, 54, 58, 60, 70, 92 f., 101, 119, 135, 137, 183.

Caird, 189, 203.
Canon, 45.
Carpenter, Dr. J. Estlin, 5, 41, 78, 102, 142, 143.
Categories, 56, 103, 108, 136, 197, 204.
Categories, Use of lower, 226.
Causality, 56.
Chhāndogya U., 23, 25, 26, 31, 32, 37, 80, 102.
Childlikeness, 115.
Christian Dogmatics, 41.
Christianity, 246.
cit, 112.
Class-distinctions, 37, 60.
Colebrooke, 73, 131.
Coleridge, 121.
Commentaries, 21, 40, 50.
Communion, 169, 236 f., 247.
Concentration, 75.
Conditions, external, 36 f., 73 f.
Conditions, internal, 38, 73 f.
Conditions, moral, 38.
Conditions, religious, 43.
Conjeeveram, 61.
Consciousness, Centrality of, 90.
Conservatism, 4.
Contemplation, 3, 38, 100, 123.
Continuity, 92.
Coomaraswamy, Dr., 249.
Cosmopolitanism, xi.
Cousin, xii.
Cowell, 131.
Creation and Cosmogony, 47, 62.
Creation of Creators, 204.
Creator, 57, 230.
Cumont, 15.
Cyclic Change, 184.

Darkness, 38, 49, 68, 91, 125, 225.
Das Gupta, Prof. S. Ṇ., xii, xiii, 3, 7, 10, 17, 22, 42, 44, 45, 47, 65, 72, 93, 94, 133, 138, 144, 152, 184.
Das Licht vom Osten, 71, 220.
Deception, 130.
Deification, 81.
Deism, 221.
Deliverance, 3, 75, 113, 172, 184.
Denotation of Words, 83.
Despotism, 25.
Destroyer, 58.
Deussen, 3, 31, 38, 39, 41, 42, 50, 72, 82, 85, 88, 89, 115, 116, 125, 126, 128, 131, 135, 140, 149, 156, 161, 173, 178, 218.
Devayāna, 58, 163, 168 f.
Development, 204.
Dewick, Rev. E. C., xiv.
dharma, 81, 164.
Discontent, 191, 220.
Discursive Understanding, 198.
Divine Companion, 236.
Dogmatism, 75, 89.
Dreaming State, 33, 48, 98, 117, 197, 213.
Dreamless Sleep, 32 n., 161, 197.
Dualism, 43, 44, 60, 63, 72.
Dunning, 233.
Dvivedī, Prof., xii.
Dyaus, 12.

Ecstasy, 20.
Egoity, 172, 220.
ēkagratā, 3.
Election, 37.
Element in Absolute, 210.
Eleusinian Mysteries, 106.
Emancipation, 68.
Emerson, 1.
Empirical Self, 123.
Epistemology, 216.
Error, 206.
Esotericism, 50, 54, 67, 73, 80, 156.
Ethical Predicates, 183.
Ethical Struggle, 212.
Ethics, 172 f., 207.
Eucken, 189.
Evangelism, 230.
Evil, 184, 196, 207, 244.
Exotericism, 54, 60, 99, 156.
Expiation, 20.
External World, Belief in, 100.
Externality, 213, 221, 232.

Faith, 125.
Farquhar, Dr. J. N., xiv, 22, 42, 43, 44, 83.
Fathers, Way of the, 58.
Fichte, 198 f.
Figurative and Literal, 87.
Finite and Infinite, 215.
Fire, Sacrificial, 13.
Frazer, 63, 139.
Freedom, 165, 185, 195, 196, 205, 213, 231.

Galloway, Principal, 183.
Garbe, 71.
Gardiner, 236.
Gaudapāda, 46 f., 53, 93.
Gītā, 7, 23, 42, 43, 44 f., 78, 127, 155, 244.
Good and Evil, 195, 214.
Goreh, Nehemiah, 11, 118.
Gough, 38, 71, 72, 115.
Govinda, 53, 93.
Grace, 38.
Greek Mysteries, 152.

Greek Philosophy, 1, 13.
Gross Body, 160.
Guru, 8, 53, 61, 81.

Haldane, Prof., 209.
Hallucination, 142.
Happel, 130, 138, 148, 189.
Hauer, 20, 26, 31.
Heat, 161.
Hegel, 88, 201 f., 213, 216, 219.
Heiler, Prof., 249.
Henotheism, 14.
Heretics, 95.
Hibbert Journal, 79, 134.
History, 190.
Holy Spirit, 239.
Hopkins, Prof., 11.
Hume, 97.
Hutton, Dr. J. A., 185, 232, 236.
hyle, 15.
Hypothesis, 118.

Idea, The, 203.
Idealism, 16, 56, 88 f., 101, 157, 215.
Ideals, Evaporation of, 214.
Identity, 28, 31, 33, 84, 110, 111, 153, 158, 159, 176, 177, 178, 193, 196, 199, 201, 208, 209, 213, 215, 217, 219 f.
Ignorance, 57, 101, 129 f.
Illusion, 47, 48, 88, 99, 100, 130 f., 193, 198, 200, 206, 207, 235.
Immanuel, 247.
Immortality, 13, 156 f., 196.
Incarnation, 244.
Indian Church, 249.
Indifference, 186, 195.
Individual Soul, 63, 67, 68 f., 91, 156 f., 179.
Individuality, 55.
Indo-European Thought, 6.
Indra, 13, 32.
Inexhaustible and Inaccessible, 120, 153.
Inexplicable, The, 144, 148.
Intellectual Love of God, 196.
Intellectualism, 108, 110, 191 f., 204, 208, 210, 212, 213, 230.
Intelligibility, 39.
Intensity, 220.
Inter-subjective Intercourse, 138.
Intuition, 35, 77, 113, 223.
Irreverence, 237.
Iśā U., 23, 38, 68.
ishṭāpūrta, 164.
Isodore of Seville, 41.
Isolation, 235.
Iśvara, 32, 57, 140, 149, 152, 154, 156, 168.
Īśvara Kṛishṇa, 46.
Iverach, 191.

Jacobi, 11, 71.
Jaimini, 42.
Jesus Christ, xiii, 238, 249.
Jñāna, 125.
Jñānayoga, 177.
John, St., 242, 250.
Joy, 134.
Juliana of Norwich, 106.

Kaladi, 51.
Kālī, 54.
kalpa, 150.
Kant, 89, 135, 139, 144, 198, 209.
Kāpālikas, 54.
Kārikās, 46, 53.
Karma, 16, 125, 160, 162, 164 f., 184, 196, 205.
karma-âśraya, 162.
karma-mārga, 54.
Karma Mīmāṁsā, 42.
Kāśakṛitsna, 43.
Kāṭhaka U., 23, 25, 26, 36, 38, 76, 80.
Kaushītaki U., 23, 32, 69, 145.
Kedarnāth, 55.
Keith, Prof. Berriedale, 11, 15.
Kena U., 23, 123.
Kingdom of God, 123, 126, 188, 238.
Kirtikar, 55, 98, 102, 108, 146, 175, 180, 188, 201, 203, 217, 223, 235.
Knowledge, Two Orders of, 43, 62, 67, 112 f., 153, 169, 192, 204, 212.
kośa, 33.
Krishṇa, 44, 127.
kriyamāna, 170.
Kumārila Bhaṭṭa, 54, 60, 93, 99.

Laird, Prof., 119.
Laṅkāvatāra, 95.
Lasitude, 220, 222, 225.
Law, 15, 195.
Law, Fulfilment of, 125.
Legalism, 186.
Leibniz, 192, 196 f.
Limiting Adjuncts, 58, 110, 128, 140, 160.
Lodge, Sir Oliver, 188.
Logical Judgement, 207.
Logos, 83, 241.
Lotze, 116, 143, 151, 166, 209, 241, 243.
Love, 196, 237, 242.

Macdonell, 38.
Macintosh, 205, 208.
Mackenzie, J. S., 249.

McKenzie, J., 81.
Madhusūdan, 245.
Magic, 18, 48.
Mahābhārata, 5.
Mahānārāyaṇa U., 23.
Maitrāyaṇa U., 23.
manomaya, 33.
manas, 161.
Māṇḍūkya Kārikā, 46.
Māṇḍūkya U., xii, 23, 34, 47.
Marett, 83.
Maruts, 13.
Marvell, 97.
Materialism, 56.
Matter, 45, 149.
Māyā, 29, 43, 47, 57, 59, 67, 70 f., 91, 119, 127, 128 f., 194, 198, 201, 203, 243.
Māyā, Relation to *avidyā*, 143.
Means and Ends, 186.
Medievalism, 41.
Mercy, 244.
Merejkowski, 148, 171.
Merit, 122, 174.
Mīmāṁsā Sūtras, 50, 83.
Mnemonics, 40, 50.
Momentariness, 92, 96.
Monism, 36, 44, 45, 46, 55, 61, 64, 100, 102, 192, 213.
Moral Substratum of Soul, 162.
Muir, 77.
Mukhya Prâṇa, 161.
Müller, Max, 1, 11, 14, 38, 42, 46, 63, 65, 71, 103, 115, 133, 135, 144, 181, 222, 248.
Muṇḍaka U., 23, 86, 87, 105, 113, 216.
Mutts, 55.
Mysterium tremendum, 2, 16.
Mystery, 31, 139, 144.
Mysticism, 106, 108, 120, 187, 221, 223, 238.
Myths, 2.

Nachicetas, 26.
Names and Forms, 29, 98, 103, 129, 157.
Naturalism, 58, 213.
Necessity, 195.
Negative Tendency, 13, 18, 24, 28, 34, 35, 45, 49, 55, 68, 112, 148, 186, 189, 207, 219, 223, 238.
neti, neti, 35, 112.
New Testament, 41, 114, 190, 207.
Newman, 3.
Nirgunam Brahman, 69 f.
Nominalists, 29.
Non-difference, 160.
Nothingness, 96, 112, 201.

Object, The Divine, 239.
Objective Qualities, 56.
Objective Reference in Ethics, 178, 180, 187.
Oldenberg, 15.
Om, 4, 83.
Oman, Principal, 240.
Opinion, 131.
Ordinary Experience, World of, 35, 48, 57, 92, 94, 113, 135, 149, 192, 224.
Organs of Sense, 161.
Other, The, 236.
Otherness, 215.
Otto, Dr. Rudolf, 2, 16, 59, 91, 198.

Pal, Mr. D. N., 52, 64, 81, 117, 142.
Pantheism, 4.
Pantheism and the Value of Life, 44, 67, 69, 147, 189, 206.
Para-Brahman, 58.
pāramārthika, 67.
parāvidyā, 30, 113, 169.
pariṇāmavāda, 72, 132.
Parjanya, 13, 165.
Parmenides, 1, 48.
Passages, Order of, 69.
Passivity, 4, 38.
Paterson, Prof. W. P., 83, 222, 225; 237, 238.
Paul, St., 125, 173.
Penance, 17.
Perfection, 172, 188, 211, 214.
Personality, 158, 216, 231, 241.
Personality, Depreciation of, 187, 205.
Pessimism, 24, 184.
Peter the Lombard, 41.
Phenomenal, 57, 96, 136.
Philosophy and Religion, 4, 5.
Philosophy, Modern, 191 f.
Philosophical point of view, 114.
Physical, Dominance of, 227.
pitriyāna, 58, 163.
Plato, xi, 1, 2, 131.
Play, 133.
Plotinus, 223.
Plurality, 55, 120, 145, 211, 222.
Poe, E. A., 143.
Polarization, 129.
Poussin, 46, 93.
Prajāpati, 14, 32.
prakāra, 63.
pralaya, 62, 149.
prāṇamaya, 33.
prāṇas, 165, 171.
prārabdha, 170.
Praśna U., 23, 56, 82.
Prasthānatraya, 39, 44, 45.

Prayer, 16.
Priest, 28.
Pringle-Pattison, Prof., 119, 120, 134, 155, 196, 202, 203, 205, 208, 209, 239.
Progress, 181, 184, 214.
Projection, 181.
Purāṇas, 61.
Purity and Purification, 38, 125, 188,
Purpose, 134.
purusha, 16.
Purushottama Misra, 118.
pūrvapaksha, 87.
Pūrvapaksha, Great, 90.

Quietism, 127.

Radhakrishnan, Prof. S., xiii, 21, 22, 35, 36, 57, 72, 78, 94, 110, 120, 143, 144, 155, 175, 177, 180, 183, 210, 245.
rāg, 10, 51.
Rāmānuja, 7, 41, 43, 50 f., 65, 84, 89, 120, 134, 141, 145, 149, 150, 157, 158, 168, 176, 187, 192, 196.
Ranade, 19, 23.
Rashdall, 175.
Realism, 45, 60, 90, 101, 106, 157.
Reality, 18, 84, 113, 140, 210, 226.
Redemption, 190, 244.
Religion and Philosophy, 216 f.
Religious Aptitude of India, 248.
Religious Consciousness, 56.
Religious Relationship, 201, 215.
Religious Test Misleading, 216.
Religious Test Superfluous, 215.
Religious Value of Vedānta, 215 f.
Renan, 191, 241.
Responsibility, 184.
Revelation, 113.
Reverence, 239.
Reward, 188.
Ṛigveda, 6–12 f., 19, 37, 130.
Ṛishis, 82.
Ṛita, 15, 164.
Ritualism, 13, 28, 58, 122, 124.
Rivers and sea metaphor, 36.
Rogers, Prof., 195, 235.
Roman Catholic Church, 79.
Rope and Snake, 142.
Russell, Bertrand, 105, 121, 209, 210.

Śabda, 202.
Sacrifice, 15, 27, 28, 245.
Saguṇam Brahman, 69 f., 149 f.
Saint, 225, 226.
Salvation, 125, 199.
Sāmaveda, 6, 19.
saṁchita, 170.
saṁsāra, 139, 166, 186.
Śaṅkara, *passim*.
Śaṅkara and Buddhism, 92 f.
Śaṅkara and James Ward, 109.
Śaṅkara, Idealistic Attitude, 88.
Śaṅkara, Life of, 51.
Śaṅkara Method, 85.
Śaṅkara Orthodoxy, 65.
Śaṅkara, Pre-eminence of, 7 f., 54.
Śaṅkara, Summary of Teaching, 55 f.
Śaṅkara-bhāshya, 65.
Sāṅkhya, 45.
Sāṅkhya Kārikās, 46.
sannyāsī, 53.
Santayana, 195.
Śāriraka Sūtras, 39 f.
Sarvāstivādins, 95.
sat, 57, 131, 149, 201.
Scepticism, 224, 225, 227.
Schelling, 199.
Scholastics, 37, 77.
Scientific Point of View, 114.
Secret Doctrine, 22, 37.
Self, Reality of, 99, 193, 225.
Sen, Mr. P. N., 7, 64, 129.
'Sentences', 41.
'Service' God, 113.
Seth, 206.
Shastri, Prof. B. K., 18, 63, 104, 119, 125, 179, 229, 231.
Shastri, Prof. K., 151, 152, 174, 183, 244.
Shastri, Prof. P. D., 17, 49, 72, 130, 133, 140.
Sheaths, 33, 58.
Siddhānta Sūtras, 87.
Sin, 244.
Sins of Ignorance, 12.
Śiva, 23, 54.
smṛiti, 77.
Social Ethics, 179.
Social Service, 126, 188, 199, 207.
Society, 124.
Solovyof, 125, 137, 179, 181, 236, 240.
Soma, 13.
Space, 56, 101, 135, 221.
Speculative Freedom, 85.
Speculative Interest, 26.
Spinoza, 75, 180, 191 f., 213, 216.
Spirituality, 36.
Śrībhāshya, 62.
Śrīharsha, 229.
Śrī-perumbudur, 60.
Śrīraṅgam, 60, 61.
Śri-Vaishṇava, 60.
śruti, 77.

Stages, Four, 124.
Subject and Object, 106, 111, 215, 232 f., 237, 242.
Subjective Qualities, 34, 109, 233.
Subjectivity, 16.
Substance, 119.
Subtle Body, 160.
Sūdras, 37, 60, 73.
Suffering, 200, 208, 244.
Superstition, 227.
Supreme Person, 59.
Sūrya, 13.
Suso, 236.
Sūtra Form, 8.
S'vetāśvatara U., 23, 29, 38, 44.
Symbolism, 36, 117, 148.

Tagore, Dr. Rabindranath, 134, 144, 155, 230.
Taittirīya U., 22, 149.
Tapas, 17, 27.
Tat tvam asi, 31, 104, 169, 216, 221, 233, 247.
Tattvabhushan, Pandit, 38, 84, 92, 97, 127.
Teacher, Place of, 37, 47, 73, 80, 81.
Temple, Bishop, 229, 244.
Theism, 43.
Theodicy, 184.
Thibaut, 42, 43, 44, 65, 67, 71, 140, 147, 160.
Thompson, Frances, 185.
Thompson, Prof. J. Arthur, 85, 115.
Thought, Centrality of, 202.
Tilak, 11.
Time, 56, 101, 200, 221.
Tradition, 4, 84, 228.
Transcendence in Ethics and Religion, 178, 180.
Transmigration, 19, 24, 122, 167 f.
Trichinopoly, 60.
Tulsidas, 241.
Trīya, 33.

Udāna, 94.
Ultimate, The, 101 f., 194, 200, 220.
Unity, Concept of, 36.
Unity, Conditions of Search, 36.
Unity of Apperception, 209.
Unity, Search after, 14, 36.
Universal, 56.
Unknowable, 35.
Unmanī, 33.
Upādhis, 129, 139, 140, 160.
Upanishads, xii, 5, 6, 7, 8, 11, 21, 34, 36, 65, 86, 116, 131, 177, 221.
Upanishads, Meaning of Name, 22.
Upanishads, Vedantic Ideas in, 21 f.
Urquhart, Margaret M., 81.
Uṣas, 12, 13.
Vaiśeshikas, 95, 96.
Vaishṇava Sects, 60, 61, 63.
Vaiśvānara, 32.
Vaitathya, 47.
Values, 183, 189, 190, 237, 238.
Vānaprastha, 6.
Varuṇa, 12, 13.
Vasu, Prof. A. C., 47.
Vāsudeva, 45.
Vasvani, Prof., 248.
Vāta, 13.
Vedānta, *passim*.
Vedānta, Meaning of Name, 7.
Vedānta, Unity of Development, 9 f.
Vedānta Sūtras, 6, 7, 21, 39 f., 50, 60, 62, 65, 85, 90, 95, 102, 116, 131, 137, 139, 150.
Vedānta Sūtras, Date of, 42.
Vedantist, Typical, 64.
Vedas, 1, 5, 6, 11 f., 37, 46, 60.
Vedas, Date of, 11.
Vedas, Fundamental Ideas in, 11 f.
vidyā, 62.
vijñānamaya, 11, 33.
Vijñānavāda, 97.
vikṣepa, 129, 140.
Virāṭ, 32.
viśeshyam, 31.
Viśishṭādvaita, 63.
Vishnu, 13, 44, 45, 63.
Viśvakarman, 14.
Vivartavāda, 72, 132.
Vivekānanda, Swami, 143, 176.
Void, 47, 48.
Vrātya, 20.
Vyāsa, 42, 54, 82.
Vyāvahārika Existence, 57, 67.

Waking Life, 97, 197.
Ward, 108, 109, 243.
Wenley, 173.
Wilde, Oscar, 224.
Will, Cosmic, 200.
Women, Place of, 37.
Word, 83, 203.
Wordsworth, 106, 186, 220, 221.
Works, 38, 121 f., 169, 188.
Worsley, 218.
Wright, Prof., 231, 241.

Yādavaprakāśa, 61.
Yajurveda, 6, 19.
Yama, 13, 163.
Yoga, 23, 222.
Yogī, 20, 45.

Zauberfluidum, 15.